TRAIL MIX

➜

JULES TORTI   Foreword by *Jane Christmas*

TRAIL MIX

920 km on the Camino de Santiago

RMB
rmbooks.com

For information on purchasing bulk quantities of this book, or to obtain
media excerpts or invite the author to speak at an event, please visit
rmbooks.com and select the "Contact" tab.

RMB | Rocky Mountain Books Ltd.
rmbooks.com
@rmbooks
facebook.com/rmbooks

Cataloguing data available from Library and Archives Canada
ISBN 9781771604802 (softcover)
ISBN 9781771604819 (electronic)

Design by Lara Minja, Lime Design

Printed and bound in Canada

We would like to also take this opportunity to acknowledge the traditional
territories upon which we live and work. In Calgary, Alberta, we acknowledge
the Niitsítapi (Blackfoot) and the people of the Treaty 7 region in Southern
Alberta, which includes the Siksika, the Piikuni, the Kainai, the Tsuut'ina,
and the Stoney Nakoda First Nations, including Chiniki, Bearpaw, and
Wesley First Nations. The City of Calgary is also home to Métis Nation
of Alberta, Region III. In Victoria, British Columbia, we acknowledge the
traditional territories of the Lkwungen (Esquimalt and Songhees), Malahat,
Pacheedaht, Scia'new, T'Sou-ke, and W̱SÁNEĆ (Pauquachin, Tsartlip,
Tsawout, Tseycum) peoples.

We acknowledge the financial support of the Government of Canada through
the Canada Book Fund and the Canada Council for the Arts, and of the
province of British Columbia through the British Columbia Arts Council
and the Book Publishing Tax Credit.

For Kim,

because without her there would be no story worth telling.

And for my parents,

who never doubted what I said I would do

(except when it came to making the bed and doing dishes).

While a picture may say a thousand words, Jocey Asnong's illustration says nearly a thousand kilometres. The vitals are all here: the official Pilgrim Passport, the iconic scallop shells we tightly knotted to our packs, the guiding arrow and unforgettable map that continues to unfold over and over in our heads three years later.

Illustrator Jocey Asnong's whimsical rendition of the Camino Frances route, beginning with the daunting Pyrenees, westward to Finisterre.

CONTENTS

– – – – –

Contents

After one last hike on our home turf, Kim and I try to calm rattled nerves with Prosecco before our flight to France the next day.

FOREWORD

— — — — —

The one phrase unlikely to be uttered by anyone returning from Spain's legendary Camino de Santiago de Compostela is: 'What happens on the Camino stays on the Camino.' Nope. You're just not going to hear that. Because here's the thing about the Camino: Once you've walked it you *have* to talk about it; there is simply no other option. Talk about it, write about it, paint a picture of it, compose music about it. You want the world to know about your Camino.

No easy task, that. How to sugar coat an 800-kilometre trek that involves tortuous climbs, exhausting daily slogs, and sleeping in bunk beds. With strangers. Who snore. Who have dubious hygiene. And not always the same strangers. Different ones every night. Try spinning that into the best experience of your life. People will think you are mad. So begins your transition from pilgrim to missionary.

For well over 1,000 years, pilgrims have travelled with little more than their faith and a wish to reach Santiago de Compostela alive so they can off-load their burdens— emotional, psychological, physical or relational—and reap a miracle in the city's elaborate cathedral. Often the miracle is discovering relief from your burdens in the company of those lugging burdens of their own. As it was in the 9th century so it is today: The Camino provides. That such a naïve ethos exists in our social-media-swamped, evidence-based world is miracle alone.

In 2003, during a fleeting conversation, I heard about the Camino. An instant eruption of goosebumps was all the push I needed to do it. It *felt* right. Didn't matter that I had never hiked or hefted a backpack. You can do a lot worse than follow your instincts. A year later, off I went. It was hard, relentless, lonely, exhilarating. And life changing. As I write this, I am sitting with a man I met on that Camino. We've been together ever since. And though I vowed never to set foot on the Camino again, I was back in 2018 to hike the Camino del Norte, one of the longest and toughest routes to Santiago.

As a couples-bonding exercise—even as a friend-bonding exercise—the Camino can't be beat. It intensifies shortcomings and strengths, both your partner's and yours. Another miracle of the Camino is not always that you completed it, but that despite your sometimes bratty, bitchy behaviour you still had a partner by the end of it.

If you have considered walking the Camino, Jules Torti's book is a great start. It will give you an idea of what to expect, what to pack and what to leave behind. (Bonus points to her for leaving distracting phones and tablets at home.) Those who have trekked the Camino Francès will recognise places Torti mentions along the way. Much has changed, some hasn't: Los Arcos's grumpy vibe has apparently not improved with time, and those chickens are still clucking in the cathedral of Santo Domingo de la Calzada. You will empathise with the should-I-stay-or-should-I-keep-going dilemma that confronts the exhausted pilgrim mulling the dregs of available accommodation options. As for the *café con leches*: Is there better coffee anywhere than on Spain's Camino?

For women, the Camino is particularly empowering. There are few places in this world where you can walk solo for 800 kilometres without the worry of being molested. Torti didn't walk alone, but with her partner Kim.

If the pandemic taught us anything it is the need to make hay. Who knows when another virus will imprison us in our homes? Who knows when our body parts will give out and render us unable to walk long distances and enjoy the grand sweep of awesome landscape the Camino affords at every turn?

What happens on the Camino does not stay on the Camino, and for good reason. The Camino is to be shared and savoured. Long may it be so.

Jane Christmas, *What the Psychic Told the Pilgrim*
JUNE 2021

Around the world we've seen caution signs for snakes, turtles, hippos and banana crossings—but never cats. Translated, this sign in Santiago means, "Let them cross."

INTRODUCTION

– – – – –

"Did you see that woman's feet?"

I was intentionally walking like a horse with blinders. I didn't want to see anyone's feet or grimaces of pain. Tiger Balm perfumed the air as Camino casualties massaged cramping calves and rewrapped tensors. What had Kim and I agreed to? It all seemed so innocent and possible as we logged our training miles on the Ferndale Flats in Ontario. Exactly, Ferndale *FLATS*.

From Saint-Jean-Pied-de-Port, France, we would encounter an abrupt elevation gain from the prairie-like 180 metres to Col Lepoeder's bird's eye view at 1430 metres. Was it even possible to walk at a 90-degree angle? Yet we were confident we could cross the Pyrenees with a few Clif Bars and some fancy climate-controlled Helly Hansen gear.

A smiley American bounced past us in a hat with flapping tails, announcing to no one in particular that this was her eighth time walking the Camino. As the day progressed, we would hear her same story eight more times as we jockeyed positions, slowed to chug tepid water and change sweat-soggy socks. The awesome trifecta of insomnia, jet lag and lactic acid hit all at once. Eight times? Like, eight failed attempts? My perfectionist self couldn't register that kind of defeat.

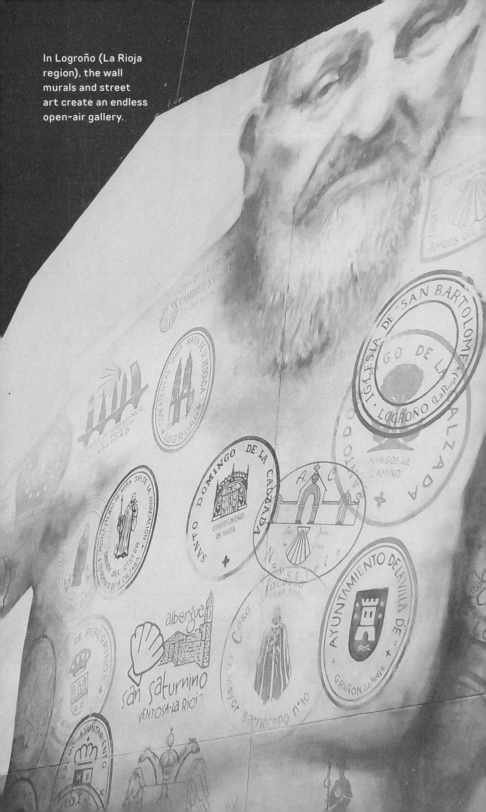

In Logroño (La Rioja region), the wall murals and street art create an endless open-air gallery.

Early Footage

- -

You can terrify yourself quite easily; very little effort is required. Just dwell on that irregular mole on your shoulder, or the way your heart sometimes flips and skips a beat for no good reason. Simpler yet, do the existential math. At 44, I'm nearly half over. All of this is the natural composition required for two things:

1. A full-blown panic attack.
2. The "inspo" (do millennials still say that?) to start getting stuff done. Like walking the Camino de Santiago.

I loathe the term "bucket list," unless it involves beer, but the Virgo in me loves a good list, so, in no particular order, this was the stuff I had to get done already:

1. Make watermelon rind pickles.
2. BOTSWANA!
3. See (not participate in) a roller derby.

4. Go ice fishing.
5. Sign up for a life drawing course
   (either as a model or artist).
6. Attend the Burning Man festival.
7. Sleep in a lighthouse.
8. Learn how to make wax seals to monogram envelopes.
9. Read *A Tree Grows in Brooklyn*.
10. Walk the Camino before my lower back decides
    otherwise.

Kim and I had been headlong and knee-deep in Botswana research. I had another year left on my ten-year yellow fever vaccination and it made sense to capitalize on the immunization with more African travel. We'd sketched out a loose itinerary and logistics thanks to a well-dog-eared copy of Lonely Planet's *Botswana & Namibia*. Emails filtered in daily from safari operators with spotty details and big price tags. Our scrambled short list of Airbnb properties, seat sales and safari dates didn't jibe, so we'd rejig everything again. And then Kim's dad was hospitalized. She flew to Charlottetown, PEI, at the end of July as soon as things flipped for the worse. At 92, it wasn't a surprise, but Earl's quick downhill slide still wasn't expected.

There were sticky elements to contend with. Should I stay or should I go? Kim and I didn't have a land line—in fact, we still only have one cell phone and laptop between us, and one vehicle. So, when Kim went to PEI, I was housebound and we could only communicate via email. I waited and paced for days, anxious for updates. When our neighbour knocked on our door before nine in the morning, I knew it had happened. "It's Kim." Anne held out her iPhone and Kim's silence on the other end was heard. Earl had died and funeral plans were escalating fast. "It doesn't make sense for you to fly out now," Kim reassured me.

Her dad's health had cast an understandable shadow of worry on our travel plans for the past few years. We were visiting remote places that would make a quick return impossible. At best, if we did learn of any trip-altering news, it would be a two-day affair to return to Canada. There's no easy way to grab a flight from Uganda when you are in the middle of Queen Elizabeth National Park in Rubirizi. What would we do if we were halfway down the Yangtze River? Checking emails became increasingly stressful and inconsistent as we liked to travel without any devices, and internet cafes have outlived their purpose in the Wi-Fi world.

While Kim shifted to the uneasy acceptance of not stalling our travels because of the "what ifs," the reality loomed the further we went down the Kazinga Channel or the deeper we went into the Bigodi swamp.

When Kim returned home from PEI, my words cut in and out like an FM radio station along a mountain pass. I hadn't talked to anyone in weeks aside from a "hello" when jogging past someone. We fell into each other's arms in a desperate way. Wine was opened and the stories flowed with a hot mix of tears. Kim said she had something for me. "For us." I certainly wasn't expecting a souvenir from the island. "It's just something small."

I unfolded the tissue paper to find two small silver scallop shells. I felt the peculiar weight of them in my hand, knowing immediately what the shells indicated. The shells were the size of a quarter and the insides were engraved with the words "Imagine" and "Wish."

"I think we should walk the Camino."

It was time.

Death always brings a sudden immediacy to life. There's an urgency to see places not seen. With ailing and aging parents, a carefree trip becomes stitched with guilt. With Earl's passing, there was an unspoken release to travel without the anchor and tethered worry.

My grandmother reminded my siblings and me on a daily basis of life's fleeting nature. "If god spares me, tomorrow I will _____ (buy that ground beef on sale at Loblaws, get my hair permed, start crocheting that Nordic knit sweater)." She was spared for 80 years and her hope for god to spare her another day had nothing to do with a bucket list of exotic places. She was happy to be spared to babysit us and fry up hot dogs, provided the humidity didn't overwhelm her. My grandmother had zero ambition to see any geography beyond Buffalo, New York's shopping malls. That was her version of international travel, and her face would be Liquid Paper white at the border crossing. Nan didn't want to be spared to see the Jökulsárlón glacier lagoon in Iceland, or the mountain gorillas in Bwindi Impenetrable National Park in Buhoma. She definitely did not want to sleep *en plein air* in Egypt's White Desert with dung beetles skittling about. She was wholly content with nabbing a "Dollar Days" sale on peanut butter and a little Arsenio Hall before bed.

I wanted to be spared to reach the end of the Camino de Santiago with my hamstrings and patience intact.

Kim is the only person I would dare walk 920 kilometres across France and Spain with. We didn't decide to walk the Camino because her dad died – it was simply time. Like fashion icon Jeanne Beker suggests, there's no good time to get a puppy. You have to just add them to the mix and the dominos will topple in a highly likely, cumulative way. Like the Camino, there's no ideal time for the general population to take a six-week sabbatical from life. The time commitment alone might explain the number of retirees and twentysomethings that dot "the Way."

There's no spoiler here. If you know someone who has walked the Camino, the catalysts are as well defined as the footfalls on the ancient pilgrimage route: Someone died. Divorce. Quit job. Lost job. For a smaller percentage, the magnetic pull to walk the Camino is undefined. And that's where we fell in line.

Kim and I had talked about the Camino more than we had about Botswana over the years. Ask any good Catholic and they will know of the fabled Way of St. James. But Hollywood deserves a bigger nod for introducing the Camino to an even bigger audience in 2010 with *The Way*. Directed by Emilio Estevez and starring his father, Martin Sheen, the film gave serious celluloid treatment to the traditional pilgrimage route to Santiago de Compostela in Spain. The plot resonated in unexpected ways and appealed to every demographic, age and nationality. The Camino seemed to provide answers. Like a unicorn, the film debuted and its magic and promise of hope had viewers move from popcorn to packing.

Sheen's character, a career-centric ophthalmologist, finds his golf game interrupted by a call from the French police. His son Daniel has died in the Pyrenees. Sheen's world shifts sideways and, upon landing in France, his grief takes a twist as he battles to understand his son's rootless, nomadic decisions. Sheen decides to walk the Camino to figure out Daniel's seemingly pointless death and, in turn, finds his own way. The motley crew he initially resists becomes fast companions, and this is where the audience sees the glittery glimmer. There's Sarah, the Canadian, desperate to walk away from an abusive husband's paralyzing grip. Jack, a chirpy Irishman, has writer's block. Joost, a jolly Dutchman, is trying to lose weight to gain his wife's affection back. Collectively, they're all trying to "quit" something by starting in a new direction. Smoking, emotional eating, judging. The stories are familiar and it would be impossible not to identify with some aspect of *The Way*. Though not every viewer cottons on to the spiritual essence of the film, it has motivated countless others from (ironically) every "walk" of life.

For Kim, *The Way* was her first introduction to the Camino, even though she was a Catholic! We watched it in my annex apartment in downtown Toronto, cozied up on the sectional EQ3 couch I'd had delivered that day. Without acknowledging it out loud, we both knew we'd see the footage for ourselves one day. We were going to do the Camino. That was 2012.

I'd heard of the Camino through a friend (and possibly Shirley MacLaine), though the idea never took root. Mag had mentioned it was something she wanted to do, but her knees were dictating otherwise. She must have mentioned the religious connection, or I tuned out with talk of Saint James, thinking it would be too holy roller for my nonbelieving self. Why would I walk 800 kilometres to the alleged burial site of the apostle Saint James? I'd only been to church with my grandmother a handful of times, and each time involved a strawberry social. And that was because god had spared her!

I loved the concept of such a physical challenge, but I was iffy about the celebrated finish line being a cathedral. I wasn't prone to visiting churches in any of my travels, short of forced visits in Quebec on an elementary school trip. So why would I suddenly want to walk all that way to attend a mass and see the swinging *botafumeiro* (Galician for smoke expeller)? It is an engineering feat in its own right, as the 80-kilo thurible is carried and swung on a pulley system by eight men. This swinging censer has been employed since the 11th century, originally intended to douse unwashed pilgrims in a plague- and epidemic-weary era. The incense is also said to serve a dual purpose as an "oration to God," or form of prayer. Of course, thanks to the grand finale scene of *The Way*, the mass has become a sold-out affair.

Is it wrong that I was only curious to see the pilgrim's mass because I'd read about the 1499 incident when Princess Catherine of Aragon visited and the botafumeiro disconnected and flew out the cathedral window? In 1622, 1925 and 1937 there were also accounts of frayed rope and hot coals spilling everywhere – but nothing as dramatic as the botafumeiro flying out the window!

I wasn't sure if I wanted to be called a pilgrim either, but I did like long walks with my gal. And watching movies over and over – which we did with *The Way*.

I shelved the Botswana guidebook and reasoned it was probably better to have a new dose of yellow fever inoculation under my belt anyway (you actually get the injection intramuscularly in your deltoid, not under your belt). Kim and I had been to Zanzibar and Uganda within the last few years, so I was satiated with Africa for a while. Barely, but for a while. We plunked in a new airport destination, backspacing "GAB: Sir Seretse Khama International in Gaborone, Botswana" in exchange for "CDG: Charles de Gaulle in Paris, France." Even the currency converter website we frequented had held our search for US dollars to Botswana *pula*. I liked that pula meant "rain" in Setswana, because rain is very scarce in the Kalahari Desert, making both the currency and rain precious and valuable. In turn, the euro conversion was even more precious indeed!

Kim set about determining essential trip math. How many days did we want at the beginning and tail end? Was a 30-day itinerary realistic? Should we build in a rest day every seven days? More importantly, if we were to start walking in September, with the elevation (and climate change), encountering snow close to Santiago was a reality we had to consider. The sun was already setting on August 15, 2018. Though we were both fit and of the same stubborn endurance level (both mental and physical), how many days did we need to train in Canada before hitting the ground running in France?

Luckily, we didn't have to beg for extended holidays from work or be constrained by constant email contact with family members. My parents were well versed in our off-grid, incommunicado ways. Kim was happily retired after 32 years at the steel mill. As the editor-in-chief of *Harrowsmith* magazine, I was in a perfectly suspended time between issues and didn't need to be accessible until November when the spring layout began to ramp up. My soon-to-be-published memoir, *Free to a Good Home: With Room for Improvement*, was in the trusty hands of the editorial team at Caitlin Press. I was free range.

But, first, we needed stuff. Everything, really. We needed sleeping bags as light as Kit Kat bars. We had to find laundry soap in the form of flyweight flakes that we could simply add to a basin of water to simulate a laundromat. Similar to those clever Listerine strips placed on your garlicky tongue for fresh breath, space age laundry flakes promise to freshen socks in the same reliable manner.

Jittery from the commitment and coffee, Kim and I began crawling through endless blogs and Camino forums. We'd both read every Camino book available, from Jane Christmas's very frank and comic *What the Psychic Told the Pilgrim: A Midlife Misadventure on Spain's Camino de Santiago de Compostela* to Shirley MacLaine's somewhat trippier *The Camino: A Journey of the Spirit*. Though the books were published in 2007 and 2000 (and the others even earlier than that), the packing list doesn't change. While there have been giant advances in GORE-TEX, packs, down and moisture-wicking clothes, you still need to walk and carry everything on your back.

However, going lightweight is a heavyweight on the wallet. Sure, there are affordable sleeping bags out there, but they are also the size of schnauzers. We needed chihuahua-sized bags that folded up into something that could double as a football if need be. It was easy to ignore the suggested sleeping bag liners to save on weight because at day's end we wanted warmth and comfort, not a skinny silk or synthetic sock to crawl into. I couldn't imagine "wrapping up" in the equivalent of an oversized T-shirt in some 15th-century, stone-walled, nun-run hostel. Even in the dead of summer I have a down duvet up to my nose and, most likely, long johns on.

Above all else we needed backpacks. Surveying our inventory, we had a Goldilocks supply of too big and too small, nothing *just right*.

We broke the bank on merino socks after several Darn Tough and Smartwool ambassadors with Camino cred insisted. At 30 bucks a pop, it was hard to believe the socks had a lifetime and stink-free guarantee. Game on! I wondered if these merino sheep were massaged like Wagyu cattle. Were they fed truffle oil and IPA beer while listening to Yo-Yo Ma or the Rosetta Stone (Learn Cantonese!)? Were these sheep an endangered species? Research would later reveal that this economically influential breed can produce 103 kilograms of wool in a lifetime. I don't know how many pairs of Darn Tough socks that equates to, but that sheep could definitely retire in the Maldives quite comfortably.

It was a pilgrimage just to track down all the required kit we needed from our outpost on the Northern Bruce Peninsula. I prayed to the Saint of Backs to keep my Tinkertoy spine together on the long-haul drives to and fro to gear shops in Guelph and Toronto. We tried on more packs than Everest Sherpas and nothing felt *just right*.

Kim and I were shifting from a walk-in closet to a *walking* closet. It would be a Charlie Brown existence for one month. Two T-shirts, one pair of shorts, four pairs of socks. We would go commando and forgo space-hogging underwear. I would sacrifice books, hoping I'd be too exhausted to notice their absence at day's end. We sighed after towelling off each time we had a shower in the next few weeks, knowing that our luxury cotton and full-length towels would soon be traded for a chamois the size of a standard facecloth.

We laid out our stuff and borrowed our neighbour's scale to see if we had reached fighting weight yet. This is the tried-and-true formula: your pack shouldn't weigh more than 20 per cent of your body weight. So, at 54 kilograms, math suggested that 11 kilograms was reasonable, but five kilograms felt much more agreeable to my spine. We also had "consumables" to account for. Water and snacks that would come and go with each day. Before we had all of our established gear (Kim was still on the hunt for a rain jacket, and I needed quick-dry pants and a space-saving fleece), we filled our temp day packs with peanut butter and cans of kidney beans. Even at five kilograms, our mini packs felt like we were carrying around small gorillas.

I was not going to sacrifice Q-tips, and an o.b. is as small as you can go in the tampon world. I tossed my hair gel aside and replaced it with a toque.

We booked our flights for September 17, hoping for a divine connection to Biarritz, France, from Paris with 45 ticking minutes to spare (otherwise we were going to be saddled with a six-hour wait for the next flight). Provided that leg was successful, we had a highly orchestrated itinerary with no room for error. Once we landed in Biarritz, we had a half-hour bus ride from Biarritz to Bayonne and a one-hour train from Bayonne to Saint-Jean-Pied-de-Port that left every four hours. Provided all pilots and drivers and backs aligned.

As soon as we entered our credit card info for the flights, it was like signing the papers to sell a house. The rush of excitement pales when you start thinking about all the crap that could go wrong in a nanosecond. What if a bat colony moves in before the new owners take possession? What if the boiler blows up?

We were hyper-focused on maintaining our bodies and I swore off any untraditional tasks. I could not be convinced to join a pickup football game (though that is rare within itself). I would not be picking up anything, really, especially after we started clocking 20-kilometre days. My chronic back issues left my nerves frayed. Could I order cortisone on the rocks? With a lime?

Wait. How much does that lime weigh?

*Back*drop

--- --- --- --- --- --- --- --- --- --- --- ---

Kim and I both had careers with big physical asks. Even with Kim's detailed serviette drawings of her workplace, I still couldn't picture the foreign steel mill surrounds where she slogged through 12-hour shifts. Instead, I visualized Slate Rock and Gravel Company where Fred Flintstone was a bronto crane operator. Her typical day (or night shift) involved the constant shuffling of 50-kilo tin anodes. She routinely dumped 23-kilo drums of chrome flake into hoppers and had the envy-inducing bicep definition to prove it.

After 17 years of being a massage therapist, I was becoming spineless. I'd roll over in the night and sound like a disassembling skeleton. It was genuinely back-breaking work. For a profession designed to resolve stress, it was also my biggest stressor. I had an average resume of injuries, most of them wipeouts from winter running or farm dog versus bike chase scenes that dramatically ended with me in the ditch. I'd suffered a concussion and saw several stars after a snowboarding incident at Sunshine Village in Banff. I had cat scratch fever (unrelated to the farm dog chase). And then I fell down stairs, top to bottom, twice. Growing up, we all took turns accidentally riding down the wooden stairs to our basement. I was able to resume normally scheduled programming after most of these bails until I turned 40 and my back talked back.

In August 2015, two weeks before Kim and I were to depart for Entebbe, Uganda, I remembered to empty the dehumidifier. It was usually something Kim did as her workshop was downstairs and there was no significant reason for me to ever go to the basement. It was a 155-year-old stone house with a bedrock floor (maybe this is why the Flintstones were my visual default setting). I had to bend in half to access the furthest reaches, removing flossy strands of cobweb from my lips as I went. I squatted and pulled out the dehumidifier bucket and froze. I heard and felt a sickening clunk in my lower back and instantly seized. The bucket tipped and flooded around me. A chill raced through my nervous system and I had to swallow hard to resist throwing up. I remained motionless, hoping that maybe whatever slid out would go back to where it normally belonged. Could I even make it back up the stairs? I was convinced I was instantly paralyzed and terrified tears raced down my face to my neck. We were leaving for Africa in two weeks!

I had locked up several of the facets in my low back, which left me bent, crooked and unable to right myself. I dreamt of medieval torture techniques that involved being suspended and stretched in shackles. Anything to uncrook me. Obviously, I made my way out of the basement, never to dump the dehumidifier again. I took a few days off work, only leaving the house to inch along to the chiropractor half a kilometre away. Kim begged me to take a taxi (as she was working), but I had to walk this thing off.

We went to Uganda (there was no way in hell I was missing out on Africa because of my dumb back), but the 18-hour flight and banging along roads with potholes the size of meteorite strikes did not help my cause. The chiro adjustments barely held, and my paranoia level was off the charts. If a witch doctor appeared, I was all in. I would have gargled ostrich eyeballs and cheetah semen if there were promise of healing.

This isn't a whiny sob story, though, just some necessary *back*ground if you will. While Kim was fretting about her predisposition for blisters, her back could be used to jack up a vehicle, leaving me to obsess over what really inconvenient, inaccessible spot in the Pyrenees my back might back out. Camino done. Like the pouting *Survivor* contestants who are the first to be voted off, it's almost worse to have your own body reject you.

Kim and I never talked about any of this. Maybe it was the whiff of superstition that kept us mum. Talking about clunky backs and debilitating blisters (which chronically end the Camino for many) might conjure up bad juju. Instead, we let our brains privately glow neon at night with worst-case scenarios. Both of us would sweat a little more than usual until the almighty Santiago cathedral was in our rear-view.

Walking together added another unique dimension to the Way. Not only were we responsible for ourselves but continuing for the other. Kim and I had already agreed that it was all or nothing. Both of us, or none of us. Yes, there are shuttle services that allow you to send packs ahead to the next town or hostel for a small fee. There are also buses that run somewhat parallel to the Camino, permitting pilgrims to bypass monotonous or taxing sections. We wanted none of that, though. No pack forwarding. No buses.

When I told my sister, Kiley, that we had somewhat spontaneously decided to do the Camino, she was naturally full of questions about our gear and training. Groomed by two decades in the Rocky Mountains, Kiley has climbed every peak and/or ice climbed it if the Banff weather was uncooperative. She knew Kim and I were hack hikers. My most recent work commute to Langdon Hall Country House Hotel and Spa in Blair was 16 kilometres return (provided I took the mucky and steep shortcut through the boreal forest to the back of the hotel). Kim didn't have the option of walking to the steel mill, as it was 50 kilometres away. Plus, her shift started at 6:00 a.m., while my start time was a more palatable 2:00 p.m.

But Kim could just crack off and walk any distance. This is what disturbed Kiley. Kim and I would set off on the old rail line trail along the Grand River in Cambridge and keep on trekking to Paris, clocking in 19 kilometres, just because. Kim would do this with her Nike sneaker laces undone. We'd wear jeans and skip bringing rain gear out of laziness to carry it. Instead, we'd pack some chilled tall boys and cold pizza if we had it, or bring two skinny granola bars. Kiley was astounded. "You guys don't even take water with you? You walk five hours and only take beer?"

I thought we would be an inspiration! Though our techniques didn't always work so favourably. On that same rail line, Kim and I turned at the halfway mark (ten kilometres) in Glen Morris, at the historic German Woolen Mill ruins. Constructed in 1867, only the stately stone walls remain. Hidden from the main rail trail, the once-secret spot has been flushed out by both wedding photographers and paranormal explorers. And by us as a convenient watering hole. We chugged our two beers, feeling the lager instantly evaporate as sweat on our forearms in the soupy August temps. By the time we reached Cambridge proper again, Kim and I had flatlined. We were starved and dehydrated zombies. The Becker's convenience store on Highway 24, at the trailhead, was like an oasis. I'm surprised we had any money on us; usually, we opted not to carry cash either. In a furry haze, I bought two neon purple Gatorades and two chocolate bars, the most substantial ones on display. Kim and I never ate chocolate bars, but I was prepared to eat the rubber off the gas pump hoses if need be.

Panting and delirious, we swallowed the chocolate bars nearly whole. Gatorade stained our lips and ran down our chins without care. "Let's not do that again," Kim said. And we didn't, that is, until the Camino forced us into the same situation. But I'm getting ahead of myself...

Once we began telling friends and family that we'd recalibrated our September trip from Botswana to Spain, pilgrims started coming out of the woodwork. What's that theory about putting something out into the universe?

A few years prior, a massage client randomly asked if I had heard of the Camino de Santiago. He had done it in 2014. When I mentioned that my partner and I were thinking of doing it, he disapproved and let me know just how much. "You definitely don't want to do it with your partner. Trust me. It's a bad idea. You'll see."

I was immediately put off (and I'm sure the remainder of my massage reflected that). Why wouldn't I take this amazing challenge on with the person I loved most? The woman I miss while I'm sleeping? I hated this guy. Leaving the hotel that night, I told Brenda, one of my colleagues, about the conversation. She stopped in her tracks and fished out the silver pendant around her neck. "This is from the Camino! My brother walked it last year!" Our chatter went in a different direction and I soon realized the connections were everywhere.

When I shared both conversations with Kim later that night, we both agreed that my client was a dork and probably divorced for good reason. And how did I not notice the silver scallop shell pendant around Brenda's neck?

I issued a bulletin on Facebook. Did anyone we know *know* of anyone who had walked the Camino?

The pings Ping-Ponged in. Rick, a fellow classmate at the West Coast College of Massage Therapy in New Westminster, British Columbia, decided to take it on after a wake-up call heart attack. Kim's co-worker had volunteered to bike a section and accompany a visually impaired rider. From high school days, Danielle said her two moms had done it and were heading back for another round. Helen, the manager of the Gately Inn in Entebbe, Uganda, had just met one of our compatriots from

Toronto. "Maureen has done the Camino! I will connect you! She was on safari a month before you two and had mentioned this trek." My sister insisted I follow her friend Sue Shih on Facebook. "She's there now! She's done different parts of it and you'll love her foodie pics!" To boot, my copy editor at *Harrowsmith* had done the leg from León to Santiago and was an instant firehose of information.

The list was random and much like a gathering of family members once removed. Kim and I collected bits from each, but our greatest resource ended up being Sarah from BC. Just after Kim's dad died, Kim and her sister, Lynne, took a deep breath and had lunch on the patio in Charlottetown's Victoria Row. Their days had been consumed with edgy, fraught hours at the hospice, followed by funeral arrangements and bank meetings. The sun smiled down and they finally had an opportunity to absorb a day at regular speed. That night Lynne sent me an email titled, "Before I Die Board." (I wondered if it was a typo. Before I die "bored"?) She had attached a picture of an art installation on the corner of Richmond and Queen Streets.

The larger-than-life blackboard read, "Before I Die..." and was a colourful list of wishes and dreams both serious and jokey. Like, "be in love," "Skydive!" "Touch lots of boobies" and "win the Nobel prize." Lynne had written, "go to Fiji/Africa," and I recognized Kim's chalk font immediately, "WALK THE CAMINO."

It wasn't written in stone, but chalk would do. Like elementary-school-era love admissions on the blackboard: "Jules + Kim, 4-EVER. T.I.D. T.I.N.D." (Translation: true if destroyed, true if not destroyed.)

In a totally Alanis Morissette "Ironic" kind of way, the woman who took Kim and Lynne's picture in front of the blackboard had walked the Camino in the spring. Kim had barely chalked the words out and Sarah said, "Oh my god! We just did the Camino!"

Emails were exchanged and, before I knew it, the groundwork was in place. Sarah and Kim were email BFFs and we felt lucky for the insider knowledge and cosmic connection.

Sarah and Kim's divine meeting in Charlottetown in front of a Before I Die... board was both prophetic and poetic in my mind. It was just the beginning of several unexpected connections (and disconnections) we would soon encounter.

Sidewalk

- - - - - - - - - - - - - - - - - - - -

"*Are we going to look gay* with matching packs?"

After a week of using our makeshift, too small and too big day packs, awkwardly filled with tinned chickpeas, stewed tomatoes and a bag of mixed beach sand from Aruba, Curacao, Hurghada and Zanzibar, we found our packs. I settled first (mostly because I was tiring of driving to and fro to gear shops). The Osprey Tempest was a 30L and fit like my favourite pair of jeans. Empty at least. I'd walked around SAIL and Mountain Equipment Co-op with their bags of sand before making this monumental decision that I'd be saddled with for a steady month. The day packs were doing more harm than good and our biological Camino clock was ticking. A few days later, Kim dropped her pseudo-pack to the ground. Trying to stuff four and a half kilos into such a small bag made it appear like a Butterball turkey strapped to her back. "Let me try your pack on again."

Minutes later she called our local outfitter, Suntrail Source for Adventure, in Hepworth (still 45 minutes away) and ordered a black Osprey. Instead of looking gay and matchy-matchy, we decided we'd look like two women with very similar great taste. Kim's bag wouldn't arrive for another week, so we took turns swapping my Osprey.

Our front step (or "base camp" as we dubbed it) resembled a whacked pinata fall-out. Punky socks dried in the sun, bras hung on the doorknob, insoles baked on the steps. The humidex had continued to climb in August and Kim launched into a new worry with heat rashes. She was already doing sock changes once every six kilometres or so and was feeling rubbed the wrong way by the merino socks that were supposed to be miracle workers. Her Keen Terradora high-top hikers left their mark and just days into training she had blisters balloon up on the tops of her toes where the Keens bent with each stride. We had read too many horror stories about blisters to dwell and Kim began applying Vaseline to her feet like a teen boy hoses on AXE body spray. Not to be braggy, but I'd been hiking in my Vasque Grand Traverse low-cuts for a few months already and was unperturbed by the extra pavement time.

"Wake, walk and wine" was our new mantra. I thought my back would be as stiff as American singer Tiffany's 1986 mall bangs with the added weight on my frame. As we increased mileage by the day, I wondered if maybe I'd been granted the super human power of being stiffness-free.

Still, I refused to do anything unnecessary or compromising. I balked at replacing the screening on our older neighbour's sliding doors. Bending was never something that came easily to me, especially after the d-e-h-u-m-i-d-i-f-i-e-r incident of 2015. We tactfully decided not to eat expired yogurt. I made an executive decision to use Dove body wash instead of the brick-sized organic bar of honey and cardamom soap that could be a game changer if dropped on either of our feet from waist level.

Of course, there were things we couldn't leave undone before truly leaving our house and property unattended for six weeks. "Did you pay the property taxes? What about that second installment on the annual sewer bill? Okay, if we are away until

November 1, we'll need to pay the satellite TV and internet bills two months in advance."

We had to put our community garden plot to bed early. After a profusion of basil, rocket greens and a healthy beet year, not much was left. The earth was cracked and Mojave-like from zero rain. We had one micro butternut squash that looked like a discount child's toy instead of a possible dinner side. Two hot peppers were still an unripe lime green, and our potential Great Pumpkin (à la Charlie Brown) didn't look like it had much more oomph in it. We opted to leave the malnourished pumpkin for our return. "We can pick it on our way home from the airport for Halloween, we'll be home in time!"

Kim squeezed in her grand finale golf round with my dad at Cobble Beach, as most courses would be closed upon our return. We had to think two months in advance and the list jumped from changing furnace filters to topping up the water softener salt to "how long can we put our last haircut off until?"

I hoped the hummingbirds wouldn't hold a grudge the following spring when they returned, as we had to bring in their feeder two weeks earlier than normal. We had house-sitters lined up, but asking them to feed hummingbirds might have been a stretch. We only had one houseplant for them to tend to, but we didn't want to press our luck with a six-week babysitting gig.

We sent in our last Coast Watchers report, part of a volunteer stint we had been involved with since we moved to the Northern Bruce Peninsula in 2016. Kim and I were responsible for monitoring the shoreline at Black Creek Provincial Park for boat traffic, beach-goers, micro plastics, algae blooms and unusual natural activity. It was an easy eight kilometres round trip to Black Creek to do the Beaufort (wind) measurements, wave direction and bird counts. We counted it as training in disguise.

In between, we learned *soupçon* Spanish. We were only going to be in France for three days, so surely we could rely on our combined high school French classes to order beer, a croissant and find a toilet.

Luckily, all good and essential things in Spanish end in *o*. For example, *corto* (small beer), *vino tinto* (red wine), *chorizo* (sausage), *bano* (toilet) and *queso* (cheese). And Camino! Outside of that, we would have to rely on old Menudo song lyrics and Speedy Gonzales expressions. I also had my trusty/rusty Costa Rica jungle sabbatical to rely on. I thoughtfully enrolled in a one-month Spanish course at Mohawk College before I flew to San José (circa 1994). My take away? *El gato es negro*. (The cat is black.) If Kim and I were super lucky, we would see a black cat drinking red wine and be able to communicate this unusual event to a local. Provided we were on the right side of the Pyrenees.

Wake. Walk. Wine.

We documented our last official WWW training day on September 16, participating in the annual Terry Fox Run/Walk along our beloved Isthmus Bay. We cracked 400 kilometres of prep in less than a month. Forty-two participants raised over $10,000 in our tiny town of Lion's Head, Ontario, alone. Kim and I completed the ten-kilometre route as though it were a true walk in the park. Our next "walk" was going to be substantially longer. We ate the free hot dogs offered post-event in a daze, like we were having an out-of-body experience. Maybe we were. The Terry Fox route was a mere ten kilometres. We had logged 400 kilometres and probably needed new hikers already. It was 800 kilometres to Santiago and another 120 kilometres if we carried on to Finisterre, the "End of the World" on Spain's turbulent Atlantic coast.

For the uninitiated, here's what you might not know about the Camino. The Way is actually a couple of different ways. The traditional and popular pilgrim route, the Camino Francés (the French Way), has a few variants as well.

On day one, pilgrims must choose between the Napoleon route across the Pyrenees or the alternate that is less of a climb and elevation gain as it winds around the base of the mountain. Camino Francés splits off a number of times depending on terrain, allowing pilgrims to choose between flat roadways or shorter but steeper ascents. There are nine major alternate routes like the Primitivo (original) route, Camino Ingles (the English Way), the Silver Way from Seville and the Camino Finisterre (End of the World) among others. They all feed in like spaghetti noodles from coastal Portugal to the south, northern Spain and France's deeper interior. The branches all align before Santiago de Compostela, especially in Sarria, where the marching population triples. Sarria is located 120 kilometres from Santiago, and those who travel (by foot or horse) the last 100 kilometres of the Camino earn the coveted Pilgrim Certificate or "credentials" (cyclists must cover 200 km). Officials in Santiago review and qualify credentials (also referred to as "passport books") to ensure authenticity of the stamps collected along the Way. I'm not sure who or why you would fake this out, but that's just the facts ma'am.

Other true facts? We had dropped $4,882.64 on gear and flights already. And we hadn't even started.

We nervously laid out our Chinook Thermopalm Hooded 10°C sleeping bags, GoToobs of coconut shampoo and conditioner, zip-off pants, quarter socks, Coolpix cam, long johns and soap packets. I pulled a tee out of my pile. Kim added a long sleeve. We eliminated a Ziploc of trail mix. Did I need two or three blank notebooks? Brevity won out. Two.

We analyzed everything. It was like an outdoorsy version of *The Bachelor* rose ceremony. What item would remain for another day? We had no other days. We stuffed our packs one last time with much deliberation and the welcome fizzy distraction of Prosecco. I put our packs on the scale and both registered just shy of four and a half kilos. The weight of the world on our shoulders!

We'd reached fighting weight. It was time to Aerosmith/ Run DMC/Macy Gray/Billy Joel it (whatever version you prefer) and "walk this Way."

Walk This Way

- -

Not to sound all Shirley MacLaine, but I'd been dreaming of frogs nonstop. According to my bedside Select Pocket Library *Dreamer's Dictionary* by Mal Thompson, frogs were symbolic of a need to engage in behaviour that refreshes the soul. The dictionary assured me that I needed time to do whatever I needed to do in order to feel refreshed. I suppose I could have drawn a hot bath and poured a glass of shiraz, but instead I cross-referenced my more mystical copy of *The Dreamer's Dictionary: From A to Z...3,000 Magical Mirrors to Reveal the Meaning of Your Dreams* by Lady Stearn Robinson and Tom Corbett and they agreed. Frogs were a good thing. Whether I saw them or ate them in my dream, they signified personal contentment and success within my sphere of activity.

September 17 would prove to be 24 hours of *activity* from the moment we turned left out of our driveway past the herds of black Angus cattle and the two emus on West Road to the halogen glow of Toronto's lit-up circuit board and tail lights.

It was a fluid day(s) of queues, customs, airport beers, a very mad dash to catch the nonrefundable flight from Paris to Biarritz and another sprint to a bus that felt like the equivalent of an hour-long Scrambler ride at the fall fair. The roundabouts and 180s had me ready to heave, and I couldn't wait to get off all the planes, trains and automobiles to simply walk for a month.

By the time we reached Saint-Jean-Pied-de-Port, it was my birthday. Fuzzy from the flights, both Kim and I had completely forgotten about it with the (GMT+1) six-hour time change. A customs agent smiled wide as he scanned my passport. "September 18. *Bonne fête, madame.*"

We landed in pure sunshine with an instant mission to locate our Airbnb at Esteban Etxea dans la Rue Peitonne de Garazi at 29 Rue de la Citadelle Nouvelle-Aquitaine. It was a marbled mouthful, so I smartly copied the address in large font in hope of finding a local who could point a finger in the right direction.

We recognized fellow road-weary travellers, ruffled but with telltale shiny gear at the ready. Trekking poles clicked along the cobblestones, guiding a hot mess of jetlagged and bloodshot-eyed internationals. It was a catwalk parade of quick-dry, merino wool and several European brands we didn't recognize but made quick note of (*Must find pair of orange Ternua hikers!). Osprey packs were a popular choice, so we felt like we at least looked the part.

It was a congruent flow of traffic along Rue de la Citadelle. Scooters, tractors loaded with hay bales, handsomely maintained Russian-issue Ladas and cutesy Peugeots and Citroëns the same size as North American baby strollers. There were no blaring horns, just symmetry.

Camino bikers were already flexing their land legs and cranking well-oiled mountain bikes past us, flipping through gears. A few Swedes weaved past with quad muscles that revealed the rectus femoris, vastus lateralis, vastus medialis and vastus intermedius like the anatomy charts in massage college.

The fever of anticipation was undeniably palpable and I gave my own quads a squeeze to make sure they were still there.

The Pyrenees pricked the fired clay sky and loomed in the way that ominous clouds do on the day of an outdoor wedding. Taunting and daunting, the Pyrenees were our first roadblock to Spain, just eight kilometres away. I forced myself to reel in my focus and take in the walled city with its fairy tale landscape. Saint-Jean-Pied-de-Port appropriately translates as "Saint Jean at the foot of the pass." Saint-Jean-Pied-de-Port is the capital of the heritage-dense Basque province of Lower Navarre. The Pont d'Eyheraberry (Eyheraberry bridge) over the Nive River is a ceremonial passage as one departs the city for the foothills of the Pyrenees and the Roncesvalles pass. It reminded me of the kind of place where Mole and Rat from *The Wind in the Willows* would have a boozy picnic with dandelion fritters and minnow pâté amuse-bouche.

It took a few passes, but Kim was the first to realize that our Airbnb address was the same place with the merry singer encouraging passersby to try his apricot shakes from a streetside window. In between whirs of his industrial blender, we were able to charade communicate that we didn't want shakes at the moment, but we had reserved a room. Luis, doing double duty as host and smoothie maker, insisted we have a sample anyway and ushered us in with grand gestures.

Inside, we felt the reliable coolness of a whitewashed stone interior. Hammocks were slung haphazardly around the space and Kim and I both had a flash of fear. Did we book two nights in a hammock? For 200 bucks? Apricot shakes or not, there was going to be a rebellion!

Instead, Luis asked us to remove our hiking boots and follow him upstairs. It was a magnificent crash pad with the juxtaposition of hammocks, canvas director's chairs and ornate chandeliers. The stone walls instantly swept us back to our own stone cottage on the Grand River in Galt. What if we just stayed with Luis for a month? I looked at the shower longingly, it could easily be found in the pages of *Dwell*. A floor-to-ceiling bamboo privacy wall (or "not-so-privacy wall" as Kim believed) delineated the massage treatment room adjacent to our chamber. Our suite had a king bed, and white curtains billowed in from our balcony that overlooked the terrace of spilling flowers and potted palms below. Dramatic foothills emerged from the plumes of mist just beyond the storied wall. Sheep bleated. I desperately wanted to count sheep and fall into a daylong sleep but knew that napping would be dangerous. Logically, Kim reasoned we should find a patio and pints instead.

On the corner of Place du Trinquet and Avenue Rinaud, we nabbed a table in full sun. Patios were buzzing as servers appeared and disappeared with trays of gold beer, plates of chorizo, pork, salami and grilled peppers.

We haphazardly ordered, understanding that we were getting *carne* (meat) of some sort and pints of Carlsberg for sure. For ten euros, we were presented with a platter of meat – enough to make Dagwood sub sandwiches for a family of six. The baguette was as long as my leg, served with a dish of butter. I'd found my ideal dietary plan and best ever birthday dinner. Nothing could make me happier than five pounds of prosciutto, sausage and shaved *lomo embuchado* (air-dried pork loin). People-watching here was like a sport, and we tried not to be smug all situated and settled with beers as a busload of new arrivals bumbled around with maps and frowns much like we had just an hour before.

My brain felt a little shrink-wrapped with the altitude adjustment and too much *lomo*.

Satiated with meat, we did a grocery store run for cheaper beer to chill for later and staked out where to buy our official pilgrim credentials. We found them for three euros at the tourist office, but they were two euros at the *peregrino* (pilgrim's) office. Our precious commodity came in a Ziploc sleeve, along with maps showcasing the undulating elevation ahead and a formidable list of *albergues* (hostels).

The pilgrim's office was jammed with twitchy arrivals bombarding a half-dozen rattled but gracious volunteers. We decided to return the next day and poked around the souvenir motherland instead. There were stuffed sheep wearing berets, scallop shell *everything*, buffs, tees and balms for every body part. Vendor stalls tempted with peaches bigger than shot puts and linear fig displays that could have doubled as art. Tiny shops selling wheels of cheese as big as our SUV's tires and duck confit were jammed with retail-rabid patrons like it was Christmas Eve.

Every door had an ornate doorknocker and we marvelled at September flowerboxes still radiant with blooms. Lipstick red roses, pink bubble gum hydrangeas and spiderworts cascaded out of every window. Skyscraper-high plane trees with scaling bark like a sycamore lined the park paths. Kitties of all colours emerged at sunset, mewling and scrapping over bits found in the garbage bins. We followed every secret cobbled passageway and stone bridge until retiring by the river with a few Kronenbourgs.

"Are we really here? Are we doing this?" Kim asked.

None of it felt real. It was a panorama for poets and dreamers. I felt like we should be drinking cognac like aristocrats. Instead we were drinking cans of beer with our flip-flops kicked off. An affectionate neighbourhood cat joined us and was very glad we had ordered a platter of meat earlier in the day.

Back at our Airbnb, apricot shake production had come to a close. There was quiet din from Luis's kitchen below our room and a bigger din outside as three pilgrims swapped stories. I had a shower hot enough to boil a lobster and flopped onto the bed that appeared softer than reality.

Semi-eavesdropping, I learned this: there was a Brazilian who was currently living in China, an unemployed teacher from Hamilton, a guy from Colombia whose responses were largely lost in translation, and a yappy Dutchman. Kim and I listened for a while but fell asleep wondering what the hell the mattress could be stuffed with. Deflated soccer balls and coconuts?

Kim found sleep before me. She already had a distinct advantage over me as she was an expert with insomnia and highly skilled at functioning on a few hours of scattered sleep. She would fare well in the hostels. I was already stiffening with irritation from the chatter from the terrace.

My body was asleep before my brain as I ran through all the beds we had slept (and not slept) in around the world. I focused on a silly bed in Egypt, in the Siwa Oasis where the pillows were like cement sacks. Our ears burned and ached for hours after we were awake and it took just as long to shake our legs and arms back to tingly life. This was luxury though. The rest of the Camino would be like summer camp for adults. I hadn't slept in a bunk bed since I shared one with my brother 30 years ago.

Something our Airbnb host had casually said to us earlier continued to bounce around my head like a housefly against a windowpane.

"The hardest part of the Camino is the social. The community. North Americans, you like to come home, shut the door and watch TV, 300 channels. It is very different here, in Europe, and on the Camino. It is not the bag on your back, it is the weight of the bags in your head that is the problem on the Camino."

And, possibly, the bags under my eyes.

Making Mountains out of Foothills

- -

Revived by a potent, milky coffee and a freshly blended peach juice, I watched the last of the fog hug the foothills before burning off. Tiny birds flitted in and out of the roses that appeared like coloured buttons along the fenceline of the Airbnb. The millennials who had chattered well into the night appeared to be on a different sleeping shift. I heard phones pinging in the night and a very early whistle of the teakettle. It may have been our host, Luis, on breakfast prep.

It was our last day to recoup and get the static out of our heads before the 24-kilometre climb up and over the horizon. I felt like I got arthritis for my 44th birthday after two days of sitting on various modes of transport. I doubted I would complain about sitting in a month's time. Luis plied us with stories in between drags of his cigarette, producing a baguette with black cherry and myrtle jam preserves. A thick yogurt followed and then a single fried egg and offer of another baguette.

The streets were fragrant with laundered sheets flapping in the breeze. Cotton candy hydrangeas seemed to right their posture with the moving sun. Kim and I returned to the pilgrim's office early, hoping to beat the mob. They had one museum-worthy desktop in the back for public use. Kim wanted to send one last smoke signal to our friends and family, alerting the wolf pack that we were going off-grid until Santiago. We would kick it old school with postcards, as per usual. Dealing with the French keyboard (as I was apparently ordained the Camino Communications Manager in the relationship) was a patience-squeezing trial. The *A* was located where the *Q* traditionally was, the *M* was on the second row beside the *L* and the *Z* was mysteriously in the first row beside the *A*. On this crazy AZERTY vs. QWERTY keyboard I couldn't access the @ symbol, making the simple entry of email addresses impossible. I opened a Google page and found a company address with the godforsaken @ symbol embedded in it and hammered out an email with more *Q*s than were probably intended. I tried to explain my hot tear of swearing to Kim, who apologized for not bringing her reading glasses with her. "The *W* is beside the *X* and the question mark is beside the *N* for chrissakes. It's like ESL typing!" My intended long and glowing Paul Theroux-esque email was immediately reduced to staccato sentences. *Had $10 euro plate of meat. Airbnb bed more like bedrock. Cheap Gouda. Cheaper wine. Xo*

With the social obligations tended to, we had other pressing chores to address. We needed a jackknife for picnics. Because we didn't trust checking a bag at the airport, we couldn't pack one of the many Swiss Army knives we had at home. Kim had to find new trekking poles too (even though she also had a pair at home), as early research indicated poles weren't allowed in carry-on. I was going to wing it with free-swinging arms.

After little debate, we had decided to do carry-on from Toronto to ensure our bags were with us (or safely stowed in the overhead bin) upon arrival in France. (Travel hack: If you're travelling with someone, split your gear evenly in your packs. If one bag doesn't arrive to your destination, at least you can continue on.)

We also needed scallop shells to attach to our packs. It's a rite of passage and widely adopted prerequisite and only two euros for such authenticity. They come in all sizes, of course, from discreet silver dollars to shells bigger than an individual chicken pot pie.

"If we lose these or they break, it doesn't mean anything, okay?" Kim reassured me. I was definitely the superstitious, heebie-jeebie type in the family and was relieved to hear this disclaimer. We chose two that "spoke" to us – orange overtones for me and a pristine white shell for Kim, both with the Cross of Saint James (also referred to as the "Santiago Cross") painted in red. (I'd yet to discover my favourite way to experience the signature cross. It would be in icing sugar atop the Tarte de Santiago, a traditional moist Galician cake made with ground almonds and lemon zest.) The cross is composed of a cross *fitchy* (the lower limb is pointed as if to be driven in the ground) with a cross *fleury* (arms that extend in a fleur-de-lys). I was ready for my *Jeopardy* debut. "Alex, I'll take crosses for $10,000." Deeper down I hoped the Way wouldn't be too Jesus-y and on that out-loud admission to Kim, we filtered into a buzzy patio and chugged two generic French blonde lagers for less than a euro. Amen. The *joie de vivre* oozed.

Adapting easily to our soon-to-be-24/7 picnic diet, we went to the local grocer for Pyrenees-worthy packed lunch items. I was making my way through all the snack-sized bags of unusual Lays chip flavours: cheese quesadilla, paprika and cheeseburger. The grocery store cruise always takes longer than anticipated when I'm involved. I want to look in every burbling fish tank at the black-knuckled crabs and *pulpo* (octopus). Even though I was clearly not in the market, I wanted to check out the olive trees for sale and touch the darling mini kiwis.

"Look at these Colombian avocadoes! They're obscene!"

Kim was stuck and overwhelmed in the cheese section. "Look how cheap this Gouda is! For two euros you can buy a round bigger than a lawnmower wheel. *And* a bottle of wine. Two euros!" We were in love with France, even if it was for only a few more blessed hours. We piled cured meats, Gouda, vino and baguette onto the conveyor belt.

We climbed the topsy-turvy stairs off Rue de la Citadelle to the namesake 17th-century Citadelle to be rewarded with a knockout view (and knock-you-out whiff of sheep manure). The French military building has been repurposed as a school and I imagined dried sheep turd fights as the reasonable facsimile of the standard Canadian recess snowball fight. For such rotund livestock, their gumball-sized pellets were better matched to a rabbit than a sheep.

Sheep with colourful dots on their bums casually posed for Instagram accounts. Years ago, an Irish sheepherder in County Clare schooled me on the pigmented rumps. They can be used for breeding purposes or to indicate a few things: an injured or ill sheep, a nursing ewe or simply as painted proof that "Hey, that ewe is mine."

We took our own tired rumps back to the riverside park to see if our little tortoiseshell cat friend (we named her Lucille) was lurking about. She was. Lucille definitely belonged to someone – she was collared but still very happy to curl up in my lap. I couldn't believe it.

Lucille wasn't an *el gato es negro*, but a *gato de carey* (tortoiseshell cat). More appropriately, as we were still in France, in French, Lucille was a *chat écaille de tortue* (a tortoiseshell).

I'm sure I anxiously petted Lucille within an inch of her life as I thought about the fast-approaching day ahead. When we returned to our Airbnb, I pulled my jeans off for the last time in exchange for the quick-dry technology of the month ahead. Luis was happy to take our jeans as clothing donations to the local church.

Kim set our travel alarm clock for 5:30 a.m.

"Can you believe we're here? We're actually doing this?"

We hugged until there was no space left between us. The only creature comfort we had packed for the month ahead was each other.

ONE

↓

Basque Country
AND
Navarra

"Buen Camino" or "good way" is
a universally understood daily
exchange of well-wishing shared
by pilgrims of all languages.

Pyrenees, Paellas and Pints

Saint-Jean-Pied-de-Port to Roncesvalles (24.7 km)

- -

"*Girls, do you want bacon?*" Luis hollered from the kitchen. The lights were thoughtfully dim as we pulled up chairs around a set table. It was squid ink black out on the terrace where we had lazed about with more punchy cups of coffee than normal just the day before.

I downed a sweet shot of pale green melon juice. Coffee barely jolted me as I was already jittery enough on my own accord. A Québécois woman joined us in the buttery light, cradling a soup bowl of flowery tea. We didn't chat beyond a pleasant *bonjour*, respecting the communal visualization of our Pyrenees crossing.

Luis slid plates in front of Kim and me. The bacon wasn't of the traditional Canadian style that we were foolishly expecting. Instead of fatty, sizzling strips, the French "bacon" was fridge-cold, and the thin folds of pork were so salty my veins instantly turned into the California water table. *Dry.* I forced down some baguette, though it felt like it was just sitting in my esophagus. Luis delivered another very fried egg once our bacon rations disappeared. Kim and I were both anxious to get out the door already and were hugging Luis goodbye by 6:45 a.m. The French woman was still nursing her tea and checking emails, cool as a cucumber.

We didn't account for the sunrise being so late.

"Is it really 6:45?" I asked Kim.

It seemed too dark – not that I was ever up at that hour, ever. Stars were still blinking and the few streetlamps revealed the milky fog that hung low over Rue de la Citadelle.

After a few minutes of unnecessary fiddling, Kim leaned in for a kiss, stabbing me for the first time (but not the last time) in the shin with her new poles. With only a few downhill steps in, I clunked the left toe of my hiker off a cobblestone, sending a hot and prickly surge through my system. We had been operating with the heightened awareness of detection dogs sniffing out contraband for the last month. Now was not the time to do a header because I was still sleepwalking.

Had we trained enough for this? When my sister was training for her first marathon, she never ran the full 42-kilometre distance until race day. Marathon training is designed to increase your endurance in a 12 to 20-week period, but the longest advised run falls way short of the 42 mark. It's all about tempo, stride, intervals, pacing, rest days. I thought this was semi-crazy, but of the half-dozen half-marathons I had run, I didn't train at all, outside of my usual daily five-kilometre loop. It was all a mental thing, wasn't it? I realize that running a full marathon with the same philosophy wouldn't be wise, but a spontaneous 21 kilometres was doable (at least in my 30s). In our pre-Camino training around the Ferndale Flats, our longest day was 24 kilometres, half-running from the obsessive deer flies that circled our heads and bare legs.

Kim broke my stream of consciousness with a loud, "Where is everyone?"

As we crossed the stone bridge over the Nive River her voice echoed in the stillness. "Is the Camino closed today?"

We expected a parade of pilgrims exiting Saint-Jean-Pied-de-Port. Kim thought we should leave even sooner than we did to get a jump on the crowd. We hadn't booked our first night's accommodations, despite the wide-eyed affirmations that we'd be dinked without a reservation. "You might have to continue on from Roncesvalles another six kilometres to Espinal if the Collegiate is full!"

There were only three options at day's end. In Roncesvalles (also referred to as "Roncevaux"), the Collegiate was the likely drop zone. With 183 beds, the hostel lottery luck was high. A smaller private hotel with ten beds, Casa Sabina, didn't answer its phone and the stately Hotel Roncesvalles would involve blowing our entire accommodation budget on one posh night. Looking around the very empty streets of Saint-Jean, Kim and I felt a little more confident that we'd have a bunk to claim.

"Let's not let the hysteria get to us."

Our time in the pilgrim's office was so brief, but it was a hotbed of panic as pure strangers swapped horror stories about bed bugs at the municipal hostels and then, of course, there was someone who knew somebody that couldn't find a place to sleep and had to walk over 50 kilometres. Everyone except us had a story to contribute, all ramping up the neuroses of day one. It was the inner workings of mob mentality!

We paused at the historic city gate, Porte Saint-Jacques, to say nonreligious prayers to the Saint of Body Parts to hold us together. The famed gateway to the walled city was added to the UNESCO World Heritage Site list in 1988. The French Way is also listed on the World Heritage list. The Bruce Peninsula, where Kim and I bought a house in 2017, is part of a UNESCO-designated World Biosphere Reserve. I suddenly felt qualified to narrate a *Heritage Minutes* doc.

My cinematic career musings continued with the sharp incline introduced immediately after the symbolic city gate like a sucker punch. I wondered if our legs would transform into Marvel comic characters like She-Hulk, Juggernaut and Mister Fantastic. For the film adaptation of our Camino experience, I settled on Robin Wright's sinewy Antiope from *Wonder Woman* as my body double. Kim leaned toward Jamie Lee Curtis and her *True Lies* bod.

"Holy hell," Kim said, feeling the same injection of cement in her calf muscles as I did. It was still so black out. I definitely needed to incorporate more carrots into my diet.

Suddenly, a flock of 40 white doves lifted into the air from a rooftop, causing me to let out my own "Holy hell!" This had to be a good omen.

"I still can't believe that it's just us! It's just weird," Kim remarked, finding a smooth rhythm with her new poles.

"I can't believe how bloody dark it is!" The road ahead simply disappeared. We moved along quietly and heard an owl's low and distinct hoot carry across the valley. We were only minutes outside of town, but the landscape had already shifted from urban to pastoral. The owl called again, eliciting shivers. A rooster sounded off and a chorus of ding-a-lings grew closer. Skinny-legged, curly-horned sheep pressed against the fence line. I thanked them again for their gift of Smartwool socks.

I'd never been happier to see dawn lift into day. It was an enchanting cantaloupe sunrise. We had climbed above the fog and shroud of the valley through pockets of humid air.

"Remember when we stayed at that bird reserve in Colombia? When we rode on the back of those dirt bikes above the coffee plantations?" I asked Kim. Here we seemed even higher in altitude already. We woke up in the clouds at the El Dorado Bird Reserve in Minca – but in this spot the clouds below us were like a dizzying atmospheric ocean that pulled in and out. We could see the Latxa sheep fully now, poking about on their stilted legs. Their wool hung in snagged shreds like candy floss on the wire fence from aggressive scratching.

It was easy to see the ice age's movement. Random chunks of rock dragged along as land caved, collapsed and succumbed to the continental carving. Kim pointed out sheep on a distant hilltop – they were the size of Tic Tacs.

By full light, we'd finally, reassuringly crossed paths with a few pilgrims. It's easy to doubt your route when you fail to see anyone for an hour. Luis had told us there would always be people ahead of us and behind.

"Always. You never get lost. You will find Napoleon route no problem," he promised.

The Napoleon route passes directly over the Pyrenees and (spoiler alert) the mountain pass is the very place where Emilio Estevez's character died in *The Way*. There was a low rumble between pilgrims in Saint-Jean of pop-up weather sometimes making the Pyrenees impassable, but it seemed impossible to us as the mercury climbed to 25°C before 10:00 a.m. I couldn't fathom anything life-threatening transpiring but heatstroke. Still, I kept in mind that real pilgrims had died on the Way or needed to be rescued from this point.

The Valcarlos alternate route was apparently less scenic but a more viable option for creaky knees. There are no shortcuts in the Pyrenees and, though the elevation gain was more reasonable, the Valcarlos variant to Roncesvalles was still a steady go at 24 kilometres.

At Orisson (eight kilometres from Saint-Jean), a dozen pilgrims were already downing coffee and trading out socks. What time did they start? Five? Many of them had headlamps still affixed to their heads, so possibly. Though Orisson is referred to as a hamlet in guidebooks, it's simply two albergues, a cafe and a welcome water refill stop. The view is startling and the coffee and camaraderie were already in full swing around the picnic tables.

Kim and I pushed on after changing Smartwools and drinking full bottles of water. We wanted to have Col de Loepeder and its 1450-metre peak behind us as solid confirmation we could do this.

We passed a surprisingly tall woman swaying along with a plastic bag. Her ginger hair blew haphazardly around her head and it seemed as though she was just on a stroll back from the corner store where she bought a few apples and a loaf of bread.

"*Buen Camino*," she called out and we returned the mandatory international salutation.

From our quick observations, there was no distinct pilgrim profile. Line a dozen pilgrims up and it would be difficult to peg the unifying connection. Curling team members? Winners of a 50/50 draw? People who rode the tallest roller coaster in the world?

We passed all ages and nationalities in Hokas, Teva sandals, Scarpa approach shoes, GORE-TEX leather-upper boots. Boots were well loved or squeaky new. There were tall compression socks, no socks, crew socks. There were countless Osprey packs, a few North Face rucksacks, Fjällräven daypacks – from 30L to 80L. But crossing the Pyrenees with a plastic shopping bag?

Our unscheduled but nearly halfway lunch stop allowed us to take in more of our compatriots as they trundled past. There were flags stitched on packs that we didn't recognize, enthusiastic whistlers, less enthusiastic hummers with earbuds, chatty Koreans and several faces hardened with focus.

"Baguette number six!" I announced to Kim, unwrapping our crude sandwiches. They were as dry as cat kibble without our usual squirts of mustard and mayo. The prosciutto was rather tough and I spat out a ball of meat that had turned into chewy bubble gum.

"How are the wheels?" I asked Kim with a smirk. It was my dad's favourite question – whether I had just run a race or finished a soccer match. "Wheels," in my dad's lingua franca meant "legs." In every phone conversation or email prior to our departure date he wondered, "How are the wheels holding up?"

"Feeling Ferndale Flat?" I pressed.

Kim was engrossed in inspecting every inch of her feet on high alert for any sign of friction.

"Actually, my legs feel good. I can feel that first eight in my shins, but otherwise surprisingly good."

While my dad wasn't overly thrilled that we were going to be offline and walking clear across a foreign country for a month, he was supportive. My mom admitted that she thought we were boring.

"I mean, you guys could have moved anywhere and you bought a house in Ontario. Kim's retired, and you can work wherever you like, Jules. If I were you, I would have gone to Europe and moved around every couple of months. You need to walk around Wales, then you'll see."

So she was supportive too, in her own roundabout way. Even though we were boring Ontario homeowners walking the Camino.

As we finished our daily baguette intake, three horses thundered up the hill, clods of earth flying behind them like a genuine chase scene. The mare had to be pregnant with twins as she was as wide as a Mini Cooper.

Setting off, we slowed to admire another chestnut horse standing stock-still in the middle of the paved path. He created quite a stir with urban pilgrims with his stoic grace and presence. This encounter was just the first of several intersections with wild and unbridled Spain.

The last eight kilometres of our day would be the most trying. It was a cruel test of kneecap stability and balance as we rode down sections of loose scree on the bottoms of our Vibram soles. I couldn't help but cycle through various pains that jumped from my gut to my shoulder to my head. Now was not the time for appendicitis or an aneurysm. It was time for a beer – that was unanimous.

The scrabbly rock was prime territory for an ankle roll. Rock and roll, indeed. The descent levelled out and the slippery slope became pavement again. It was a peculiar high, entering Roncesvalles. One of survival. It had been a steady seven hours on a never-ending cocktail of adrenalin and euphoria.

The Collegiate appeared behind a break of fir and oaks. A large group had amassed in the grassy area next to the path, pointing fingers, checking watches and looking possibly disgruntled.

"Shit. What if the Collegiate is full?" Kim said.

"We don't know that. And I don't remember passing 178 people today." I liked to reserve my panic for situations that were 100 per cent confirmed.

Passing the group, we overheard a loud talker on their phone, explaining that the Collegiate doors were closed until two o'clock and then it was first come, first served. A queue had already begun in the shade and Kim and I fell in line. The process was seamless as soon as the doors opened. Volunteers ushered us in and asked that boots be shelved in the designated room that was already potent with past feet and sour insoles.

"English? Credentials?"

Our first stamp was applied with a firm slap of ink on paper. "Breakfast too? Fill in this form. Pay here. Remember, lights out at ten o'clock. Doors locked."

The Collegiate Church of Roncesvalles was constructed to care for and protect pilgrims and is one of the few (and largest) that is open year-round. It would be our inaugural experience sharing a co-ed dorm room with 60 of our non-closest friends.

A gruff Dane in the lower bunk across from me piped up, "This is the nicest one on the Camino. It goes downhill from here." Such sunny optimism on day one!

I was impressed by how fluidly the system worked. It was a steady and congruent flow of Japanese women in floppy hats, a few solo Dutch dudes and twentysomethings with man buns flip-flopping to the showers at the end of the wing. We leaned toward beer first and showering later, when the crowds thinned again for the nearby church service and dinner.

We "made" our bunks, which consisted of a shake, fluff and quick uncrumpling of our sleeping bags. Starchy pillowcases were provided for 12 euros (each), along with a breakfast token for Casa Sabina in the morning. On our way out we stopped to take in the vending machine inventory on the lower level of the Collegiate.

"Oh my god, you can get everything from Wagon Wheels to spaghetti Bolognese!" I couldn't believe the selection of curries, Swedish meatballs and instant noodles.

But we were in Spain and vending machine spag Bol seemed almost sacrilege, although Kim was tempted. Behind the Collegiate, we found refuge at the break-the-bank Hotel Roncesvalles. The beers were still reasonable considering the venue. However, our beer bill was soon going to ring in higher than our first night's sleep. At four euros each, the Estrellas remedied our thirst and daylong jitters. We clinked our glasses with such enthusiasm they should have split in two. We toasted our friend PJ, who had recently discovered she had 1 per cent Iberian ancestry via one of those mail-away spit tests that analyze your DNA.

"To PJ! We're in the Iberian Peninsula!" Kim announced.

"Are we?" I wondered.

"Close enough."

We cheered to Kim not having an asthma attack at Col de Loepeder. We celebrated not having appendicitis or forgetting our baguette sandwiches at Luis's place.

"Do you think that woman with the plastic bag made it?" I asked.

From our vantage point on the patio of the fancy-pants hotel, we could see pilgrims hobbling into the village, some already bandaged and limping. The sheer willpower! At 44, I felt like I was left with no excuses watching sturdy silver-haired women and men with sculpted calves pass by.

The sunshine was uninterrupted as we checked out the village too. Aside from La Posada, there were only a few games in town. We filed into Casa Sabina where the beers were still four euros a pop. Looking at the menu, the kilometres caught up with us.

"Hey, we *are* in Iberia!" Kim exclaimed, noticing paella Iberian on the menu for 12 euros. We figured it would be an expensive night as everyone was funnelling into one spot and many started their Camino on the leeward side of the Pyrenees, skipping the guaranteed defibrillator of the mountain pass from France.

The paella pan was delivered and devoured. The mix of savoury butter beans, snappy green beans, fatty chorizo and *pollo* (chicken) folded into buttery Arborio rice was a miracle, really.

Still managing to walk in a forward direction, we dropped into La Posada for a nightcap. Kim easily found us seats as most everyone had filtered out and were probably wisely sleeping. We were too wired though. Or so we thought. After two glasses of Tempranillo and a steamy shower, Kim and I fell asleep in our bunks like we were drugged, oblivious to our 60 coughing, sneezing, shifting, snoring roomies.

Found Bras and a Beer Truck

Roncesvalles to Zubiri (22.3 km)

The first rude awakening came at 3:30 a.m. A fire alarm blared through all three floors of the Collegiate. Like most, I couldn't decipher if it was a wake-up call or an alarm. It was both, I guess. The classic response from the bedraggled was none. Swearing in multiple languages could be heard, followed by sleeping bag hoods being cinched. A few feet shuffled past, ready to evacuate. I wasn't ready to move yet. My sleeping bag was like a magic carpet to nirvana.

Two hours later, when Kim tapped me from above, it was time. We survived! I fell asleep in such a haze of Tempranillo that I forgot what we had done earlier in the day and what was ahead. My body felt miraculously intact. A bit weary, but I flexed my quads a few times and they responded favourably.

The Dane across from me moaned like a wounded animal and spilled out of his sleeping bag and stood upright to give his mostly bare but hairy body a big, healthy scratch. His yawn sucked the air out of the room and he managed to follow it with a yawn-song of sorts. Moments like these helped Kim and me hone our packing speed efficiency.

Exiting our floor, we passed through powdery and floral zones. Other bunk sections had their own animal smell, and this had nothing to do with gender. With boots segregated on the main floor, it was amazing how punky a few pilgrims were after just 24 hours.

Downstairs I elbowed Kim immediately.

"There's the plastic bag woman! She made it!"

She was preoccupied sorting through a bin of clothes and, as we neared her, she pulled a bra out of the heap. Shamelessly, she held it up to her chest and smiled like a Cheshire cat. We hadn't made eye contact, but she was quick to share, "I totally forgot to bring a bra. Can ya believe it?"

I couldn't. I wake up and have a bra over my head before my feet hit the floor and I don't even have boobs to speak of. This woman definitely had breasts that were in need of a bra – how could she forget? Did she also forget a backpack? Is that why she only had a plastic bag on her person in the Pyrenees?

"I'll take this and…this." She held up a neutral black T-shirt.

I asked, "Is this a lost and found?" I wondered if this woman should be helping herself to someone's valuable bra. When you only pack two of everything, a single missing sock can turn a day upside down.

"Oh no. This is a donation box. Take a look! There's some good crap in here. I guess people arrive here after the first mountain cross and unload a bunch of shit. Too much weight, you know. Hey, where are you guys from?"

Kim and I kept it simple with "near Toronto," but Cheri-Lyn was from Toronto so pushed for an exact address. In the span of three minutes she condensed her story and told it in seemingly one breath. We learned this: She was a lawyer. In between jobs, tired of the racket. Bought her boots on a whim at Yorkdale Mall.

"I tried on one pair and walked around Yorkdale in them on Thursday." She had decided to walk the Camino just four days beforehand. Kim and I felt like we had made a rushed decision with our one-month turnaround, but bra-less Cheri-Lyn had spontaneity in her DNA.

"I thought what the hell, I just need some boots. Paid my rent, bought a plane ticket and here we are."

Her frank charisma made me smile. "So what's with the plastic bag?"

Cheri-Lyn laughed and shrugged. "I'm forwarding my stuff, man. It's cheap. A couple of euros and you don't have to kill your back."

She seemed in no rush to get walking. I apologized for our anxiousness to get a move on and genuinely hoped we'd see her again.

We returned to Casa Sabina, where breakfast was being served in quick installments. Toast was already waiting on plates in front of the only two empty seats at a group table of rambunctious French women. Smiling politely, we ate our cold toast competition-style, ready to strike off. The coffee was frothy and chuggable, so we were out the door in sub seven minutes.

"Holy crap, it's dark!" This would become my daily observation as I stumbled over something, always a minute in. Kim was well suited for the early wake-up calls and instant high performance. I felt like the kid with staticky hair on end, strawberry jam on the side of my face, wanting to have a small cry because I was still tired.

I took the blame for the decision not to bring headlamps. "We won't be walking in the dark, that's for sure!" I was thinking of nighttime darkness, not encountering morning dark. Wasn't the sun up at home at this time? We had two Petzl headlamps at home that would have been very ideal. Not to mention the solar flashlight that our 1 per cent Iberian friend, PJ, had given us. Instead, we had one lousy penlight that Kim would use at night to check the alarm clock. Forever a clock checker from working 6:00 a.m. shifts, Kim saw it as her unspoken duty. She would wake us. If the schedule were left to me, there would have been a whole lot of, "What? It's eleven o'clock?" I've always loved sleep and luckily chose a profession that permitted big sleep-ins. The fact that I went to bed before nine the night previous was historical. It was the earliest I'd fallen asleep since age 6 – and I definitely wasn't walking 24 kilometres or drinking a gallon of beer back then.

Thanks to the multiple headlamps and camera flashes ahead of us, we narrowed in on the main attraction. On the main road out of Roncesvalles, a landmark sign beside highway N-135 elicits both a thrill and a full body quiver: "SANTIAGO DE COMPOSTELA 790."

Breakfast chatter revealed that the second day was relatively flat and shaded. A rest day after the punishing Pyrenees.

"Did you hear about the woman from New Zealand who missed the turn and walked 40 kilometres? You should see her feet!"

It was amazing how fast-talking points like this spread. Like chicken pox, it ran wild. I couldn't help but think of that childhood game, telephone, where you whispered a message to the person beside you and then it had to be passed along the chain. By the end, this woman from New Zealand would be simply overzealous. "Yes, she walked 100 kilometres on the first day and found a horse named Peanuts who once lived in Egypt."

We hadn't heard about the New Zealand woman's feet until we were eating toast. The only proper conversation we'd had was with Cheri-Lyn about her bra situation.

As I followed Kim into a tunnel of trees, there was a dull roar of conversation all around us. It seemed like all 180 pilgrims had emptied the Collegiate at once and were jammed ahead of and behind us with clicking poles and cameras. It was a huge contrast in just two days. Would it be a nonstop parade all the way to Santiago? I'd seen magazine spreads of Everest and Kilimanjaro where climbers were queued up like Costco shoppers. Was this the Camino?

I thought of the last email I'd received from one of the book publicists I frequently networked with from Greystone Books. *What the Psychic Told the Pilgrim: A Midlife Misadventure on Spain's Camino de Santiago de Compostela*, by Jane Christmas, had been published by Greystone in 2007. Corina, my publicist pal, knew the author and had deliberated about walking the Camino with an intimate group of friends. She wrote, "I actually think that it might just be too populated for me…sort of like Everest without the dead bodies."

I hoped Corina wasn't right (though she often was).

The landscape rolled out flat – that is, once I could actually see it. The ice age had applied a heavy rolling pin to this region after the Pyrenees. We still had to dodge shiny Glosette-like sheep turds, skinks and slugs fatter than breakfast sausage links. One willy-nilly foot plant on a slippery slug and you'd be flat on your back. And backpack.

I loved the soundtrack immediately. Cowbells mimicked wind chimes as they clinked and the sound reverberated across the pastures. Kim pointed out more strands of sheep wool attached to the barbed wire.

"It reminds me of mini prayer flags," I said.

Both of us were still in that pinch-me phase, Kim's walking poles quickly becoming pointer sticks to indicate magpies bouncing on rooflines.

Two hours in, we were ready for a sock change and a shared tortilla. These tortillas! Expecting a North American version of a tortilla shell with some surprise inside, our bigger surprise was learning that the Spanish tortilla is like a dense, cheesy, buttery, crustless cousin to a quiche. This one was layered with thinly sliced onions and potatoes and was dangerously good. We'd logged maybe nine kilometres – hardly enough to warrant the calorie load of the tortilla.

Over our last slugs of gorgeous coffee, I referred to the trip notes I'd made at home. Hemingway's novel *The Sun Also Rises* makes mention of Burgete, and at Hotel Burgete the piano bears his signature. Kim and I had totally blown past Burgete already. I had it listed as three kilometres from Pamplona, not three kilometres from Roncesvalles. Obviously, I was still sleepwalking and night blind. Oh well. I preferred his *Green Hills of Africa*. In the frenzy of logging kilometres and wrapping up our Canadian life, any reading time I had was scattered. I'd shelved *The Sun Also Rises* so many times that I agreed to let the sun set before finishing it.

Satiated with our new go-to breakfast order, we entered what would become a daily reel of wonder. Wild raspberries, rosehips like crimson jewels, lilting sunflowers, curled knee-high ferns and majestic plane trees that I wished we were surrounded by at home. I was taken aback by the true wild that remained despite the foot traffic that pounded through on a daily basis.

Don't be fooled – there were still hills to contend with. Hills steep enough on the "flat" section to blow an aorta, or certainly push any plaque from your arteries. I questioned our dietary intake – the increased cured meat quota alone was slowly transforming me into a (happy) human margarita. But then a beer truck appeared like an oasis in Alto de Erro. A beer truck! We only had three kilometres to knock off before Zubiri, so we gladly took a time out with chilled cans of Felsgold pilsner (which Kim renamed "Feelsgood") and two hard-boiled eggs for three euros. Kim remarked how civilized the Camino was feeling.

According to our refugio and albergue list, Zubiri had six options to investigate. I keyed in on the Río Arga Ibaia, figuring it was near a *río* (river) and there were 12 beds versus the 60 at El Palo de Avellano. Crossing the Romanesque bridge and river, the hostel was the first that everyone would see, so I assumed we'd be out of luck. Perhaps it was a case of reverse psychology? Pilgrims assuming that it would be full and not bothering to enquire?

We grabbed bunks for 12 euros each, opting to pay the additional three euros per person for breakfast as we were slim on Clif Bars and takeaway coffee was simply nonexistent in the super sleepy villages we passed through.

As Kim set up camp, I read bits of history to her about the Puente de la Rabia.

"It actually means 'Rabies Bridge.' Back in the day, they believed that if animals crossed the bridge three times, they would be protected from rabies." I continued, amused. "Get this! In the 15th century builders discovered the embalmed body of Santa Quinteria – the patron saint against rabies! Ooh – and there was a leper hospital in Zubiri too, but there are no remains of that."

"Okay, Ms. Tour Guide, want to stretch out and have a few beers by the river?" Kim asked.

"Well, we should cross the bridge again so we don't get rabies."

So we had our rabies-combatting beers with a growing and thinning group of catnappers and yoga posers. Arriving pilgrims walked directly to the river's edge and kicked off dusty boots, wading in like it was Mecca. The sun was July hot and our grassy crash pad was the best anti-inflammatory around.

The hostel was kitted out with all the necessities, so it made sense to eat in. We decided to take advantage of the oven (and not fight over the stovetop that was already bubbling with water for pasta and fry pans oiled for fish). A supermarket frozen pizza and bottle of vino tinto made for an instant, cheap date. We were joined by Miriam, an energetic outreach nurse from Vancouver on a "marriage sabbatical" and Gudrun, a smiley 73-year-old Dane who enlightened us on all things Denmark over shared bites and sips in the kitchen. Miriam wiped away tears as she told us she'd be flying back to BC the next day, from Pamplona. "I must return to work."

"You will be stuck with me then," Gudrun offered, plying us with more wine. "I go slowly slow, but I will find you here and there."

And we would.

Pinchos and Pods

Zubiri to Pamplona (21.1 km)

6:00 a.m. Baguette slab. Jam. Glacial coffee.

The lactic acid had found us. It was *galactic* acid, actually. It was another bumbly walk for the first two kilometres out of Zubiri through woodsy tunnels, trusting each footfall would carry me forward not sideways. We would be landing in Pamplona, the city with the largest population along the Camino Francés.

The first jarring juxtaposition was the giant hum of the Magna magnesium quarry. Fully visible from the trail, it was a rude interruption to our so far scenic dream sequence. Just as I was startled by the flock of doves taking to the sky departing Saint-Jean, here a gaggle of cranky geese ran at a chain-link fence and almost dropped me to my knees. They were like junkyard dogs, yapping and quacking with an unprecedented anger. I wondered why the homeowners would consider and continue such a set-up. It wasn't even seven o'clock and these geese would wake the long dead Saint of Rabies!

Once my legs stopped feeling like stiff baguettes, I was able to appreciate the contrasts of Chinese money plants, pungent junipers and long-standing apple orchards. It was such a jump in vegetation. Suddenly, we were cutting through a swath of grass two metres high. It was like a corn maze – when I lost sight of Kim, I hollered ahead for her to stop for a photo. We popped out of the maze single file and were parallel to the Arga River with a songbird serenade in our ears.

Dan the Man's pop-up appeared much like the oasis of the beer truck did in Albo de Erro. Dan was fundraising for a kids' school trip to Norway. Kim knew already that I wanted a boiled egg. I'm not sure why this was my new thing, but I bought them at every turn and Dan even had a shaker of garlic salt. Dan had bananas (say that ten times) and coffee brewing, all for a donation. Pilgrims desperate for a caffeine fix filed in behind and explained to anyone that was listening that this was a *donativo*. Apparently, we would find these pop-ups all along the Camino. Good!

Before entering the walled city of Pamplona, we were flagged down by a profusely sweating man wearing a lot of red.

"You don't want to continue. It is mayhem. Very crowded. You'll never find a place to stay."

"Why?" I asked.

He explained that a huge festival was going on in town and everyone was drunk already. Perfect!

"There will be no hostels to take you, but the municipal, here, over there, it is available." Sounded like a heist to both Kim and me. We thanked him for his concern but carried on and turned to see him convincing three Korean women to turn around to safety.

He was honest about the party. It was full throttle the moment we entered the city gate. The San Fermin fest was honouring the city's first bishop – or that's the short and sweet version we were given. The streets were stuffed with impromptu bands with tubas and balloon vendors managing 100 helium-filled foil unicorns and princesses. Tables were groaning with bottles of vino and elaborate *pinchos* (bite-size snacks characteristic of Basque country). In between, kids hoofed soccer balls and revellers carried glasses of beer into the streets, dropping them whenever and wherever they were empty.

It was difficult to imagine the running of the bulls...here. Where?

We attempted our successful reverse psych philosophy employed in Zubiri of checking the first hostel we found for availability. Albergue Casa Ibarrola was a step up in price (18 euros plus breakfast), but it was slick. Directly off the main street (Calle Carmen), the albergue's design motto explained everything: "A modern concept for the oldest of the roads." The sleeping "pods" on the second level were part of a 24-hour quiet zone. Once inside a pod, you could pull down a blind, enclosing your space into a super private, 100 per cent dark chamber with plugs to recharge actual batteries and your own. The cubicles had a locked safe and private light. The showers had rainfall showerheads, and every inch of the space was carefully curated. Boots here. Packs here. Much like kindergarten, everyone followed neat suit and the disruption of pilgrims shuffling through bags in the early morn was completely eliminated, since the backpacks were intelligently located outside of the washroom doors and away from the busy kitchen.

The inn dated back 300 years, but the contemporary touches eliminated all of that in a spoiled space for just 20 pilgrims. The manager scanned our passports with his phone and, using the Aloha2 app, we signed the screen with a finger signature.

Emulating Japan's "capsule hotels," luxury ship cabins and the international space station, pods ensure the highest degree of rest. Kim and I laughed at the offer of "a differentiated offer for those who want to live the party in a comfortable, economical way and in the heart of the party." Yep. That was us.

We showered off the day's dust and joined the vibrating throng outside our albergue, amazed that we had locked in such a cool night's sleep. That is, if we didn't get carried away with celebrating the first bishop!

It was trying to fully absorb anything but the fever of the crowd and exuberance of the Spaniards in broad daylight. Everyone was drunk already. We ducked into a few chocolate shops to admire the artwork found in the displays (Chocolate high heels! Chocolate olives!). The bakeries were like galleries too, with sugary palmier cookies and glazed, pillow-like croissants. It was the kind of place where you wanted to lie down and exclaim, "Take me now!"

Weaving through the parade of giant head puppets, firecrackers and bangers were exploding under our feet.

"Look at these pizzas!" I pulled Kim back to check out a half-dozen pizzas in a window, topped with full-length wieners.

It was a beautiful chaos – like the running of the bulls down Estafeta Street, except without bulls. We grabbed pizza (not with wieners) and beers, which ended up more on us than in us with the crowd jostling.

Even though we'd already walked over 20 kilometres, we walked a few more, going round and round the streets in the dizzy spirit of San Fermin. We bought the same plaid bandanas that were knotted around everyone's necks from a pub as patrons filtered in and out with wine from other bars. "Guess they don't do inventory on their glasses," Kim remarked.

Stores were crammed with tchotchkes: snow globes, bull "balls" bubble gum (which I bought for my dad) and bull everything, really. It was like Niagara Falls on retail steroids.

The quirky bit was the sudden influx in Senegalese men in gold chains, flashing wide smiles. While the rest of the crowd was wholly Spanish, 100 per cent of the vendors selling African-beaded bracelets and knock-off Louis Vuitton bags were from Senegal.

"Madame, please buy for my babies at home. Please, a bag."

I explained that we were walking the Camino and a purse just wouldn't do. Practicality and function were of the utmost. I didn't bother to explain that I'd never carried a purse in my life, because he felt it really suited me, but he granted Kim and me a pass for our spiritual commitment and wished us a genuine "Buen Camino."

Purse-free, we found seats inside Bodegón Sarria, a Michelin-recommended resto. The glass displays were mesmerizing, and there were a few surprises in our ordering as the menu was vague. It was a divine lineup of pinchos (with blackboards also referring to them as *"pintxos"* or *"pinchus"*): squid, eel, octopus. Many were presented on slices of baguette, but Kim had had her fill of bread.

"Babe, we have a lot of baguette days to go!"

We made our way (amazingly) back to Calle de Carmen and our albergue to test drive their promise of the highest degree of rest. It was already eleven o'clock. We were not abiding by good pilgrim behaviour.

Full Moon Werewolf Wine

Pamplona to Puente la Reina (23.8 km)

The knock on my cubicle screen was probably evidence of why aquariums request that patrons don't knock on the fish tanks. Was I inside the international space station? Did I run with the bulls last night? I still had a bandana tied around my neck confirming my attendance of some event. I could still taste squid. Octopus? Something.

"It's time, babe," Kim whispered.

Leaving Pamplona was a challenging obstacle course, dodging rolling wine bottles and shattered glasses. The streets that were stuffed with fiesta goers a few hours ago now revealed the remains.

"Oh my god," I said to Kim, recovering from a skid on a wet pizza box. "It's like a garbage pinata exploded on this street."

"No kidding! And look, it doesn't end!"

We crossed an intersection of endless beer bottles and garbage running in two more directions. Despite our foggy heads, we were glad to have landed in Pamplona for such a crush of people and frivolity. I'd seen the papier-mâché giant head puppets in documentaries, but to see them appear several feet above the crowd was a disjointed marvel. They represented nobles, peasants and historical figures – none of which we recognized. We did learn to recognize the blare of the marching band as a signal that the big heads were coming. Children had mixed reactions, either wailing in sheer fright or dancing along, rave-like. We did neither, but I knew I filmed extensive footage on our camera. Hopefully, we still had a few megabytes left for photos for the rest of the trip.

Exiting the city was a slow slog on the lopsided sidewalks, with a few U-turns to find the supposedly obvious shell symbols that were supposed to define the Way. Maybe we were just parched from the previous night, but upon leaving the city's pavement, we immediately entered Sahara-like conditions. Everything in our midst felt as dry as crackers and just as dehydrated as us.

A feisty solo pilgrim named Clara approached us with a pack that could have fit both of our bags inside. She needed a pack animal to accompany her! She was panting as much as we were.

At first it was just a direction confirmation on her end as she had been wandering about in a few wrong directions already. Pamplona was tricky to exit, especially with the rolling bottle terrain and racket of trucks vacuuming up glass like street-sized Roombas.

"Did you check out the festival last night?" Kim asked. At breakfast we'd already heard grumbles about the ruckus and noise that apparently permeated earplugs. A woman from Ohio had a headache from it all – and she didn't even participate. It would have been a shame to bed down early with a cup of tea when Spain was going absolutely gaga outside the albergue doors. This was history! If we were going to have headaches, I wanted it to be from participating.

Clara had been out too and was woozy from white wine that she swore turned her into a werewolf every time she drank. She had a string of funny remarks and I hoped we'd all keep stride for a while. When I asked about her massive 65L Osprey pack, she agreed that it was a bit much.

"But I have tins of tuna and mussels and I'm carrying some meaningful stones. And half a bottle of wine. Hey, I've already forwarded my waterproofs (rain gear) and bug spray to the end!"

I was quite certain that tins of tuna would be available at some point. And, really, how much did you have to love tuna to ensure a ready supply? I said she'd make a great contestant on Monty Hall's *Let's Make a Deal*, but the North American reference was lost on her. And then she lost us on her rendition of a spirited playground song about a cheeky magpie. It reminded me of that merry "Kookaburra Sits in the Old Gum Tree" song.

"So what part of Australia are you from?" I asked, ready to share that we had a lovely friend from Noosa on the Sunshine Coast. They would get along famously with werewolf wine drinking and magpie songs.

"Australia?" Clara stopped in her tracks. "I'm from England!"

Kim covered for me, explaining that I wasn't a morning person and that I was still waking up. Which was true, but I was going to lose my Girl Guide Accents badge rather quickly. My head still felt full of crumpled crepe paper.

Clara was definitely a "friend at first sight." She amused us immediately with her mission to quit smoking on the Camino, as she lit up and hauled a long drag. "I know, I know."

She had an old-school Canon 35mm hanging around her neck. "This thing alone weighs about four pounds," she said, readjusting her pack. "Sorry guys, I need to get back on my own pace, you're too fast for me."

"We'll see you ahead, then," and Kim and I motored on, rehashing the funniest Clara bits as we walked parallel to a cycling race and a whiz of spandex zipped past us. Did all Spanish men have Tour de France legs? Shaved clean and all sinew, these dudes were all blood cells, granite and Gatorade.

A spine of 40 wind turbines grew larger as we climbed the Alto del Perdón grade. A strapping, shirtless guy bounded down the rocky path without hesitation, a loyal dog hot on his heels. I couldn't imagine running full stride on such questionable terrain! A small, unattended, trailside, pop-up donativo offered a random inventory of two beers, some grapes, cut pineapple, a handful of almonds (nutcracker provided), potato chips and a peach. There were interested takers, but Kim and I carried on, still working on the calories of our breakfast baguette.

Kim had her head down, and sweat was stinging both our eyes like jellyfish venom.

"It's the sculpture, Kim! Look!"

Equally surprised, Kim said, "I can't believe we're here already!"

Here the iconic metal sculpture made most famous by *The Way* provides selfie/hashtag/Insta gold. The band of pilgrims on foot, horse and donkey creates a necessary pause. Surprisingly, the same energy company that oversees the mighty turbines erected the sculpture. An inscription reads: *"Donde se cruza el Camino del viento con el de las estrellas"* (Where the way of the wind meets the way of the stars).

The wind on the ridge was full throttle, but we found Clara, tucked in behind a rock, lighting a smoke.

"I know! I know!"

We asked if she could take our picture and then swapped cameras to take hers. She found a group of lanky guys to walk with and they were content to flake out for a bit in the sun.

We pressed onward, into the "bowl." The gentle descent into Puente la Reina also meant an ascent in temperature as we left the Pamplona basin for the Mediterranean clime favoured by vintners.

"Well, at least we didn't miss the sculpture," I laughed. (It would be impossible, really.) In Pamplona we never did find the bust of Hemingway near the Puente de la Magdalena. We successfully found the party though!

And then we found Limonada N&N in the historic town of Obanos. The only scribbles I had about Obanos were about an annual play called *The Mystery of Obanos* that retells a legend that involved a brother stabbing his sister, and then, full of remorse, building a hermitage to serve pilgrims as penance. I documented this because the play involved casting 800 villagers – which meant everyone in Obanos! I forgot about this entirely as Kim and I took turns sharing sugar-laden lemonade from the entrepreneurial stand's miniature host. He was probably 10 or so, and with his stiff two-euro lemonade menu, this kid would have university tuition (PhD even) in no time. He was equal measures cute and charming, even when he had to disappear inside to make another batch. Our lemonade intake was probably the equivalent of our Pamplona beer guzzling.

He stamped our passports in a hurry to make way for a new customer puffing his way up the hill. Total gold mine. Just like the beer truck and Dan the Man's hard-boiled eggs with garlic salt, this kid's lemonade was a true lifesaver. Part of the magic of the Camino is the unexpected. That's why we wanted to walk without phones or tablets, free range. Yes, we had done some research before we left about things to walk absently past (like Hemingway's bust and the piano bar featured in *The Sun Also Rises*), but we were walking without maps or a guidebook to indicate where the next ATM or water station was. We only had to eavesdrop for a few minutes at any coffee shop to learn of the conditions and amenities ahead. We were surrounded by CNN correspondents and meteorologists eager to share intel. The same coffee shop informants were also on their phones, reserving their next bed. Kim and I didn't have that privilege and were disappointed that such a traditional, ancient pilgrimage route had already been marred by technology and hostels accepting phone reservations. We had a hard copy list of hostels and albergues – that was it. Couldn't we all just walk and arrive on the same page?

It was an ever-changing terrain into Puente la Reina – a treadmill of serrated rock and then golf ball-like stones. Then we were picking our way through granite bowling balls, slippery scree and pavement heaved up by the pulsating veins of century-old tree roots. There were cobbles, dodgy gutters and cracked earth that hadn't seen rain for years. There were shady umbrellas of olive trees and dill-like plants that were being consumed by dozens of land snails.

We slowed to look at the squeaky clean and buffed parade of vintage Porsches, Jags and MGs that had congregated as part of a Camino driving tour. The annual fall rally attracts international enthusiasts. Kim stopped. "What? We could have driven this?"

After splitting off a major road, we cut through tidy, linear market gardens ready to win fall fair ribbons. There were baseball-sized tomatoes, curly peppers and cactus pears in all directions. Kim and I had lunch on the move (not from garden helpings, tempting as it was). We bought carne empanadas that would have been more savoury after 30 seconds in the micro, but they hit the spot. Our appetites were rather nonexistent. I expected us to be like prehibernating bears, ready to consume 10,000 calories in any form each day. We were strangely experiencing the opposite, barely able to finish our palm-sized empanadas. As we slung our packs back on, I said to Kim, "Ugh. My T-shirt totally smells like those squid pinchos from last night." We were ready for a laundry day.

In Puente la Reina, we made a cobblestone beeline for Albergue Estrella Guia because it had "*estrella*" (stars) in its name and because there were only eight beds. The Santiago Apostol had 100 and R.P. Jakue had 85, while Padre Reparadores had 96 spots for five euros. Estrella Guia was 15 euros each (including breakfast). Kim and I were grateful and fully aware of having the luxury of not having to sleep bare bones at the municipal albergues each night. They would do in a pinch, but I also liked to stay in places with a little personality and less than 200 steaming boots at the door. Many pilgrims are drawn to the municipal hostels because there's a promise of instant community. The kitchens are inviting and communal, and if you're looking for friends, that's the ticket. For couples, introverts and independent travellers, any albergue advertising less than ten bunks often indicates more privacy and a similar mindset. Or so we assumed so far.

At Estrella Guia, Natalia ushered us in with whispers and asked us to remove our boots in the corner. It smelled intoxicatingly good (not removing our boots – it was her hostel space that smelled good). The scent was identical to the Pullman Hotel G we stayed at in Bangkok a few years before. Kim and I almost said it at the same time. "Pullman G!" It was a beautiful blend of sandalwood and vanilla.

"Please, choose a card," Natalia insisted, fanning them out on her desk. She told us she was Brazilian, saving me from another misstep in accent guessing. She told us many things, all in one breath. She opened Estrella Guia 40 days ago. She had walked the Camino with her husband and knew she belonged here. "Please, what does your card say? It is your word card, something to think about on your Camino."

She oozed colour and good – I worried that she might be a little too extravagant for Kim, but Kim played along.

"My card says...patience." She rolled her eyes while Natalia's eyes lit up with an "aha!" I chose "love," which seemed fitting and earned me a wink from both parties.

Love and patience. Yes.

Angelic music, like a heartbeat, murmured in the background.

"I do Ayurvedic massage too," Natalia advertised. At this point, Kim and I were terrified of stretching or massaging any part. We were both steadfast of just "muscling through" and stretching at the very end. I swooned at the idea of a massage but was also painfully aware of how treatments can remove essential and protective muscle guarding. Guarding can be a positive, protecting your body from injury. We declined the massage offers but asked if Natalia had cold beer instead.

"Canadians, yes? You are same!" She did have cold beer and there was a donation bank that looked like Clara's camera on the counter that we could deposit money into.

Natalia twirled us about the rooms and brilliant murals depicting her love-laced life with Juan. I kinda felt like I'd smoked some Northern Lights Kush. The space was a collision of IKEA meets Brazil meets Zen temple meets peace pipe. Throughout the tour, Natalia shared her sparkly philosophies and reminded us that it was nearly a full moon.

"It is best to buy a bottle of wine and enjoy it on the terrace. Full moon. Very magic."

We wrestled Natalia into trying to hold the room that slept three as a private room for two, and our plying and willing worked. It would have been rather awkward to have someone in the bunk above the lower double, but we were becoming accustomed to the fluid boundaries of the Camino.

Natalia stamped our credentials and coloured them – ensuring we wouldn't forget her. Everything about Natalia and Estrella Guia was hopeful and the product of making dreams come true. Right down to Kim and I having our own room and being able to share the same bed. Few hostels and albergues have private rooms to offer, so this was a lucky night for us.

We flip-flopped down to the river behind our hostel and laid flat in the grass, wholly entertained by a string bean pilgrim doing sun salutations. She was the epitome of pureness: eight glasses of water a day, oatmeal and probably probiotics.

"We should start doing yoga," Kim suggested as she finished her can of beer.

"Now?"

"No, when we get home. Maybe."

I returned my gaze to the magnificent six-arched Romanesque bridge over the Río Arga that we had been chasing. A statue of the Virgin Mary once stood at the middle of the bridge. Legend tells that a *txori* (little bird in Basque) would land and clean the Virgin's statue face, and how this was considered to be a good omen by the townsfolk. However, during the Carlist wars, an unwise count poked fun at the txori and the town's love affair with an obsessive bird. Two short weeks later the count was defeated in battle.

Little txoris flitted about the immaculate riverside gardens and it was hard to pull ourselves away for some paella, but siesta hour was lifting. The streets were already surging with hungry and thirsty pilgrims.

The main street was already in shadows but still warm from the day's sun. Damien, a French twentysomething with spellbinding husky blue eyes, joined us. William, also from France, joined our table and launched into his precise plan to walk the Camino in less than 20 days as he was meeting a boat on the Atlantic coast. He would be sailing from Morocco to South America for the next two years. His life story and appetite were a lot to take in. It was a spectator sport, really. Kim and I shared a paella and donated our full baguette to William, who ate spaghetti Bolognese as a starter, followed by pork chops with rice, then a cakey dessert and jug of wine. William was greyhound skinny and ate like the world was ending. I liked that we didn't have to worry about a two-way conversation. His monologue was like listening to an audiobook over paella.

More pilgrims were crowding in, eyeing our table, so we disbanded and returned to our hostel with werewolf wine and made our way to the terrace.

"Clara!" She was there, legs propped up, smoking. We shook hands with a Swede named Sara, Nashville Matt and a tall guy from Iowa.

We all tracked the full moon's shift toward the river Arga until Clara said, "Oh my god, it's one o'clock! This bloody wine! I tell you!" We were transforming into devil-may-care shore leave sailors instead of pilgrims.

Spoiled Rotten at Chapitel

Puente la Reina to Estella (21.8 km)

We didn't see Clara or any of the full moon rooftop gang at the breakfast table. Kim and I had a quick coffee and were thrilled to have a sweet substitute for the customary breakfast baguette. Croissants! Marmalade! Satiated, we crossed the six-arched bridge that we had lazily laid under seemingly hours before. Constellations were still clinging to the sky's belly.

With the slight incline of the bridge I was impressed with my back's involuntarily participation so far. Everything felt good and in the groove. Kim had found her rhythm too, mastering the removal and addition of rubber tips to her trekking poles while in motion – with only a few accidental stabs to me when I followed too closely.

We were on a dirt path as brick red as Prince Edward Island in no time. Kim sighed with the unexpected terrain change by removing her rubber tips, again. Fields of seeded asparagus, peppers and vineyards in the distance appeared like verdant quilts. It was a sharp and sudden transition into the olive and wine region and the vines were absolutely groaning with grapes. The Navarra region is known for its well-defined transitions in soil and crops every 25 kilometres. I didn't need a drone's aerial view to confirm this.

It seemed more arid – perhaps it was the increased presence of cacti and iguanas. We stopped to inspect the apocalyptic number of land snails mowing down the unidentified vegetation that looked like wild and woody dill. At a quick glance, the tall reedy plants appeared to be laden with white berries. To the trained eye, they were snails, and it was a total invasion.

Foraging goats risked their lives straining to reach low-hanging olives on a trailside cliff. They clung by mere hooves to a dodgy purchase of clay, desperate for the higher branches and oblivious to the tumble they'd take, all for a simple olive.

Ant trails bisected the Camino route several times. Distracted with taking photos of the snails, I soon found myself being silently trampled by ants marching up and over my hiking shoes. Hundreds moved along in a vibrating, determined mass. Kim remembered witnessing ant parades in the olive plantations in Santorini, and I had flashbacks to Monteverde, Costa Rica, where the ants came marching one by one, hurrah, hurrah, right into my rudimentary kitchen. They were on a mission and entered by the door, scaled the wall, kept a tight line across the ceiling and were out again through the grass thatch.

Hopscotching over the ants, we noticed the first pop-up of the day, nestled in the shade of the olive trees. There were warm cans of Coca-Cola by donation. It was only 10:00 a.m. and there were several thirsty takers. Kim and I passed but recognized Gudrun the ol' Dane in the olive trees.

She raised her arms in dramatic disbelief. "Girls, no Coca-Cola? Look at this view and beautiful shade." It was a really sweet set-up, but we had ants in our pants and were eager to get to Lorca for a proper coffee jolt. A few kilometres later, Albergue de Lorca's blackboard menu easily lured us in with mention of tortilla *patata* (potato).

We had dust up to our knees already. I snapped the ankle of my sock and a plume of dust arose, like Pigpen from *Peanuts*. Laundry would be imperative, as we had really pushed the limits of the Smartwool "stink-free" guarantee. I had been wearing my two pairs of quarter socks on rotation for seven days. The last two hostels had zero clothesline real estate left, so we kept pushing our wash cycle.

Today we could feel the burn, on both cheeks. Butt and face! The sun was powerful, and with so many lizards underfoot, it felt like a desert passage – but one with huge reward. Kim and I had banked a few days in our itinerary for semi-impromptu rest days. Estella's wine region beckoned and we thought we should be culturally responsible and visit a few wineries en route. We were lucky at Natalia's hostel to have a room to ourselves, but the bathrooms were still a shared affair. It was time for a bunk-bed-free night and an en suite for two, not two dozen. However, most hostels have an abrupt checkout time and, unless you are ill or injured, they don't cater to two-night stays. The hostels that were lax often didn't have a private room to offer and reminded us that there would be a big shuffle of pilgrims from five to eight o'clock, eliminating any hope of a sacred sleep-in.

Our only option was to go big and Hospederia Chapitel on the left bank of the Ega River provided. We apologized for the dust cloud that followed us in as the polished and perfumed clientele brushed past us with a frown. Adjacent to the 12th-century San Miguel de Estella Church, the opulent three-storey hotel is purely boutique with just 14 rooms. The espresso aroma from the lower-level Spire Tavern in Taberna Chapitel filtered seductively into the lobby. We squeaked in without a reservation for one night, opting to move over to the thriftier but slick Agora Hostel for the second night. We'd be out in the glow of the streetlamp light by 6:00 a.m. the following day, so it didn't make sense to blow another 105 euros on such a precious, limited sleep.

Our room was a dream. We canned the air conditioning immediately in favour of opening the church-side windows wide. At the side of the church, a fortress-like staircase wound around an unexpected rocky escarpment known as "La Mota." While the exterior of this Estella church is an "OMG" showstopper – even for the nonreligious – St. Michael's Church has earned unsavoury fanfare from a botched restoration of the statue of St. George at Navarre. Naturally, images of the Christian martyr slaying a dragon on horseback went viral – for the wrong reasons. The *New York Times* headline asked, "Is That St. George or Tintin?"

The 500-year-old sculpture was unrestored to the tune of 32,000 euros. Amateur restorers left St. George with poorly painted pointy eyes and a cartoon-like pink face, much like a Playmobil character. The company and church were both fined 6,000 euros for their not-so-handy handiwork.

I loved the odd claims to fame that *Estella la Bella* (Estella the Beautiful) boasted about. It's a wealthy town built on wool and leather, but it's best known for its suckling pig. It was on every other menu, including our room service options. It was suckling pig or lamb entrails – guts for 13 euros. While Kim industriously washed almost an entire week's worth of dust out of our socks, I read aloud from the hotel menu.

"Maybe you would like curdled milk with honey and nuts? Frozen whisky cake?" (That actually sounded enticing). "Or listen to this combo: broken eggs with black pudding and breadcrumbs, cheese and ham with a fried egg and French fries."

"Sounds like Spanish poutine," Kim said, hanging our valuable socks in the window from a precarious hanger with the few clothespins we had.

Every inch of our room brought so much comfort. I pulled on yet-to-be-worn quick-dry pants, not because of the temperature but to wash my shorts for once. The king bed and lounge chairs still had beams of afternoon sun toasting them. I could have fallen asleep for three days in the chair alone.

With laundry drying (and hopefully not falling to the sidewalk two floors below), we thought it best to keep with our tradition of finding a sunny spot along the river and watching the world go by. Everything was shuttered for siesta, save for a South-Asian-operated variety store on the edge of town. We grabbed a sleeve of my go-to lomo and a small jar of skewers threaded with pickled onions, olives and gherkins. I poked at the display of blackened peppers on the counter and naively asked how *caliente* (hot) they were.

The shopkeeper kindly offered me a sample in a nontaunting way. "It's a gift." The area is also known for their piquillo red peppers and wild mushrooms, so I was happy to sample the local, authentic fare without having to buy a two-kilogram box.

"Holy hell!" One bite and my lips lit up – and not with a smile. This pepper was the equivalent of fishing a glowing ember out of a fire and immediately placing it on my tongue. The owner shrugged and very casually popped an entire pepper in his mouth. I was certain smoke was coming out my nose and ears with every breath. For the next hour, I could have fried an egg on my tongue. I was human Sriracha.

"Gracias for the gift," I offered, swearing on the way out of his store.

We rode out the siesta on a set of stairs that led to a boarded-up house. Ducks paddled past and switched sides of the river as two shaggy dogs made their presence known, eager for any handouts – pork or pickled onion skewers? Dismayed, they took flying leaps into the river.

Kim and I wondered aloud about the rest of our rat pack.

"We'll get off track with everyone by staying here two nights. Maybe we'll catch up again, but that's the weird thing about the Camino, hey?" Kim said.

She was dead right. Unless our current group took a rest day somewhere soon, we'd be on different itineraries and might not see Cheri-Lyn to ask how her new lost and found bra fit. Gudrun was our version of "Where's Waldo?" as we'd spotted her a few times throughout the days, but Clara was probably a goner. She had no timeline or return ticket to worry about, so we guessed she was still at Natalia's, sleeping off her werewolf wine. Her hope was to get back to England by Christmas, so she had a lot more rest built in than we did.

We returned to our room to absorb all the pleasures of a big grooming session. We shaved, tweezed and enjoyed the social time-out and glasses of Tempranillo in our window. Some late arrivals were cruising through. I say "late," but Kim and I were probably always the earliest arrivals, landing at one or two in the afternoon.

After our spa session, we made our way to the plaza in hopes of something other than suckling pig and firecracker local peppers. We read a dozen menus that were all lacklustre. Spaghetti *and* fries? Together? Pasta with nuts and roquefort sounded like a stomach cramp. The traditional "pilgrim's menu" that was offered in most towns wasn't our caloric speed either. For guys like William, walking 40 kilometres a day, a spaghetti Bolognese starter and pork chop entrée might be what dreams are made of. For us, we never ate three-course. At home, there was never dessert. Salad was often the "main" in our house.

A bit frustrated by the limitations of such a big town, we returned, somewhat defeated, to an American-styled diner in the main square called Cruji Coques. It had a jukebox, framed LPs on the walls and Formica everywhere. Despite the oozing Americana, the concept was apparently genuine and inspired by a typical Catalonian dish, *"coca de recapte." "Recapte"* translates as "the provision of things to consume or use." It was a little bit lost in translation, but we understood the appeal of the trendy, crunchy, wood-fired pizzas like the *fungi* one we had. It was extremely tempting to steal the cute axe that the square pizza was served with for cutting the slices, but we were concerned about pack weight and possibly being arrested.

We fell into bed at Chapitel, narrowly remembering to bring in our prized laundry. Our bodies were unsure of what to make of the comfort. There was no set alarm clock. No sleeping bags! No overhead bunk for me to crack my head on in the morn.

It felt strange but totally wonderful. Could we afford to increase our nightly accommodation budget by 90 euros?

Sommeliers for a Day

Rest day, Estella

Though our bodies didn't permit us to lie longer than 8:00 a.m., we were blissed out in a giant bed with real sheets and a duvet instead of a worm-casing sleeping bag.

I nipped downstairs and ordered *cafés* from the Spire Tavern while Kim set up our sunny perch in front of the hotel window. We had picked up pastries from a nearby bakery the day before. I knew they were going to be celestial as the brown bag was ready to bottom out from the lard content. Laced with cinnamon and sugar, the cakey squares were a curious, sticky mix of fried dough and wafer.

"Another coffee?" I asked.

Kim leaned back in her hotel-issue robe with closed eyes. "Oh yeah."

Even though we'd only been walking for five days, everything was fast forward and slow motion all at once. We'd knocked off nearly 115 kilometres (and probably five more the night we roamed around Pamplona). Sleep had been fleeting and seemingly decimated with each hostel stay.

I returned with another tray of velvety coffee. Normally, we'd be nearly ten kilometres in.

"Do you miss running?" Kim asked.

"I thought I would, a lot, but walking the distances we are each day, I think it's a pretty satisfying substitute for running. It's probably good for me to switch things up for a bit."

The whole-body funky fatigue of walking that we were experiencing was unmatched, but I had long been hot-wired to run. When we were training, I subbed our 20-kilometre walks for running for fear of pressing my luck, adding more unnecessary kilometres to my wimpy back.

Any runner will nod along in agreement, recognizing that inert need to run. It's been a 20-year-long part of my daily minutiae. Running was my litmus test and confirmation that I was okay, healthy. There are very few gaps in my running history and they are qualified. I've been known to run with a train track of stitches in my groin (hours after receiving them) and 24 hours after a big sidewalk flip that resulted in a concussion. A bigger trip in a construction zone on Spadina in Toronto led to X-rays to ensure I hadn't split my patella (kneecap) into ten pieces. I didn't, so that was my green light to run again the next day, despite my skinned hip and knee and seized shoulder. Even though I couldn't kneel on that knee for an entire year.

Kim was well aware of my stubborn streak and addiction to running. On Zanzibar's west coast, I tried my best to navigate the fondue-hot temperatures when the tide was out, running on a coral shelf littered with black urchins and oceanic potholes. In Caye Caulker, Belize, I zigzagged the dirt road and ran across the airport strip with Kim on my heels, keeping pace on a Pee-wee-Herman-styled three-speed. The only time I didn't run was when a pride of lions (Murchison Falls, Uganda) or Egyptian militia in Cairo dictated otherwise. Even in the Congo, during a volunteer stint at a chimpanzee sanctuary, the woman I was staying with, Chantal, kindly bought me a membership to the golf course – so I could safely run. Provided

I dodged the sunning snakes on the back greens that were two metres long, and the occasional Callaway ball.

Kim and I have a longstanding joke (and promise) that she only runs for last call.

"It's awesome that we can walk together. That guy I massaged at Langdon Hall? The one who said I shouldn't walk the Camino with my partner? That still bugs me. I mean, this is an incredible experience – why wouldn't we share it?"

Kim said, "I know! But there are a lot of single walkers out there. And even the ones who are walking with someone – often they're not."

It was a peculiar phenomenon. We'd seen several pairs of twentysomething friends, two German brothers and one married Dutch couple. They walked tandem, but the brothers and friends split throughout the day and we'd see them solo, ear buds in.

I couldn't imagine walking without Kim – or ahead or behind her for that matter.

"Shall we go walk through some vineyards today?" I asked.

Even though Navarra is known to produce some of Spain's best fruit-driven rosés, the ancient region also produces a lot of Tempranillo, Cabernet Sauvignon and Merlot. Rioja tends to overshadow Navarra on North American shelves, but having walked through most of Navarra, we were able to witness (at ground and grape level) the shift in climate and soil 100 kilometres south from Pamplona and the northern mountains to the drier continental centre and now Club Med climate.

The concierge was able to arrange a driver for us, as surprisingly there were no formal established tours in the area like Ontario's Prince Edward County or Niagara-on-the-Lake. I had assumed we could land in Estella and latch onto some tourist bus or shuttle and take in three or four wineries in the afternoon. "We can take you to Propiedad de Arinzano, it is closest. Each person pay ten euros plus driver. Maybe." The driver fee hadn't been determined and it would be a 30-minute drive, one way.

Kim shrugged and said, "We're only here once, let's do it. How outrageous can the taxi be?" It was a big part of why we chose to have a rest (wine) day in Estella too. We had been drinking bottles of red for two euros since we arrived, so it was like we had been saving money anyway.

First, we shuffled over to the Agora Hostel that we had peeked in at upon arrival to Estella. It had a cool Scandi meets industrial vibe, with reclaimed wood furniture and stencilled lockers. It was the kind of space we would live in quite happily. The cheery Aussie behind the counter informed us that Agora was in its second year of operation. It was super-hip and squeaky clean with an Icelandic soundtrack. The communal kitchen, with its jumble of mismatched leather, red and robin's egg blue metal chairs, looked like the ideal place to pop open a laptop and write a book.

When our wine taxi honked, I felt oddly guilty jumping in a vehicle. So un-Camino like! But once we drove into the meticulous grounds of Propiedad de Arinzano all was forgotten. We learned a lifetime of wine intel from our private guide, Julian. Kim and I had been to dozens of wineries over the years, from Kix Brooks's (of Brooks & Dunn fame) Arrington Vineyards south of Nashville to Prince Edward County's artisanal vegan winery situated in a storied 1805 barn, Karlo Estates. We'd tried cashew wine in Hopkins Village, Belize, and tempted fate with some roadside wine bearing a Great Wall of China label (中国长城葡萄酒有限公司) along the Yangtze. (China had experienced a blindness epidemic that was traced back to illegal bathtub vodka.) Most wine tours are a shuffle, trying to squeeze in some elbow room to swirl a Merlot while a bored server rhymes off details about the terroir until the next mosh pit sloppily pushes in. Here we were engaged and learning.

Kim and I were the only guests at Arinzano's 355-hectare property. It sits like a jigsaw piece between La Rioja and the Bordeaux region. Designed by Spanish architect Rafael Moneo, the winery is monastery-like. There's even a medieval "Ham Room" where visitors can sample 100 grams of 100 per cent acorn-fed Iberian ham and a glass of rosé Hacienda Arínzano for a stiff 45 euros (the amount we had shelled out for two bunks at Agora). Julian kept ducking into the shade, wiping his brow with a handkerchief.

"I'm from France, I find this heat so unbearable!" he apologized.

We wandered through the prized rows and noted the difference in vines that had been heavily pruned to produce just one coveted bottle. Julian pointed out a vine that had been pruned to produce a dozen bottles. Typically, it takes one kilo of grapes to produce one bottle. "Shall we try?"

We were eager after the tease of seeing such an abundance of grapes. Crates of just-harvested grapes from the 128 hectares of planted vines were ready to be processed and we snuck in ahead of the forklift to the cool of a room lined with barrels. They were American oak or French and each barrel lasted three to five harvests. The age of the tree used to make the barrel influences the taste of the wine as well, so each glass is a precious dance and miracle to recreate.

Barrels can speed up the aging process of wine too, often by two years. We worked through our samples of Chardonnay, Tempranillo and a Merlot. Julian magically drew the samples out with a metre-long glass siphon.

"This bottle retails for 80 euros," Julian casually informed us.

Kim nearly coughed her mouthful out. Arinzano produced 250,000 bottles a year. The math involved had too many zeros for me to figure out, but they were probably doing okay. We would *not* be buying a bottle for our dinner at the Agora Hostel though.

"Each barrel?" Julian pointed, "They range from 800 to 1,200 euros. Each." Some of the barrels are baked to infuse flavours like vanilla and cinnamon. "They are very porous, so the barrels absorb the flavours well." We were absorbing the barrel flavours just as efficiently.

The wines here are classified as bona fide *vino de pago*, which is a unique designation awarded to individual vineyards or estates, not an entire region. In 2017, there were 17 *vinos de pago* in Spain. It's a lengthy process as it takes ten successful harvests to qualify.

We lingered with a glass and took in the vineyard's sleepy setting. It was a treasured day, but we knew that in no time we'd be following the River Ega out of town. Glowing from the terroir, we returned to Estella and learned that our tour fee included the shuttle ride. They were new to tourism development and vineyard tours, so it was a temporary trial that we lucked into. We suddenly loved the winery even more!

With a picnic of cheaper Iberian ham, Gouda, roquefort, olives and some buttery crackers, we found our same spot along the river's edge and watched new dogs frolic with a school of giant trout. Muscovy ducks cruised past and I laughed at Kim, who had to turn her head.

"Ugh, their heads are so gross," she commented, wrinkling her nose.

Muscovy ducks have warty, pimply, red skin surrounding their eyes and beaks, making them rather off-putting, despite their popularity with chefs as a lean protein that tastes similar to veal.

"And that Iberian ham is gross too. It's so fatty it's making me gag."

When the sun dipped for the day in the wake of an orange sherbet haze, we returned to our hostel with leftovers and found seats downstairs to enjoy our thriftier wine purchase (3 euros versus 80). Sue, a warm Aussie who lived on a sheep station in New South Wales, was happy to share a glass and her story. She was staying in Estella for a few nights to recover from an unpredictably taxing Reiki session. We knew we wouldn't see her again, so we enjoyed the fleeting time and offered her our acorn-fed ham. She was reading *A Year to Live: How to Live This Year as If It Were Your Last* by Stephen Levine.

I was worried that Sue knew it was her last year alive, but she answered my nonquestioning/questioning facial expression about her book choice.

"I'm a mental health nurse," she explained. "This is the kind of stuff I read to ground myself again." We left Sue the last pour of our Crianza wine and settled into our curtained-bunk capsules for the night. I charged our camera, grateful for the plug adapter I'd pinched with permission from Chapitel. When the concierge presented a box with left-behind adapters, I was happy to up my request from borrowing one to "can I have this?" In my Pamplona fog, I'd left the adapter plugged into my international space station capsule. I did remember the camera attached to it though.

It was the pattern of the Camino. You gain a few things (adapter, bra, wine appreciation) and lose a few (Clara, adapter).

The Wiener Pizza Fiasco
Estella to Los Arcos (21.6 km)

Breakfast at Agora was an elaborate affair. We pushed our departure back to take advantage of the spread that wasn't available until 7:00 a.m. Muesli! Yogurt! There was also Iberian ham and cheese, but we stuck to the Swiss mix.

Our sleep had been somewhat exasperating. How did we get assigned to the sleep apnea demonstration room? I'd never heard such noises – and mostly from the women! I missed the lovely confines of our Chapitel walls and 300 square feet for two.

The horizon was a promising bright cantaloupe as we followed a spotty lead of headlamps that veered off to a surprise trailside forge in Ayegui. The blacksmith at La Forja de Ayegui had a huge, welcoming bonfire crackling and snapping away, and the warmth was appreciated on our goosebumped bare legs. I'd heard rumours about the blacksmith's coveted passport stamp – it was a Camino must-have.

We admired his tiny, lucky horseshoes and scallop shells, in addition to larger works that weren't backpack-friendly. For the blacksmith, he was a prime example of location, location, location. Everyone stopped, hoping to find a weightless, one-of-a-kind, take-home treasure.

"Ready for some vino?" Kim asked, rubbing her hands together in front of the fire.

We were totally on track, following the exact proposed itinerary we had emailed my parents and Kim's sister. I had highlighted this day and provided a link to irache.com with many asterisks. ****LOOK FOR US ON SEPTEMBER 26th AROUND 8AM!! We'll be at the wine fountain!!!****

The Bodegas Irache website has a 24-hour-a-day, 365-day-a-year webcam trained on La Fuente (the fountain). If we were on pace, we'd be there first thing, less than three kilometres from Estella. The actual wine museum didn't open until 10:00 a.m., but, curiously, the fountain has a free pour of red wine commencing at 8:00 a.m.

Legend has it that monks received weary pilgrims who came to the Irache monastery hospital in the 11th century with a hospitable glass of wine. Wine was thought to be restorative, much like the Irish iron-rich cure-all, Guinness.

In the '90s, a fountain was installed for pilgrims to keep history free flowing. Obviously, it is the only wine fountain along the Camino, otherwise Kim and I might not ever finish. Each day, the fountain is filled with 100 litres of young red wine "to quench the pilgrim's thirst and make their path more bearable."

I wasn't exactly thirsty for red wine at 8:00 a.m. but took a happy slug from the communal glass at the landmark fountain and waved wildly at the camera in case my parents were awake at 2:00 a.m. in Ontario to tune in to my wine fountain debut.

There are actually two taps at Irache – one has water. A unique but essential part of the Camino is the frequency and free provision of potable water along the way. Towns and villages along the Way have accessible taps for locals and pilgrims alike to fill bottles with safe drinking water. However, they are not always exactly where you would desire or expect them to be. So, if you are travelling map-less like Kim and I opted to, keep a few swallows on reserve.

The cantaloupe horizon quickly gave way to a denim-blue-sky day. It was a flat and temperate walk and a supposed easy leg before our first 28-kilometre day into Logroño. I spied the food truck first. This was not something I expected to see on the Camino ever but was happy to engage in. We had a jar of six olives and some broken crackers, but with a hot, cheesy tortilla and cold beer on offer, we were sucked in. Naturally, there were no posted prices and the beer ended up being a huge gouge at four euros. Kim balked and gave the food truck owner a "tsk tsk" for capitalizing on the good nature and journey of pilgrims. He had a good soundtrack (Eurythmics) and it was the best tortilla we'd had so far – but we wouldn't tell him that.

The last 12 kilometres into Los Arcos were without shade or pop-ups. The village itself had a weird vibe. Maybe the food truck's prices had miffed us, but everywhere we turned the few albergues or hostels available were advertising prices designed to soak pilgrims. They were lacklustre, dated and dingy spaces with either cranky or nonexistent service. None included breakfast. We looked at four and turned our noses up at each one then turned around, wondering if we had missed something. Our trusty accommodation sheet listed two hostels in Los Arcos, but there were several more of questionable standard. On the outskirts of town, we decided, begrudgingly, to book the Los Arcos Pension for 50 euros.

"There's no sense walking back, babe, we've seen everything." Kim was right, but I wanted our trendy Agora Hostel esthetic.

"Agora was cheaper, way cooler and included muesli! This place makes me want to take Xanax," I said.

We did have the luxury of another private room with pistachio green walls and a tiny balcony overlooking some scenic rubble and a few deserted houses.

"We're in a really sketchy quarter," I said to Kim, surveying our grim neighbourhood. A grizzled, crease-faced guy in an ill-fitting tank top smoked a hand-rolled cigarette. He was perched on a chair near-collapse a few doors down, but otherwise the place was disturbingly vacant. Not even a feral cat.

Did we miss an evacuation memo? There were a few villages we had passed through that had a distinct Armageddon quality. Where was everybody? The population had completely vanished without a siesta or Sunday to explain the vacancy.

Our socks needed another suds bath after so much dust. Kim hung our precious cargo on the derelict balcony before we struck off to investigate the nearby dimly lit Hotel Monaco. So this is where everyone was! There were probably 20 men drinking red wine inside. We had an awkward beer and decided to move on, magically finding the ladies bar where all the wives were playing cards and betting pennies. It was such a juxtaposition. The barkeep had an app on his phone that he encouraged us to speak into. The app flipped English to Spanish, or attempted to. He was bored by the current clientele, who played 20 rounds of cards before finishing a small glass of beer. We watched a few tense rounds, mesmerized by the focus and commitment of the players.

"Well, shall we investigate dinner?" I asked. We guessed this would be an ordeal too, given the establishments we had visited so far.

We walked the main road into Los Arcos to the bitter end. Here there were several vending machines that looked way more tempting than anything we'd passed. We turned on our heels, pilgrims still chugging in behind us. We weren't gloating, but we'd already found a place to stay, hung a load of laundry, drank two beers and walked the perimeter of the town four times.

A bakery-slash-fruit-stand seemed promising when I spied flatbreads in the window. "They really love their wiener pizzas here, heh?" I said to Kim. "Actually, I'm going to take a picture of them, the one I took in Pamplona was fuzzy." I zoomed in on the slices and the whole wieners. My dad would *love* this pizza.

Suddenly, there was a torrent of aggression. High-pitched Spanish yelling directed at me. I had no idea what was going on, but surely I wasn't involved. The shop owner punched an angry finger at the hand-scrawled sign an inch below where I took a picture.

"NO FOTOS!"

I apologized and explained that I genuinely didn't see the sign. It was a bloody hot dog pizza, not a picture of CIA passwords for Christ's sakes!

"Give me your camera."

I felt the warm spray of her hostile spit on my face. She was furious and I was somewhat terrified for my life. Kim's eyes were bigger than mine.

"Ah, no, you can't have my camera."

"You delete! Delete those pictures!" Holy hell. Was this woman on the run, or what? We had just bought the camera about a week before our departure, to have something more compact instead of our bulkier Canon. I was worried I'd delete every picture I'd taken so far.

This woman was not relenting. I would not be allowed to leave the premises until I deleted the wiener pizza photos. When I was in Entebbe, Uganda, I had a similar encounter with two police officers who wanted me to hand over my camera. The coppers thought I was taking surreptitious photos of the president's house – meanwhile, I was truly, innocently, taking a picture of a giant marabou stork in the dumpster (not even in the direction of the presidential palace). I held my ground, though I walked away quite sure I was going to be shot in the back and dead over a marabou stork.

Argh. Dumpster storks and wiener pizza. I had to learn to be less fascinated by things!

I tentatively pressed the trash button on the camera, praying to Saint Wiener Pizza that 100 kilometres of our Camino weren't going wayward. I could feel the snitty woman's garlic breath hot on my neck.

"There. See? Okay?" (I sound all bossy here, but I was quivering and still apologetic because we wanted to buy slices of pizza.) She stomped off, satisfied, just in time to yell at another unsuspecting woman. Three German girls walked in and were squeezing peaches at the front of the store. Again, it was the dreaded pointed finger and a "NO TOUCH!!!!" sign that was missed. Apparently, this woman needed bigger signage. I thought the German was going to cry.

"Don't worry," I assured her. "I was just yelled at for taking a picture of her wiener pizza."

We ordered two zucchini pizza slices, certain they would be spit on when we turned our backs. "We should see how much her wine is," Kim said, and I followed her with the pizza in a plastic bag down the four stairs to the shelves of wine. I was yelled at again for having a bag on the lower level.

"I *hate* Los Arcos," I said. We couldn't blow out of that town fast enough.

La senda de los elefantes (The Elephant Walk)

Los Arcos to Logroño (27.6 km)

I unfolded my body parts in the dim pixels of our stark, hospital-like room. The bed left me feeling like a piece of human origami. We split a litre of peach nectar and yogurts we had to slurp without spoons.

The first four kilometres were super dark as we left our dingy digs at 6:30 a.m. A black cat hurried across the road – our first true *gato negro*! The cost of my college Spanish crash course was redeemed.

Somewhere before the ten-kilometre mark we split through Torres del Río and kicked off our boots to enjoy a supreme *café con leche*. The coffee in Spain! Our Cuisinart drip at home made a great cup but failed to touch the magic that purred out of the shiny espresso machines that surely cost as much as a small car.

"*Torta de txantxigorri!*" (Note: This is definitely not how I pronounced this, but I attempted to in my excitement as I held it up to Kim across the aisle.) The divine breakfast pastry we had in Estella now had a formal name we could ask for (maybe).

It was prepackaged but looked identical to the fresh bakery's squares. We grabbed two and could barely finish a shared one. It was just as superlative deserving as the first one we had from the Estella bakery. It was a holy trinity: *torta*, café and summer sun. I scratched a reminder in my notebook. If we were to share our itinerary with anyone, we'd tell them to skip Los Arcos and make a beeline for the charms of Torres del Río instead. In particular, Hotel Rural La Pata de Oca with its dramatic stone wall terrace dripping with tiers of full-bloom purple and fuchsia pansies.

The leg to the walled town of Viana was as dry as a cracker. The ground seemed impossibly arid. What could the farmers grow? Rocks and mortar? Upon entering the town, there was an immediate jovial buoyancy in the air, unlike the thundercloud of Los Arcos. Cute cafes and patio chairs beckoned, and no matter how caffeinated I was, it seemed necessary to have another here. Our plan was to lunch in the old bunker-like stone wine cellar at Casa Armendariz, but the cellar was closed for a private function. I begged to just have a look, but even looking was closed, apparently.

Instead, I queued up in a jammed deli, while Kim stood out of the way with our packs. There's nothing more obnoxious than being boofed with a pack inside a cafe, and I was surprised at how many pilgrims still entered markets and pubs with them on, forgetting their safe clearance range. Kim had been hollered at in Venice, climbing onto a water taxi a few years back with her backpack on. She had an added sensitivity about it and always ensured we weren't annoying or toppling displays with swaying water bottles and clipped-on sandals.

I ordered two baguettes (whole wheat, finally!) with tuna and was handed a pincho with a crosscut of chorizo and a garlic clove. I was like a magpie, taking note of all the pretty things: green olive-studded buns and egg-washed braided loaves, jars of pickled oranges. Pickled oranges?

We took our picnic into an empty courtyard and snapped open cans of beer. "Did you order an egg sandwich?" Kim asked, opening the parchment paper.

"No. I ordered two tunas. You have egg?"

"Yeah, egg *and* tuna. Weird."

The combo actually worked, and we agreed to duplicate it at home. Kim was a firm believer of mayo marrying well with everything.

The town was so perfumed (beyond our egg and tuna sandwiches). It smelled exactly like clove cigarettes. Geraniums painted all the terraces a brilliant and tidy red. Spaniards with shiny-coated, oh-so-obedient dogs strolled elegantly past; both human and canine at the ready for a *Vogue* cover shoot. Kim let out a cough as she shook a cloud of dust from the knotted-up fleece attached to her pack.

"We're starting to stink," she announced.

It was true. Our newness had been snuffed out in the Navarra region.

The Camino split through endless vineyards and century-old olive trees, all in perfectly organized Virgo-pleasing rows.

The earth was even more cracked and parched here, stippled in sections with tiny mauve periwinkles. I half-expected to see a burrowing owl or horny toad. By the time we arrived in the bowl of Logroño, the capital of the famed winemaking region of La Rioja, our tongues were hanging. It was a giant crater, surrounded by mountains and a buttery haze. We had four kilometres on pavement that seemed to soften our Vibram soles as we made our way to the town across a chocolate milk–coloured river.

The 28-kilometre day resulted in Kim nursing the onset of shin splits with a six-pack on a park bench in the town centre. Ice was hard to come by during siesta, so she smartly improvised while hydrating. On the opposite end of the bench I elbowed an intermittent charley horse that inconveniently kept grabbing my left quad. It can be a mental trap, dwelling on every cramp, microtear and twinge. I was already hyper-focused on my back and took great efforts to be mostly ergonomic and measured in my movements, though many of the lumpy bunk beds erased such efforts. It made sense to take advantage of the local medicine as approved by the monks who dispensed wine to pilgrims way back when. We had already learned it was a helpful sedative too – a little inoculation from the snoring mass and early sleeping bag stuffers and shufflers.

"This is where the best bar-hop street is," I told Kim, reading the short notes I'd made on the area. "We also have to look for a gastrobar and *vinoteca* (wine collection) called Tastavin and find the huge mural with Camino passport stamps near the river."

After a little lubrication, we checked into the Albergue Santiago Apostol, purely by chance. There were seven listed in our pamphlet and on our way to find the mural we found this jaw-dropper. As the former caretakers of a 155-year-old stone cottage, Kim and I were magnetically drawn to anything carved out of rock. This albergue was drop-dead gorgeous, with exposed timber beams and a massive cathedral ceiling that carried whispers up and away. There was a slick locker station to lock and recharge phones, and a staffed bar and kitchen area that was bright and Icelandic with simple red chairs and world maps in typography geography.

After a flip-flop walk through nearby Parque del Ebro's elaborate and trippy murals and some prerequisite salami and Gouda, we lazed about before heading to Calle Laurel, the nightlife epicentre with 60 bars and restaurants. They weren't kidding.

Locals joke this is "*la senda de los elefantes*" (The Elephant Walk). Falling under the spell of the street's energy, frivolity and too much vino might leave the uninitiated walking on all fours, elephant-like. Aside from a few pilgrims in their Dri-FIT, quick-dry best, it was largely locals – on a weeknight! Didn't everyone have to work in the morning? We had to walk nearly 30 kilometres, but that was all we really had to accomplish by sundown.

The parade of bonhomie was contagious. Why couldn't we have this in Canada? Like Pamplona, the glassware was free range. You could walk from one establishment to the next with your glass, or leave it behind on any table. It was different than Pamplona in that the streets were immaculate. Six women from Milan, all in white with gold knuckles and necks heavy with Cartier joined the mix, fearlessly drinking red wine in white on a tailgate-party-crowded street.

Kim and I grazed and sipped all the offerings. Bacon croquettes, baguette bites with soft quail eggs and pickled onion. We found Tastavin (another Michelin-recommended restaurant) and tried the prettiest offerings topped with phyllo-wrapped shrimp, sweet tomato jam and soft cheeses.

For anyone needing reward or justification to walk 30 kilometres, this was it. We returned to our hostel before ten, unelephant-like (or so we thought).

TWO

La Rioja
AND
Castilla y León

And sometimes on the Camino, there are no explanations for what you see. This hive-like structure spiked our curiosity, especially because there was no story to explain it.

The Angel's Share

Logroño to Nájera (29.6km)

- -

In our absence (imbibing on Calle Laurel), our hostel remained mostly empty, which decreased the number of potential snoring company greatly. We were well rested and found a quick and easy rhythm, though there was even more pavement to pound on to get out of Logroño.

The pleasant surprise was slipping into a park and curling around a reservoir lake dotted with ducks. The sun was just lifting and burned orange through the pines. We loved the instant immersion from urban infrastructure into deep forest, pastoral land and Rioja's signature red earth vineyards (66 million gallons are produced here each year). There are over 500 wineries in Rioja, making Ontario's Prince Edward County a tiny tot operation.

We passed more white asparagus than I'd ever seen before. I think I'd had it once – canned possibly? Our family had a healthy supply of green asparagus that grew wild along the train tracks behind our house. Unpicked, the wild stuff was great to fashion whips out of and my cousin Dustin and I seasonally returned home with equally welted bare legs from cutthroat fights.

It was 28 degrees on September 28. I couldn't believe it. Of course, we packed for all potential elements on the Camino, but Kim and I were expecting a quicker transition to pants and fleece. We crossed fingers for double-digit autumn temps and the mercury delivered.

We cut through the massive Don Jacobo vineyard, watching pilgrims ahead of us sampling the wares from the vines.

"Imagine how many grapes they lose to people walking the Camino," Kim said.

"I know! People are treating those vines like a grocery store aisle."

We had tried grapes with permission from the vineyard in Estella but felt guilt in freeloading – pilgrim status or not. Yes, there is the "angel's share" (a whisky reference that refers to the percentage of liquor that evaporates in the barrel's aging process), but what was the pilgrim's share in Spain?

Our first stop was 13 kilometres in, just after Navarrete. Here *bodegas* (underground cellars) suddenly appear like magical hobbit doors. I thought of my grandmother's punky root cellar, the smell so distinct in my olfactory. I could see the bags of potatoes with their eyes sprouting into curly anemic worms. My siblings and I would only nip in for a can of contraband CPlus or root beer. It was always a hurried visit for fear of being locked in.

We were among surreal paprika red crags now. Crickets clicked like playing cards stuck in bicycle spokes. Locals called out, eager to sell their clay pot inventory and chestnuts. Kim and I shared halves of a salami sandwich and torta that mostly flaked to the ground with each bite as a random duo played guitar and an accordion at the edge of the forest.

"Let's get some chestnuts!" I said.

In Toronto, I often bought chestnuts from the Asian grocer on Bloor to eat on my way to work. They were soft and sweet, like sweet potatoes but easier to eat on the move. Kim tried one and was happy for me to finish the rest. Bonus! Instead, she bought an empanada from a Somali guy who was prepping for a vintage car show that weekend. In between setting up mechanical bulls, he was bagging up golden empanadas.

Arriving in Nájera, we checked into Puerta de Nájera, mostly because it was close to the river. It looked palatable enough until we paid and went upstairs. The bunks were jammed in to capitalize on more pilgrims. We'd be sleeping like sardines and probably have a frosty shower. Steam was billowing out the adjoined washrooms like an active volcano. A frazzled woman with a short towel barely covering her middle let us know just how gross the experience was.

"Watch out for the hairball in that far shower," she cautioned. She was right. That hairball was about ready to crawl away. There were 35 people, six toilets, four showers and two sinks. For ten euros, we just wanted a hairball-free space. It was the middle of the afternoon and everyone seemed to be lingering inside, so we dropped our bags and left, whipped first by the spray of a lean Chinese man wicking a T-shirt out. The clothesline was sagging and somebody was moaning in a lower bunk while listening to Pachelbel. A Swedish cyclist had ice on his knee and was yapping into his phone, which increased the volume of everyone else's conversations. We became quickly and inadvertently acquainted with a co-joined friend couple from Michigan who were Ping-Ponging between separate dorm rooms to discuss that night's dinner and tomorrow's elevation.

On the opposite side of the river we found a little solitude and watched a loyal border collie show off his Frisbee prowess. Patient locals were pulling in crayfish in baited baskets – and then an unexpected water snake slithered in, creating a high-pitched reaction from all the men within radius.

After a glass of vino tinto and a few cod and queso croquettes and more chorizo with garlic cloves, we scrapped the idea of an official dinner. We weren't ready to return to the mayhem of our hostel yet. In the dying light we wrote postcards (well, I did, Kim made suggestions for content). I kept my eyes trained on a nearby church spire with a stork's nest suitable for Big Bird, even though I knew the population migrated to Africa in the summer. The nests were a pure marvel on their own. I smiled as an elderly man bent like a question mark passed us, carrying a very vocal birdcage. Nothing like a nice walk with your birds at night.

A local, eager to make conversation, asked us in hand gestures and charades if we were walking to Santiago. Our comprehension was poor on both ends, but, regardless, he offered us a cluster of green grapes with a grin.

Our angel's share, with permission.

The Chicken Church
Nájera to Santo Domingo (20.9 km)

- -

"If you've ever wondered about hard-boiling an egg in the microwave, I can tell you it doesn't work."

As Kim and I laced up our boots, a 60-something woman in a tie-dye Buff was perspiring from a very thorough cleaning of the microwave. "The thing just blew up."

"Well, on an up note, this will be the cleanest this kitchen has ever been," I offered. Looking around, an exploded egg was hardly obvious in a grimy kitchen with a cluttered counter with questionably "washed" dishes and a sponge that looked like it had been found in a scummy pond.

I'm sure she wanted to laugh and agree, but she was too flustered and said no to my offer of a lemon yogurt from our four-pack.

"Thanks, but I've totally lost my appetite now."

I offered the yogurt to Matt, a guy we'd met the night before from Tipperary, Ireland. (Yes, it is really a place, not just an Irish song lyric!) He was pulling on socks and readying for the day.

"No. I'm too fat for the Camino already, thanks."

I drained a chocolate milk drinking box with a not-so-compatible lemon yogurt, but it was still better than an egg explosion and empty stomach. Kim and I were eager to ditch the hostel and escape the chatty Michigan couple that wormed their way into every conversation, eye contact or not. We also wanted to clear the room from the snoring wildebeest that rumbled Kim's bunk all night.

It was a Sedona-like departure, with rusty red craggy canyons and a waning moon lying low in the navy hammock of the dawn sky. A pop-up shop with cubed watermelon and bowls of figs appeared just as our craving for something snacky did. We'd been on a smooth tractor track for most of the morning, cutting through endless vineyards, rustling wheat and wild poppies. There was a restorative coffee stop in Azofra and then another sprint from "Michigan Squared" as we dubbed them. Even though I longed for a savoury tortilla, my nerves frayed a little with their chatty presence. Being social *and* anti-social are equally tiring!

The vineyards eventually thinned, giving way to undulating hills and a wall of square hay bales stacked at least nine metres high. In another classic demonstration of juxtaposition, in Cirueña, the Rioja Alta golf course appeared smack dab in a total ghost town. I snapped a pic for my dad of his golfing buddy (Kim) beside the fourth hole that ran parallel to the Camino. I lost Kim for a moment as she stared off into the rolling greens with yearning.

As we arrived in Santo Domingo (naturally during siesta), tour buses trundled past by the half-dozen. Neatly pressed and perfumed Italians milled about the deserted streets. We found a sun-warmed bench away from the sudden masses in the elaborate, but dizzy, diagonal-stone-patterned Plaza de España (Spain Square). I opened a bag of fried-egg-flavoured chips, which were wonderful, although opening the bag was the equivalent of an instant fart. I wanted to apologize to the kerchiefed lady two benches away.

It was a monumental day. We were actually visiting our first church on the Camino. Even more surprising, it was at my request. The Santo Domingo de la Calzada is known best for its live chickens that are kept in the cathedral.

Legend has it that a German family en route to Santiago stayed with a farmer and his family in Santo Domingo. The farmer's daughter, already at a distinct disadvantage to not be born in the times of Tinder, Christian Mingle and Plenty of Fish, put the moves on the teenage son. He rejected her advances and, as bitchy revenge, she surreptitiously hid several items of silver in his backpack and then openly accused him of stealing. Without CCTV surveillance to back his nonguilty plea, the boy was hanged. His parents continued to Santiago with an even greater weight on their shoulders and stopped on their return to see his body. But they discovered he was still alive, hanging by a noose! The parents were exuberant and demanded that their boy be cut down as he was innocent. This is where shit gets real. The magistrate shouted, "Why, he is no more alive than this roasted chicken I'm about to eat." The roasted chicken then somehow stood up on the magistrate's plate and was brought back to life, feathers and all, and crowed with delight.

The current-day chickens (which work on rotation) in the cathedral are said to be descendants (of the resurrected fowl, of course). Don't shoot the messenger here.

For three euros each, the chicken cathedral visit was a bit of a lunch bag letdown. I expected them to be more interactive, maybe at eye level. Instead, the chickens are housed behind a glass window, five metres above the pews. A bus group had oozed in, crowding out any vantage point, so we had our look from afar, somewhat disappointed after such a tall tale.

Adjacent to the cathedral was a post office museum display with vintage Morse code equipment, even more vintage *correos* bikes and heavy canvas mail delivery bags. Perhaps the early genesis of Uber Eats? The further we crept into the displays, the creepier they became.

"I would love this for our bedroom!" I said to Kim.

"Oh god," Kim laughed, taking in the larger-than-life painting of Jesus being circumcised in front of a hundred townsfolk tuned in to the procedure reality TV-style. There was also a 10,000-piece puzzle on display that we agreed would have taken enormous effort to complete. Probably just as long as the oil painting of the circumcision.

The gift shop was a bit of a horror, with chicken *everything* à la carte. There were chicken egg timers, chicken chocolates and stuffed chickens wearing tiny satin soccer jerseys. ¡Vaya España!

We celebrated (coincidentally) with deli chicken from the local grocer.

"What if this was one of the chickens in the church?" I asked Kim.

She was quite positive that the church chickens were reincarnated. If the legend had anything to do with it, they were probably reincarnated as German boys. I pointed out a whole pork leg for sale for 39 euros. There were several dried legs on a shelf beside the jars of olives and boxes of crackers. I imagined my kid sister having a big wail seeing these. On the flip side, I was always magnetically drawn to the gross and unusual. At Calbeck's grocery store in my hometown, the deli section always had fat and purplish cow tongues tightly wrapped in cellophane on display. I could never resist the pull of a good squishy cow tongue poke.

Curiously, on our way out of the grocery store, an actual 90-kilogram pig on a leash (and its owner) crossed our path. Santo Domingo's vibe was beginning to lean toward the bizarre.

That night we stayed in Abbaye Cistercienne. We would be the last guests as the abbey was closing for the season the very next day. Kim was happy to score some left-behind Caesar dressing for our plain mixed greens in the communal fridge. I found four Starbucks single coffee sachets too and palmed them like drugs, small gifts from the Camino chicken gods, I presumed. This place had to be better than the 220-bed Casa del Santo.

The floors of the historic abbey were topsy-turvy like a funhouse. Initially, a tired and gruff nun showed me a room with three beds. Hello, awkward night! But, conversely, we could luck out and have the room to ourselves. It was another Camino gamble, but I already knew we would rather sleep with 12 people instead of one interloper. Kim was starting to unstuff her sleeping bag when a stout Polish man entered our room and took up residence on the empty bed. I gave Kim eyes and eyebrows that suggested, "SNORER" and told her I'd be back in five minutes. I had read that there were 32 beds in the place, so why did the nun cram this guy in with us?

The nun had already lost her patience with me for some reason and was less than thrilled to see my mug again. "Are there any other rooms? Beds? More private? *Private-o?*"

She scowled and huffed and I followed on her heels up the stairs, again. Her breathing was laboured and I hoped my privacy request wouldn't be the end of her. Or me, if she toppled backwards on the crazy tilted staircase.

On the top floor, the nun creaked open a door and threw her hands up in that universal, "Are you satisfied now?" kinda way. The room had five super single cots, all sloping downward, ensuring an embolism by morning. Each bed had a red plaid lumberjack blanket on it and a pillow sized for a chihuahua.

"This is perfect. Beautiful!" I thanked her, biting my tongue.

The 16th-century Gothic building with baroque facades was exactly the kind of place you'd want to play hide-and-go-seek in. The courtyard was marvelous and the massive stone fireplace inside the dining area made us long for a fire, even though it was still sweltering in the shade.

The abbey housed the tombs of three bishops – the founder and his two nephews. We didn't see them, but there was an eerie presence that night (which could have been due to all the blood rushing out of my head from the mattress angle).

Mary from Prince Edward Island

Santo Domingo to Belorado (22.9 km)

- -

In the morning, after a very failed attempt to make grilled cheese sandwiches on a stick pan (definitely not a no-stick pan), Kim and I met Mary MacPherson. I'd seen her the day before in a violet "I'm an Islander" T-shirt.

"I bet she's from PEI," I said to Kim.

"Why? There are lots of islanders around the world."

"Yeah, but the logo looked like PEI. I'm sure."

Sure enough, Mary MacPherson and her T-shirt were from PEI, where most of Kim's extended family lived. They fell into easy conversation, comparing landmarks, recipes and family trees. Within minutes we learned that Mary was from Stratford, where Kim's parents had lived. Mary knew Kim's dad! The natural reflex question from Mary was, "How is your father doing? I heard he wasn't faring well this summer." My heart ached for Kim and pounded a little harder as I watched her face fall.

It was the first time Kim had encountered that question on the Camino, and everything was just on the surface for her. Mary was quick in her response, recognizing the telltale silence. She hugged Kim and reminded her of what a kind man Earl was. Mary, unbelievably, lived on Rosebank Road, about a five-minute walk from where Kim's parents had lived.

The very small world tightened a little. Of all the times we had been to Stratford, we had never crossed paths with Mary. Instead, we met on the Camino, in little ol' Santo Domingo, in an old abbey kitchen with crappy frying pans.

The extended sunrise was an unfiltered cream soda pink over fields and fields of sunflowers with heavy heads. The lavender blooms of rose of Sharon trees coloured our way until we moved into tall stands of whispering corn husks. At home, blooms of any sort would have long succumbed to summer's end and the first grip of frost.

Passing tied bundles of age-old grape vines for sale, I finally asked what they were for.

"Lamb chops," the man replied, bouncing an ashy cigarette between his lips.

I figured it was a lost-in-translation moment, but when we stopped for coffee in tiny Redecilla (population maybe 150, if that) a guide-toting pilgrim from Germany informed us that La Rioja is known for lamb chops cooked over the embers of old grape vines.

Aha. In the same moment I realized that Spain had really great coffeehouse soundtracks. I was distracted by an old Gwen Stefani track as it transitioned seamlessly to Carole King's "So Far Away." We *were* so far away and somehow still inexplicably knitted to our fellow Canadian alma mater.

Shortly after our welcomed coffee perk, we encountered a distinct decor change in the last 20 kilometres. Homes that followed the path of the Camino now had hippie-style beaded curtain entryways. The cafes did as well, and only the habituated knew how to emerge with a café in hand without dragging a string of beads through the milky foam.

"The vending machines here are crazy!" Kim remarked. I pointed out one that offered hot burgers *and* Oreos *and* beer. We both stopped to examine the pharmacy offerings of another. "Look! There's everything from lip balm to Tiger Balm to condoms to Compeeds." (Compeeds are a Denmark gel plaster product that was sold to Johnson & Johnson in 2002.) "They even have 24-hour Compeeds available!" Kim said.

The slow-motion leg into Nájera had unknowingly left her with an ember-hot blister under her fourth toe. The New-Skin we had cautiously packed was more nuisance than help, and a Rotterdam pilgrim well versed in blisters offered a Compeed to Kim. She decided immediately they were the stuff of miracles as she was able to walk without issue and the blister softened on its own accord and reabsorbed. Kim had been watching horror flicks before we left on how to resolve a blister with a knotted thread remedy. I chose to ignore the YouTube tutorials with crossed fingers. I could do cow tongues and hoofed pig legs, but not blistered human feet.

As we walked, we stocked imaginary vending machines in our heads with all the stuff we were craving. Strawberry Pop-Tarts. Maple-glazed doughnuts. Pogo sticks from the fall fair dunked in mustard. Fig Newtons.

After hours of hay-stubbled fields and melt-your-ice-cream-cone heat, we enjoyed the silent surprise of watching hot air balloons lift into the indigo sky in front of us. In Luxor, Egypt, Kim and I had hot air ballooned over the Valley of the Kings at sunrise. It was an experience we were glad to have had, but mutual risk mitigation led us to agreeing to *never* do it again.

"My god, I can't believe we did it in Egypt! What were we thinking?" Kim said. It was a dicey adventure from the get-go, especially because we both had chronic diarrhea from some murky sugarcane juice we drank in Cairo a week before.

For those who haven't ballooned, you go from ground zero to a mile in the sky without blinking. When you land, you begin to question the merit and reward of riding starry-eyed in a propane-powered balloon in a highly flammable, oversized wicker basket.

Following the balloons' slow sweep into Belorado, we couldn't book into Hostel B quick enough. Just three months old but situated in a 180-year-old house, the hostel was incredibly hip, with an inviting lounge area softened by leather poufs and floor cushions and colour-punched pillows. There was a small *mercado* (store) kitted out with the usual suspects: jars of white asparagus, salami, Gouda, instant noodles and microwave meatballs.

We splurged on a private room and finally succumbed to this thing called a siesta. It was a shadeless day and we were knocked out from the heat and kilometres for a solid two hours. A "Sunday party" raged in the alley outside. It was difficult to navigate the siesta rules. Any other day it was a complete city/village shutdown from 2:00 p.m. to 5:00 p.m., and the bars and restaurants didn't open until 8:00 or 9:00 p.m. Except on Sunday?

Satiated from our siesta, we did our usual private room shower and shave and had sundowners in the plaza with pilgrims on the same REM cycle. We opted for a Hawaiian pizza to go in order to enjoy our private room further. While waiting, we were offered crispy noodle-wrapped shrimp. My new favourite thing.

As we tipped back malta beers, we smiled at the familiar faces on pace with us. It was the convergence of a growing "Camino family." Admittedly, Kim and I kept to ourselves much of the day, but we had enjoyed conversation with Felicity and Louise from South Africa. Mostly we were wondering how we could secure gigs picking olives on Felicity's farm.

There was a still-nameless woman from Rome who had stayed at the abbey too, and we enjoyed sharing colour commentary as she bounced past in her skirt. She had such a tiny frame and such an enormous sack! We waved to "Irish Jack," whom we'd met in Nájera, in the hostel with the hairball shower. He was wearing his "uniform," as we all were. He told us that it was the same checked shirt he was wearing at his office job just the day before he decided to quit and do the Camino. He kept close company with a smiley, blonde, ponytailed woman from Barrie, Ontario. Michigan Squared passed by as well, but they were on a tight agenda to attend mass, so the coast was clear for us.

With our pizza box in hand, we retraced the Paseo del Animo (the Walk of Courage.) There were handprints and footprints of famous people (not known to us) and pilgrims past. I took photos of dumpsters painted with talented renditions of superheroes as church bells sounded across the plaza.

"I still can't believe what we're doing. We're here, in Spain. On the Camino. We are actually doing what we said we would," Kim said. "And they have Hawaiian pizza in Belorado!"

Today's Entertainment: John Deere and Friends

Belorado to Agés (27.7 km)

- -

We jetted out of the very bijou Hostel B on a chocolate milk and cakey chocolate muffin high with nearly 28 kilometres ahead of us. We passed through villages still sound asleep (even the dogs) through the Oca hills. The earthen trail narrowed into a goat path and then widened into a four-lane logging road/fire protection swath through the fragrant pine and oak woods.

"This is the last water fountain until San Juan," we were warned by a nimble man in a Tilley, unaware of his spotty sunscreen-smeared face. "There's nothing for the next 12 kilometres." There had actually been nothing 12 kilometres before either. We were lucky to find coffee and slabs of wet, cheesy tortilla in Villafranca. Tosantos's only cafe was closed, and Villambistia and Espinosa were apocalyptically silent. There were no services whatsoever.

In San Juan de Ortega we pulled in behind a half-dozen handsome horses that we had practically kept pace with since the last village. The colossal monastery was a pit stop for everyone. Rumours were swimming around about full occupancy at the hostels in Agés, and many pilgrims were opting to queue up for the 68-bed refuge instead of continuing on another four kilometres. There were only two options in Agés, a third had shuttered awhile back. Kim and I ordered a pint at the tiny beer counter beside the monastery to debate our night's sleep.

"So the municipal albergue has 36 beds and El Pajar has 34. Or we have a guaranteed spot here," I said.

There were probably ten people holding ground with their backpacks, waiting for the monastery to open for business at 2:00 p.m. Even if everyone on horseback was intending to stay, there was still time to opt in and queue up.

"There's nothing here, though, except the monastery. And this bar," Kim nodded to the barkeep. There were some bags of chips and slices of cake on offer, but that was it. The monastery probably had a pilgrim's dinner, but there would definitely not be a Hawaiian pizza in our future.

"Let's move on. It's only 12:30," I said.

Kim agreed to push on through the tumbleweed town and finished her beer like she was in a contest. "I'd say this was a one-horse town, but there are actually six."

Laughing, we made way for more fretting pilgrims who filtered in, debating the familiar "should we stay or should we go" dilemma. Every slice of available cake on the counter was scooped up, locust-style.

Forty-five minutes later we entered the town proper, which had a small grocer and restaurant. I couldn't wait to say, "I haven't been here in *Agés*." Though the pronunciation was probably much different than my joke.

We found El Pajar de Agés easily – there were only a few buildings on the main street. It was hardly full and we shook our heads, disappointed that we allowed ourselves to get swept into the alarmist talk at the monastery.

We checked in, dumped our stuff in a generic but sufficient room with eight bunks and found our own sunny siesta quarters on a park bench behind the main drag that cut the cool wind in half. It had been a super simple walking day, but the high winds left our cheeks hot pink. The temperature had dropped a little, so I was happy to still have a toque on. Normally, I peeled down within two hours of walking, but every time I thought about unzipping my fleece, minutes later I was zipping it up again.

Kim and I ate leftover pizza that we had bundled up in toilet paper (dual purpose), completely enthralled with the local entertainment. Three men stood around a revving John Deere, discussing logistics. Where should they unload the split wood in the bucket? There was a lot to say about this and, as the tractor purred into action, the wood was dumped nearly on top of the parked car and yelling ensued. Wood was tossed into another pile with a frown as the chubbier of the three stood, unhelpful, simply holding two bunches of grapes.

"Check out the guy with the grapes," Kim said.

It was like he was blankly watching television instead of these two real live men sweating it out. On the flip side, Kim and I were blankly staring at the man with the grapes.

Eventually, all the wood was stacked and the man shuffled inside with his precious grapes. We tucked in too and made reservations for the blackboard-advertised pilgrim's menu, with a few requests. Instead of the spaghetti and meatball starter, we asked for the pumpkin soup side, and instead of pork loin, could we have the other starter of mixed salad? We split a generous paella main between the two of us. The portion sizes were above and beyond and the ceramic jugs of wine that were included in the meal were medieval size too. Were we going into battle?

We caught up with Felicity from Capetown again and chatted more about her olive farm. Each year they hand-picked seven tonnes! Felicity was solo, her walking companion laid up with inflamed joints and blistered feet that weren't finding the Camino agreeable. Felicity was nervous that her friend might choose to fly home, as she wasn't finding any relief with rest. Her enthusiasm and commitment had thinned.

Kim and I had talked about this so many times. It's such a disconcerting commitment, choosing to walk the Camino with a partner or friend. How do you synthesize continuing solo? Do you bus a few legs to cut back on the mileage? Stall a few days? Continue direct to Santiago with a promise to return and walk the missing sections?

We didn't know the answers either. Felicity decided to turn in early and we felt her heaviness and uncertainty.

We were wide-eyed at eight o'clock and the dining area had long cleared out. The hostel was small and the staff was eager to wipe down tables and close up shop.

"Should we go to that tiny bar on the corner?" Kim asked.

"Yeah. Everyone is in bed here."

There were three women sharing rice and chicken legs at a round table just inside the door. As we milled about, waiting for service, the youngest said we were welcome to join them. The cranky waiter was perturbed that we didn't want dinner and hastily brought us wine. The conversation with animated sisters Ang and Lucy, and Lucy's daughter Rose, flowed as easily as the wine did.

"Shall we share another bottle?" Lucy asked with her beguiling Kiwi accent.

"Of course. I tell you, if any of my math or history teachers were from New Zealand, I would have learned something," I confessed. I liked collecting friends with accents, especially Kiwi, Australian and South African.

The girls would be stopping in Burgos the next day, as their work schedules didn't permit the luxury of carrying on to Santiago. Rose, however, was giddy about carrying on to Greece to hang out on a yacht with her friends for a week. Her mother shook her head. "She's the youngest and here I am, heading back to work while she goes on a Contiki!"

Again, we were crestfallen to lose the company of three women we found such an instant connection with. Was this our fate? We hadn't seen Clara since Puente la Reina and were probably completely off track with our itineraries by now. Was it because our time together was condensed that the kinship seemed so sweet? I found it hard to believe that another month with these gals could turn sour, so I gave up on making a philosophy about it all and enjoyed their precious presence and honeyed laughter. We let the true-blue All Blacks fans know that we expected a Māori haka dance when we parted ways.

Walking back to our hostels together, we stopped at El Pajar, warm from wine and the day's wind, to say goodbye. We realized the Kiwis were staying at the same place – in our room! None of us would sleep a wink that night, though, thanks to the restless guy with a stuffed-up nose on the upper bunk beside me. His nocturnal sounds were a cross between a moaning dog and a creaking door in a haunted house. They were so inhuman that I intentionally lay awake, dead curious to hear what sound he would make next.

Marzia's Philosophy
Agés to Burgos (22.3 km)

The Kiwis were still stretching and yawning when we left. Those gathered in the cramped hostel lobby gathering poles and boots said it was four degrees out. Four! It was already 8:00 a.m., so I was happy to be leaving with a bit of soft sun on our backs as it was the first morning we could see our breath. The sky was like a giant Etch A Sketch with a dozen jet streams criss-crossing in the powder blue atmosphere.

A hot cocoa IV would have been a dream as somebody had flicked the wind machine on high. Soon enough we'd be navigating an extremely rocky trail that seemed blasted by meteorite strikes. A few wobbles helped increase my core temp. It was a stability test for our ankles and a focus test for my sleepy head.

Eating dense curried rice and veggie-stuffed pastries that could have doubled as doorstops, we passed through Atapuerca, a UNESCO World Heritage Site. More than 90 per cent of the prehistoric humanoid artifacts found in Europe were unearthed here. Excavations had also revealed a new species believed to be cannibalistic – *Homo antecessor.* I swallowed the last bites of the dry pastry, hardly surprised at cannibalism being a more popular dietary choice in the area.

The walk into Burgos was increasingly industrial, akin to 90 minutes of walking through Scarborough's scabby, lacklustre outskirts. We hadn't seen any markers or arrows and hoped we didn't have to retrace a single step backwards through such dullness. It was a big pavement day into central Burgos. We kept our eyes trained on the only other pilgrim we'd seen for seemingly hours – a smiley Chinese teen who could be spotted at 50 paces. He had a tin cup clipped to a carabiner on his pack and it swung wildly to and fro, clinking with each footfall. Kim didn't know how he could stand it. We couldn't as followers! We passed him, but one short coffee refuel stop had us tailing behind him again.

Clink. Clink.

I felt sorry for the Kiwis, knowing this was their last day on the Camino. And what a bore! After such halcyon days, they would depart with the belching industries and chain-link fences stitched in their minds.

At El Pajar I had pocketed a brochure for a hostel in Burgos that looked promising. There was no price tag on it, and in such a large city its location could have been way off our intended track. At the stoplight, I asked Annette Bening's Burberry-scarf-wrapped doppelganger for directions. We were close! The hostel was near Río Arlanzón and, according to Annette's enthusiastic charades, we had to cross the river or use a trampoline.

Hostel Burgos was super slick for 16 euros each, including breakfast. And the hostel brewed its own beer in-house! It was successfully running with the industrial vibe that was totally unlike the "industrial" manufacturing wasteland we had narrowly made our way out of. The orange palette and wood pallet seating with neon cushions in the lounge were a fun twist. I browsed the stack of freebie books – apparently only

Dutch and German pilgrims were reading on the Camino. The sole English offering was *Fifty Shades of Grey*. Pass.

Our room was a Jenga pile of bunks. We could hardly bend in any direction and there were only four of us in the no-vacancy, eight-bunk room. Feeling claustrophobic, we made a hurried exit for our routine riverside park bench beers to people watch. Kim and I lived in a town with a population of 600, so people watching was a big deal.

"Did you see her feet?" Kim asked.

This was her famous question and my famous answer was always, "No!"

"She was on the bunk below you. The Korean woman? Her feet were a mess. They looked like raw meat."

"Gross. Stop," I insisted. Kim had been blister-free since her minor scare and now this woman's feet had her on high alert all over again.

"She had an entire plastic bag of bandages and gauze strips. She won't be walking tomorrow."

Kim and I had talked about taking another rest day, as Burgos was a popular stop. We both felt solid, though, and agreed to just keep chugging. While our extra day in Estella was pure bliss, it felt odd to fall out of the rhythm.

It was easy to see the draw for a rest day here. There were marvelous museums and cathedrals, irresistible bakeries and cafes pumping out the sweet aroma of ground beans and cinnamon-laced fried churros. The candy shop was a cloud of icing sugar and intricately wrapped "OMG" moments. Every restaurant spilled out onto a trendy patio space where the beautiful sipped Perrier through straws and picked delicately at minimalist plates.

By the river, century-old sycamores lined the promenade. It was a Chanel runway. Men confidently wore pencil-legged salmon chinos, just-pressed purple button-downs and red sneakers. All the men in Burgos were either gay or really dapper.

Well-heeled women wore silver and gold New Balance sneakers and sequined spandex. Suited men sped by on motorized scooters and old-timey cruiser bikes. And the dogs! It was the Westminster Kennel Club Dog Show! Springer spaniels, Frenchies, dachshunds and Yorkies with tiny bows pranced and cantered past. Eventually, pulling ourselves to an upright position, we asked a bookstore owner for a cool bar recommendation. She sent us to Norte GastroBar and it was exactly what we wanted. It was like drinking a beer in our old stone house, but with a vintage motorcycle parked inside. We nursed Mahou Negras the colour of motor oil and a bowl of hot and spicy nuts. Norte doubled as a smoothie bar, and as quickly as our bartender poured pints, she was whirring Nutella shakes and offering dried kiwi pieces to a hyper toddler in mini high-tops.

We picked up Brie, Pamplona salami, some pickled peppers and a baguette for a picnic at our hostel. It was like sitting inside an IKEA kitchen showroom. Marzia was quick to join us, invite or not. She was a big, fun-oozing personality from Italy who had been on the move for the last three and a half years. Most recently, Marzia had lived with the Hare Krishnas in Australia before opting out of the money-free existence. She had her yoga and scuba creds, so, when she needed to, she picked up jobs long enough to get her to the next place. Like South Korea. Like the Camino.

"Now I'm working on my philosophy." I liked that Marzia said this out loud. She was engaging because she was so whimsical and frank. "I've done the Camino before and I've decided now is not my time. I'm going to take the bus to Santiago and then head to Muxía. I'll spend three weeks there instead. You totally have to go to Muxía after Santiago, trust me."

We offered her a glass of wine in exchange for the entertainment and enlightenment.

"I'm always establishing self-challenges. You know, like 12 hours of silence, no social media, no drinking." Immersed in solitude, she discovered "it's all about being what you want. If you want love, you need to BE love to attract love."

She wanted to tell us more about her philosophy, but she was still working on it. "You two totally need to go to The Alchemist too. They have communal pasta nights and everyone sings in the kitchen. They do these gorgeous lavender footpaths. Totally chill."

I made a mental note *not* to go to The Alchemist (though I adored the book). Singing in the kitchen was my biggest nightmare. I hardly liked ordering burgers from Lick's in the Beaches in Toronto. I don't want my order sung to me, let alone to sing for meatballs and noodles.

At the bottom end of our bottle, Marzia said we would hate her in the morning. "My alarm is going off at three a.m. to catch the bus."

We didn't hate her because of that. We mildly hated her for hitting her snooze eight times before shuffling her way out of our shared 9 x 7–foot bedroom.

THREE

The Meseta

With each region, there is a distinct shift in architecture, evident in roof materials, walls of mud or stone and doors like this medieval entrance.

A Spanish Happy Meal
Burgos to Hontanas (31.4 km)

- -

It took 45 minutes to exit the urban bones of Burgos into suburbia, and then, just as sudden, we were in the dry-as-Melba-Toast desert of the Meseta. The wind was full tilt as we followed a rutted farmer's track through 25 kilometres of leaning blonde hay and a queue of turbines spinning at warp speed. Our training in the Ferndale Flats served us well! The zero-elevation scape of wind-whipped pastoral vistas felt like home. Some pilgrims actually voluntarily skip the Meseta due to its reputation of being a monotonous mental grind void of shade.

I was still yawning hours later from Marzia's alarm but enjoying every bit of the no-shade zone. It was October, so our days would presumably get colder. I'd only worn my pants once, and only so I could finally launder my shorts. (Or Kim could launder them, to be truthful.)

The last 11 kilometres became trying. "I feel like I have full body tendonitis," I said to Kim.

"I feel like my feet have been through a meat tenderizer. These stones are so jagged they're going right through my soles."

"The reprieve is ahead, babe." Our last distance was quiet but noisy with self-talk, as Hontanas seemed like an oasis evaporating as rapidly as our water supply.

There were four albergues in Hontanas. Some pilgrims walked like missiles, unswerving, focused on one target: the next municipal albergue. Generally, municipals were the cheapest option at five euros and always had a kitchen. The amenities were Spartan, while a few more dollars usually earned you a pillowcase, a pouf or a showerhead that didn't feel like a horse with a prostate issue pissing on your head.

Albergue Juan de Yepes was at the top of the bowl that Hontanas sat hidden in. Though I was always tempted to see all the hostel offerings, to ensure that we were choosing the coolest one, Kim was fading. I didn't suggest walking any further for fear that we'd have to double back to Juan de Yepes anyway.

"Look," I said to Kim, in an effort to pull her out of her tired funk. "They even have beer on tap. And a cute pantry!" The shelves were stocked with all the pleasures: dates, olives, walnuts and bananas.

There were a few taps at the counter where I filled out the reservation paperwork and stamped our passports. How civilized! I booked two beds and ordered two pints in one swoop. The courtyard was sublime and we were quick to capitalize on the two vacant extended loungers. I had butt chafe (it's a thing!) from sitting on so many wooden barstools and benches, and the cushions made me sigh out loud.

Our perfect perch was sunset central with an unobstructed view of the 14th-century Iglesia de la Inmaculada Conception and its giant bell that gonged on the hour. Kim washed a few items and took advantage of the clothesline and Beaufort scale, where 80 per cent of pilgrims' clothes and socks had already blown to the ground.

There was a seductive waft of paella in the air that mixed with the sunbaked limestone terrace and just-washed hair.

Several clusters were hobbling in. The hostel's outdoor communal footbath transformed into a human version of a watering hole, not unlike Tanzania's Ngorongoro Crater. On my way back from juggling another round of beer I noticed that the terrace was beginning to resemble a M*A*S*H unit. Blisters, iodine. A German guy's heel was practically falling right off. It was a total gross-out show.

"Should we forage for dinner soon?" Kim asked.

"Not after what I just witnessed." Of course, Kim craned her head, almost eager to see the horror.

We gave up our front row sunset seats when a stream of chattering bats left the belfry of the church and scattered into the encroaching night. It was easy to decide on dinner with only two options in town. I asked a local about the general store and when it might open up.

"It hasn't opened in three years," he grinned, revealing more gaps than teeth in his smile.

There was a sliver of a moon crawling across the sky as we had a laugh over our "Spanish Happy Meal." For four and a half euros we were served a burger, a healthy helping of fries and a glass of wine!

"I think there are more ounces of wine in our glasses than ounces of burger in our buns," Kim commented, holding up her one-centimetre-thick, steakette-style patty.

"You're right, but I think this is the best thing I've ever eaten." I could have eaten two. About once a month I have a very hungry day for no particular reason. The burgers triggered flashbacks to my emergence from the Costa Rican jungle after a three-month volunteer stint when I was 20. After a steady feed of rice, black beans and canned mackerel, I matched the appetite of my mate, Tomas, in San José and ordered two Whoppers at Burger King. *Two* Whoppers! I still can't believe it. To boot, I had a blueberry shake. And fries. And parasites, but that's another story.

Our room was surprisingly quiet when we returned. Everyone was equally wiped out by the heat and the kilometres of the day. A Swede still carried on a phone conversation from his top bunk, sharing a story from the "Camino Radio" (gossip grapevine) about a pilgrim who had broken his leg falling out of the top bunk at a hostel.

Sleep came fast and heavy for me on the lower bunk, while Kim slept a little more cautiously on the upper tier.

Bunk Bed Break

Hontanas to Boadilla del Camino (28.5 km)

- -

In dawn's melon-coloured cobwebs of light, we trundled past the restaurant we had our Happy Meal at the night before. A glowing digital LED sign indicated a brisk five degrees Celsius. We'd start with toques and mitts but be panting in a 30-degree preheated oven in no time.

Before the ten-kilometre mark the hill loomed. Kim saw it first. "Oh god."

We were snaking toward Alto de Mostelares, but it was possible we were veering left, not over. I should have known after nearly two weeks on the Camino that if there was a hill or mountain, we were probably going over it.

The caution sign indicated a 13 per cent grade, and it was felt sharply in the calves. As a runner, I've always found uphill climbs so much easier than the descent, which loads your kneecaps in an uncontrollable way.

A bouncy group from Italy had just barfed out of a tour bus at the bottom of the grade. They all had poles and visors pulled low, energy bars in hand and sleek little day packs. They smelled so clean, just laundered, like a Dove commercial.

"Have they come up for air?" Kim said, huffing a little.

I was huffing too; it was so early for this kind of ask. Three women behind us yapped and yapped like they were at a cocktail party. Their voices carried and rang in our ears. They were too far behind us to slow down and let them pass, so we pushed on faster.

Luckily, the group had its first scheduled pit stop at the top of the hill and we were happy for the solitude of our own footfalls again. Kim tried her new zigzag technique that she had spied another pilgrim doing on a descent. I followed suit, although I zigged in too tight of a pattern and was on Kim's heels. The slalom approach definitely worked, lessening the impact on my quads. The charley horse that kept biting me had dulled and disappeared. I'd totally forgotten about it and was impressed that the steep 18 per cent descent didn't physically remind me.

We passed San Anton church, one that I had made special note of. San Antonio (not to be confused with Saint Anthony, who is the patron saint of lost things) is the patron saint of animals, and on January 17, pet owners in Spain bring their animals to be blessed on this sacred saint's day. Though I am more familiar with the blessings of St. Patrick, I immediately liked what I read about this St. Antonio guy too.

I was surprised the Meseta had such a bad rep. There was an imposing pre-Roman castle (Castillo de San Esteban), a 13th-century Gothic church and a 16th-century behemoth with carved skulls along the wall.

We didn't really stop again until Itero de la Vega, 20 kilometres into our day, where the familiar dirt road eased into smooth pavement. We'd found a rhythm on the 20-kilometre legs with coffee and a tortilla two hours in and sock changes then and once more with a beer and baguette around the 13-kilometre mark.

Today it was a park bench picnic of cured salami, Brie and crackers. The Brie had melted perfectly in my pack, like it had been under the broiler for a few minutes, making spreading easier. I just needed a little sweet and tart lingonberry jam and some crushed pistachios.

Rolling into Boadilla like tumbleweeds, we couldn't believe how sleepy it was.

"Helllooo?"

There were three sleeping options. The municipal hostel looked both tired and frightening. I feared we might walk away with tetanus or something. It looked like it should be condemned. Behind door number two, the lobby area of the next hostel was so jammed with pilgrims desperate for lunch that we didn't have the patience to wait. I wondered if we could shimmy up the church spire and snuggle up in the massive stork's nest.

It was another six kilometres to Fromista, and as much as we wanted to keep walking for alternatives alone, we decided to see just how much the fancy-pants Hotel Rural En el Camino would be. The elaborately carved entry door alone was intimidating on the wallet. Kim flapped around in the air-conditioned, marble-floored lobby as I waited for an employee to appear. A pursed-lipped woman was lingering over a glass of red wine the size of an egg cup, watching a Spanish game show on blare-level to override the sound of a vacuum somewhere nearby.

I felt like a true Pigpen, leaning on the counter, a sweat-soggy baseball hat turned backwards. A short woman in a hairnet with ruby red lipstick appeared. She was so short behind the counter I would have missed her completely.

"Hola. How much for a private room?"

I didn't bother requesting one bed, as most queen beds we had encountered in Spain were two singles pushed together, which we would do anyway.

"Forty-five euro."

I was stunned and slapped my Visa on the counter. The other two hostels were no longer an option in my mind. As I signed, she filled two bowls with salty potato chips. An odd welcoming gift, but I accepted them and she pointed to the beer taps.

"We'll be back," I promised. "After we drop our gear." The room was opulent and so shiny. So clean! I tiptoed around in my socks, leaving powdery dust everywhere I went. Once my socks were yanked off, I caught a glimpse of my legs in the full-length mirror and laughed at the dirt lines.

"Ohmygod, look how filthy we are!"

We needed a break from the bunk bed routine. It was strange living so "packed up" all the time, but we had learned to be efficient. Whatever we were wearing the next day (T-shirt one or two, green socks or purple) was tucked into a corner beside our heads. Water bottles were pre-filled the night before, and with a shot of yogurt, we were out the dark door after stuffing our sleeping bags away.

Kim took full advantage of our extra square footage and emptied her bag to revisit what might be at the bottom. Rain jacket. Pants. Pack cover. We had our bags' contents memorized, really.

You'd think we'd be fighting over the shower, but both of us were eager to laze about in the courtyard, even with the rings of dust around our ankles. The ruby-lipsticked employee issued us chip refills and Viking-sized pints. My forearms were quivering.

Two equally dusty cyclists from the UK pulled into the courtyard where we had camped out, and we surreptitiously watched them navigate about 30 white sheets hanging on the hotel clothesline. The couple smiled and said they too were ready to guzzle a beer. They had rented bikes for 16 days and had the pressure of reaching Santiago on a stiff deadline.

"Walking *has* to be easier," the wife confessed. Kim and I agreed; it would be. While cyclists can opt for paved routes, there were purists trying to bike the traditional Camino. Kim and I have both biked a lot and it would be a foolish assumption to think riding the Camino was an easy ticket. The terrain was pure evil in sections, and on the single-track goat paths pannier bags would be clipping tall grasses and snagging bushes. The elevations were heart-stoppers to begin with, but trying to crank a bike up the serpentine trail *and* pass pilgrims every few feet?

Kim's friend had talked about biking the Camino with her vegan wife. Every day we came up with convincing reasons why they should never attempt it. There were so many other swaying factors too. I'd noticed a few bulletin boards with vegan Camino maps hanging from pushpins. It would be a tough go – even for the most flexible vegan or vegetarian. If you haven't noticed the repetition of salami, Iberian ham and chorizo lunches and dinners here so far, well...

The Camino attacks at every angle. It's debilitating for light sleepers or those who like to sleep in. There's zero privacy. Sometimes you have to shit in a very open field because there are no trees or even a blade of grass to hide behind. If you love sleeping in, you'll be cranky. It's a total no-go zone for control freaks and/or those who can't operate on any variation from three square meals a day. It's nonstop baguette, sour T-shirts, a snore fest and lights out at 9:30 p.m. But, somehow still, above all else there's extraordinary in the ordinary. I loved that our only obligation was to walk to the next village and feed ourselves. And then do it all over again. I also loved that we were staying at Hotel Rural. Unfortunately, beyond potato chips, it no longer served dinner. We had to shuffle back to the jammed joint next door and squeeze in. Pilgrim's menu it was.

Kim and I split the meal. I had the savoury white bean soup starter, which came in a cauldron suitable for an entire family. Kim had the main, a fried piece of hake (fish). We both picked at the iceberg and tomato salad and passed along the custard doused in cinnamon to the razor thin guy beside us.

In the sanctuary of our own room we showered obnoxiously long. I couldn't imagine how anyone who didn't go to summer camp or have siblings could survive the Camino. Bunk beds, and dinner with a dozen. It was a lot. As Luis warned us in Saint-Jean, "The hardest part of the Camino is the social."

Marzia reminded us too of how the Camino experience is distilled. It wasn't her own philosophy but a theory that floated around.

"The first part is totally physical. Then the Camino becomes mental in the Meseta. The heat, the unchanging landscape. It grates on you. And, finally, the last half, it's spiritual. You'll see."

An Unconventional Convent

Boadilla del Camino to Carrión de los Condes (24.5 km)

It was a frosty six degrees as we circled around the tiny town in the sleep-drunk wee hours of morn. And by tiny, I mean a population of 70. Of that population, Kim and I only saw three genuine residents – including the woman drinking egg-cup wine while watching game shows in our hotel lobby.

In our Camino scavenger hunt we picked up a Canadian couple from Calgary, equally baffled about how to exit the hamlet. Round and round we went, walking minutes down a few tractor paths only to return defeated. Colin had his map and two guidebooks at the ready, while Cathy shone her headlamp around like a searchlight.

Two Germans made an abrupt left 30 metres ahead of us and we kept watch until their headlamps dimmed. Colin shrugged, "Well, at least there will be six of us if it's the wrong way."

The first six kilometres to Fromista along the Canal de Castilla disappeared without notice as we fell into the same pace as Cathy and Colin, swapping hostel horror stories and Canadiana. The sky was still dark denim by the time we crossed the dam complex and stopped for a routine tortilla and coffee in Fromista. We joined amiable locals already saddled up to the bar for 8:00 a.m. sangria and beers taking in the morning news on the telly. While it seemed too early for beer, it was also too early to visit the Fromista Cheese Museum with its patchy hours of business.

We split company with our countrymen, opting for an alternate route along the Ucieza River. Colin informed us that the trail wasn't as well marked, but given the choice it sounded more appealing than walking along the gravel shoulder of the highway into Villalcázar. The road into Carrión would run parallel to the road again, so we bid them adieu for the hinterland and babbling brook.

The skinny river was lined with even skinnier poplars and trembling aspens. Birdsong volume was on high. European robins look dramatically different from *our* American (Canadian) robin, as their distinct rusty orange breast plumage runs up their necks and over their eyes. They are particularly friendly and one seemed to tag along with us as we walked.

Flies swirled around our heads and tried to sit in our ears. Coincidentally, they seemed to appear along the Camino at the same time as the tour buses, two days previous.

We passed a stout Irishman who looked and sounded a lot like Mr. Magoo but with an Irish lilt and calves as big as my head. He was thrilled to see us, as he had been hobbling along, convinced he was on the wrong track. Kim gave me our top-secret signal to get a move on before being sucked into conversation. She waved the flies away from her head and said, "I have to keep moving! These flies!" I agreed and took off, hot on her heels, despite wanting to stop and write down the name of a cool albergue with tipis that I could see in the distance. "You can Google it later," she said. I laughed at how very social we were both becoming, practically jogging away from people to maintain our solitude.

It was a long, flat haul into Carrión. Trickles of sweat felt like lemonade in my bloodshot eyes.

Cathy had asked if were staying at the Espíritu Santo convent that night. "It's famous for the singing nuns. They put on a concert every evening; it will be lovely!"

I wasn't entirely convinced, but I did like the *Sound of Music* when I was 7.

At the convent, the nuns barked out instructions. I've had kinder experiences going through customs in China or Thailand. The eldest was strict and saucy, wagging her finger at all the misdoings going on in the entryway while she checked in the pilgrims ahead of us.

Exasperated, she yelled at Kim and another woman for not leaning their walking poles along the designated wall. Again, the finger pointing. A man clearly wilting from the heat was hollered at for leaving his bag in the spot he did.

"Jesus!" I said to Kim. "I'm almost afraid to stay here."

It was five euros for the pseudo-military experience, and we were surprised to learn we'd be sleeping in actual beds, not bunk beds. The co-ed dorm room slept 20 or so and it was the largest display of gaudy floral duvets I'd ever seen. We claimed beds at the opposite end of someone who was clearly ill, nose blowing and coughing as we entered. A few beds were already occupied with napping pilgrims. The guy behind us was scolded for putting his backpack on the precious duvet cover.

We decided to put on our flip-flops and leave the convent before we were forced to polish pews or buff the stained glass.

Carrión was a livelier town, but, again, siesta impeded our hopeful plans. The Museum of the Nativity Scenes was closed. I was intrigued by the niche weirdness of such a museum. It reminded me of the folksy Byggðasafnið Hvoll in Dalvík, Iceland. The Icelandic museum was established as a tribute to one of the tallest men on the island, Jóhan Pétursson, who was seven feet seven inches tall.

On par, the nativity scene museum housed displays from Ireland, China, Italy, Niger and Bhutan, among others. The collection is over a thousand strong. I had looked forward to seeing the mini scenes inside a bottle and on an iron spike, as advertised. One was apparently created inside a sunflower seed! To me, this was much more fascinating than singing nuns, especially if the cranky one was a choir member.

Kim was okay with skipping the rock concert, confident that Colin and Cathy would give us the full report. Disappointed that the nativity museum was a bust, we embarked on my second mission for Carrión: to search for the holy Patxaran. Made from blackthorn or plum-sized sloe berries, the digestif is sometimes mixed with cava and called a "San Fermin" or traditionally enjoyed on the rocks. Patxaran (in Basque language) or *pacharán* (Spanish) was on my edible Spain checklist for historical purposes. The elixir dates back to the Middle Ages and was served at royal weddings in the 14th century.

"We've had the Iberico pork from the acorn-eating pigs and hake fish. Might be tough to find the wild boar. Oh, and I think that Tetilla cheese, the one shaped like a breast, is in Galicia," I said to Kim, reviewing our to-eat list.

Kim was accustomed to my crazy to-eat lists. It led us to camel stew in Egypt, elk burgers and fermented shark in Iceland, Cheez Whiz waffles in Caye Caulker, Belize, peppercorn beer in Quebec City and duck wonton pizza in Shanghai. These among other questionable things – and the odd fried insect.

The Spain list was incredibly tame in comparison: spider crabs, *vieras de Santiago* (scallops grilled in a brandy sauce) and the likes of *kalimotxo* (or *calimocho*), an iconic Spanish cocktail that's simply red wine mixed with cola.

We found a bar that served Patxaran shots for two euros. It was a sweet syrup, kind of like sambuca's gentler cousin. Wine was even cheaper here for one euro a glass, and each glass was served with a free plate of spicy potatoes and a few toothpicks as cutlery. We stood at the bar's edge watching local kids hoof a soccer ball at a younger boy trying to ride his bike across the square. Kids these days! A lanky Dane introduced himself, recognizing the telltale attire (and unquenchable thirst) of a pilgrim. Cimmy had been walking since May 7 – from Denmark! This put everything into perspective for Kim and me. This guy had been walking for five months! This is not uncommon to hear, but it was the first time we'd met the actual person whose story and mystery was carried from one end of the Camino and back again.

Back at the convent, the kitchen was a hectic mess of amateur chefs frying up slabs of schnitzel, while others jockeyed for burners to boil water for eggs and noodles. We nodded to the group of Koreans we had smiled at a few times that day. They were clustered around a dinner that consisted of two tubs of ice cream and two six packs of Amstel beer.

Kim and I had a bag of greens, a jar of white asparagus, tuna and what we presumed was a dill yogurt dressing. There were offers of leftover schnitzel (not ice cream, that was decimated like hyenas discovering carrion), but we passed and retreated upstairs to our elegant dorm room. It would be a restless sleep, even though the beds had proper sheets and coverlets. Most nights it was a symphony of nylon sleeping bag shimmying punctuated by zipper adjustments.

Halfway with a Tutu

Carrión de los Condes to Terradillos de los Templarios
(26.6 km)

We were happy for the alliance of Colin and Cathy, who fed us so much intel from their trusty guidebook the day before. Though we skipped their nun recommendation, we heeded their advice to load up on snacks, as there were no shops for the first 18 kilometres. Relying on pop-ups would defeat the surprise of a pop-up, so we were okay with carrying nuts, small tubs of coconut yogurt, and granola bars (that tasted oddly like penicillin).

It was a warmer start at nine degrees, and the long, flat gravel road ahead was the kind that inspired runaway-dog-on-the-prairie-type jokes. Like, if your dog were to run away, you would see it running across the fields three days later due to the flat, treeless scape. Still, void of trees and terrain, it was difficult to find the trail markers again. Had they painted them on the sides of moving cows? Runaway dogs?

The Camino palette had shifted to yolk yellow and ochre. It was a total dustbowl and the dirt devils swirled behind tilling tractors on both sides of the trail.

We had some added baggage and were hopeful to catch "Roma," the sweet Italian woman we had met back at the abbey in Santo Domingo near the famed chicken church. In the dim light of the dorm, she had left super early, unaware that her signature skirt was on the floor at the end of her bed. Roma normally had spandex capris on with her "tutu" over top. Kim and I usually found her later in the day when she stopped for a longer rest over lunch. She was legging 35- or 40-kilometre days in an effort to compress her walking calendar into 25 days or less.

Kim spied Colin and Cathy ahead first. Cathy was nearly six feet tall and her silhouette was easy to spot in the barren scape.

"We hit the halfway mark!" Colin shouted.

"We did?" I replied, doubtful.

I'm not sure if we high-fived or sighed at the thought of another half to go. We'd logged 400 kilometres before we left Canada, so I was feeling a bit like Cimmy who had been walking since Denmark. It was halfway, but really the math indicated we'd already walked the whole way. Unofficially.

While I was CEO of Finding Weird Things to Eat, Kim was the mathematician, adding our mileage. When I ran half-marathons, I rarely wore a watch or looked at the mileage signs. It was easier just to keep steady and run uninhibited. I also have this theory about sleeping naturally and not succumbing to an alarm. Luckily, few of my jobs have required a start time before noon. Left to my own devices, testing my natural sleep patterns is still a dangerous go. In other words, thank god for Kim.

But what if we were to walk and sleep as long as we could? As long as it felt comfortable? The 790 km sign to Santiago in Roncesvalles still haunted me. I'm more of the "don't tell me, I'll just keep running or walking without knowledge" sort.

Kim is very measured, though, and these sorts of details are necessary for her. I rarely look at a clock when I'm working, walking or running, but she is Big Ben. Throughout the day at home, she will randomly announce the time – not because we have to be somewhere, just because. It's a cute and quirky thing.

I was surprised she missed our halfway mark, though it crept up on us so fast. Admittedly, we were entering that inevitable chronically groggy and mentally foggy stage of "Where did we sleep last night? What was the last town we were in?" It would take us five kilometres of serious concentration to piece it together. The days were blurring with the steady visual void of landmarks. It was hay, tractors and cornflower sky. Repeat.

There was a pop-up along the way, despite the warnings to stock up, at the ten-kilometre mark. It was the first terrible coffee we'd had, though the molten-hot temp was welcomed. The plastic cup it was poured in seemed ready to melt in my gloved hand. Kim spied Roma; her back was turned to us as she stretched. We pulled out her tutu skirt and asked if she might be missing something. Kim held up her skirt and the hug was the kind you'd give someone who'd found your lost dog.

"I didn't even know! I would have been so lost without my skirt!" Roma was so gracious and belly-laughed when we said it didn't really suit our style, otherwise we might have pinched the lost skirt and kept mum. (Cheri-Lyn would have kept it for sure.)

A group of guys were eating sandwiches in monster bites and drinking beer already. It was such a merry time on the Camino, any time. Kim was reminded of her shift workdays. When you've been up since 4:30 a.m., you're technically eating your lunch by 8:00 a.m.

We blew into town after passing a stand-alone albergue that had chickens on a rotisserie. It was hard not to be lured in by the intoxicating smell permeating the air, but we pressed on to get further along our way. At J. de Molay, we paid for bunks, not so enthusiastic about the jammed rooms once we located them. The place resembled the aftermath of university frosh week, with drooping clotheslines and dropping bodies. The distinct draw here was the sunny rooftop terrace – and we quickly retreated to the hidden space with beers and pinchos of pickles, pickled onions and bites of tortilla on baguette slices.

As we watched weary pilgrims parade in, Kim and I formed blueprints for our ideal hostel. We would have designated soundproof chambers for snorers. Early risers could have their own room. Why couldn't rooms be designed by departure times? Though the Camino was largely conflict-free, increased swearing was predictable from 5:00 a.m. onward when the "squirrels" would begin rustling and packing up. Seemingly, the squirrel set would unload their entire backpack contents and proceed to slowly (and painfully) wrap each item in rattling, crinkling, eardrum-vibrating plastic bags. There would be rooms for those who wanted to chat and have a big ol' tea party. Kim and I had attended a cheesy Valentine's party years prior where singles were encouraged to wear pink glow sticks around their necks, while couples indicated their relationship status by donning blue. If you wanted to be a socialite on the Camino, could you please wear a pink glow stick and join the squirrels?

We put our selectively social pink on when we saw Gudrun for the first time since Estella. She hugged us tight, like a long-lost comrade. The heat was eating at her energy levels, but she was still full steam ahead with her enthusiasm.

"Let's have a bottle of wine together!" Gudrun had found solid company in Teresa, a twentysomething from Germany. Sometimes they walked apart, with Teresa pushing ahead, but at night they reconvened and chose to stay at the same hostels and cook meals together.

"Tonight, pizza!" Gudrun exclaimed. Kim and I ordered one to share – the kitchen was pumping them out every few minutes. Teresa opted for the pilgrim's menu and surrendered her jug of wine to the three of us, choosing to have a coffee with her soup instead. Gudrun ordered a pizza too, which was smart for leftovers. Except Gudrun ate the entire pizza herself! Kim asked her if there was a dog under her side of the table. For such a tiny woman, her appetite was enormous. The last time we'd seen her, she had a bag of spinach, noodles, six pieces of fruit and a baguette. And that was for one sitting.

I said to Kim that it would be nice if there was an app where we could check on people we'd met along the Camino, to see where they were along the trail. Kim laughed, "It's called texting."

Oh yeah, there's that. And we didn't have a phone anyway.

Baguette-Busted Retainer

Terradillos to Calzadilla de los Hermanillos (26.4 km)

- -

I decided on my Camino memoir's placeholder title in Terradillos around 3:00 a.m. *Hostile in the Hostels: Near Murder on the Camino.* After several hours of mansnoring to the max (the kind that makes your ear's cochlea recoil), the Swedish foursome continued on their oblivious way. The night before, I'd watched in amazement as they sniffed out extra blankets from another dorm room and made forts out of the bunk bed frames. They created private and wholly efficient fabric walls around the lower bunks for their wives. At 6:00 a.m. sharp, the leanest one – in his tighty-whities – flicked on the overhead lights. There were eight of us in the room, but apparently four were ready to go. "We're up, so you're getting up," seemed to be the neon message.

The Swedes shuffled, shifted and stretched. The women emerged from their forts. One of them had spent a solid ten minutes doing something annoying with a plastic bag. Like the token old lady trying to break into her Werther's Originals in the movie theatre for half the movie.

Retaliating in a slightly passive-aggressive way, I slyly turned off the overhead light when I left to use the washroom down the hall. On my way back, I noticed the light had been turned on again. I casually turned it off. Wasn't IKEA Swedish for "common sense?" I was at a loss for these four. One of the Swedes flapped over and illuminated the room once more. As I packed up, just an arm's length away, I flipped the light off one more time for good measure. Tighty-whitie (whose tighties left nothing to the imagination) pounded over in his bare feet and turned it on again.

Before this drama, Kim had snapped at the woman in the lower bunk adjacent to mine. She had her lamp on red-light mode, but still! Kim had the alarm clock above me and could see it was 4:30 a.m. This woman had already bedded down when we came up from dinner and was crinkling every noisy thing she had in her possession. We only had so much gear in our packs – what the hell could she have been playing around with for so long? There are only ten things max in everyone's pack!

"ENOUGH ALREADY!" I heard Kim huff in her direction. The red light of her headlamp cast a glow on the room's ceiling, as the woman tried to place where the growl came from. I snickered and was proud of Kim for asserting herself. It was ridiculous. Between the four o'clock squirrel and the Swedes, we were wired upon exit. And we still left before the Swedes.

We "blew our stink off," as my grandmother always suggested I do as a kid. In our hurry, though, I forgot our tube of conditioner in the shower. I blew my stink off but felt bitchy again, blaming the Swedes and the squirrel for ruining my attention span. Kim didn't use the conditioner at all, but my hair would be like the hayfields if I didn't replace it.

It was a watercolour sunrise and my rage (and proposed book title) dissipated in the glow. It was another morning of jet stream art, streaking the sky like a child's wild uninhibited painting. It would be a day of frustration, though, right from the get-go. We were jockeying with a small Asian man who kept stopping to take pictures with his iPad. We'd stop out of courtesy and he'd wave us ahead. In no time, he'd be on our heels, pass us and then stop again. It was a lurching walk and at the stone bridge leading to Ermita Virgen del Puente, Kim said, "Let's stop and change our socks or something."

I helped Kim slide her pack off to the ground.

"For crying out loud!" she said.

Our "friend" decided to stop too. As soon as Kim switched out socks, he was ready to carry on as well. We let him make tracks, but he had already stopped to photograph a sunflower.

"It's gonna be one of those days," Kim said. I thought of Marzia and her analysis of the Camino. We were still in the mental portion and very ready for the shift to spiritual.

Before noon we were in medieval Sahagún and found a patio near the arresting Arco (arch) de San Benito, with its dramatic lions and giant coat of arms. We were starved and internally cranky.

We hovered inside the deli, waiting for the owner to acknowledge us. He carried on a very colourful conversation with a striking woman and paid no attention to our presence. Finally, her phone rang and she stepped outside. Gruffly, he asked if we wanted coffee. We asked about sandwiches, seeing that he had all the fixings under the deli counter.

"Yes, sure, no problem. Salami? Parmesan? Olive oil?"

We said yes to it all and watched him prepare the open-faced baguettes with flair.

"Thirteen euros," he said, sliding the plate our way.

"Thirteen?" I frowned. Maybe he meant three euros.

Kim's jaw dropped. "That's like 20 bucks Canadian. Twenty bucks for the same sandwiches we've been buying for two or three euros along the way."

The guy stiffened his lip. "You ask for salami. You want Parmesan. You want herbs and oil." He slammed his hand down, disgusted that we contested his steep prices.

"Now what?" I muttered to Kim, worried this guy was going to go ballistic.

She shook her head. "Like I said, it's this kind of day."

We reluctantly paid for the sandwiches, herbs and drizzled olive oil and all. "Next time we ask how much first," Kim suggested.

"Yeah."

It was an expensive lesson but reliable future indicator. If a restaurant or bar, anywhere in the world, doesn't have a blackboard menu including prices, the prices are probably going to be outrageous. Dejected, we took our seats, reminiscing about the time we'd been stiffed in the White Desert in Egypt. The hotel owner wanted 20 bucks for two tall cans of beer. Twenty American dollars! I had a good hollering session with the owner and was eventually granted a price reduction when I squawked to our driver about the overcharge.

"But he says you two had a shower and used the toilet."

Kim and I couldn't believe it. "Oh c'mon. Look at us! Do you think we had a shower? And we definitely didn't use his scabby toilet!" I looked at the door handle and murky bucket and crossed my legs. Instead, we took awkward spots in the living room around the coffee table with the Donald Duck tablecloth, while the Quran blared on the scratchy black and white TV. The only thing we would do in this man's hotel was drink a beer. The most expensive beers we had drunk in the world.

We laughed over the ordeal and remained grateful that our biggest setback on the Camino so far was an overpriced baguette. The most expensive baguette we'd have in the world.

Two bites in, I felt the wire on my upper retainer break and lift off the brackets behind three of my front teeth. I felt a sickening rush of anxiety and fished my tongue around, hoping to push the wire back in place. Ironically, I had busted my lower retainer in Egypt. (But that time I thought I had somehow swallowed it in the night and it was perforating my stomach

Listening to the tinkle of cowbells echoing in the valley below as the sun rises into the clouds above the Pyrenees.

Crossing the mighty Pyrenees divide between France and Spain.

(*Top*) Praising the sheep for the merino wool in my quick-dry socks in the Pyrenees. (*Bottom*) Wild horses thunder across the Pyrenees.

Riverside in Zubiri, miraculously intact after crossing the Pyrenees.

(*Top*) Getting into the bunk bed groove at Albergue Rio Argo Ibaia in Zubiri. (*Bottom*) The iconic sculpture at the summit of Alto del Perdón in Navarra, 12 km from Pamplona.

(*Top*) Wind turbines churn adjacent to the sculpture, along the spine of the Erreniega Range. (*Bottom*) En route to Villafranca del Bierzo, in the dust of horses to our next vino tinto and bunk bed stop.

(*Top*) A pilgrim oasis—Panaderia Las Cuevas in Atapeurca. Cafe con leche and croissants to fuel the next leg to La Faba. (*Bottom*) The Meseta's famous arid, oven-on-broil landscape.

Whenever Kim and I doubted our direction for a moment, an arrow would serendipitously appear.

Another day begins in the pink warmth of dawn in Galicia.

This kitten is catnap-ready with a dream catcher around its neck for good measure.

(*Top*) Venison stew in the clouds at Foncebadón's mountaintop
La Tab. (*Bottom*) Portuguese moonshine and frog toss with Nigel,
the Brit barkeep in La Faba.

(*Top*) Official greeter/security at Pensión Rural A Casa De Carmen in Barbadelo. (*Bottom*) A familiar sight – cows and horses living in the lower level of farmhouses near O Cebreiro.

(*Top*) Our Vibram soles alight upon the official engraved landmark in front of the famed Cathedral of Santiago de Compostela. (*Bottom*) Arriving in Muxia for a few days of restoration.

(*Top*) Beach day in October! A sight for sore thighs in Praia de Lourido, Muxia. (*Bottom*) The Faro de Muxia (lighthouse) and Costa de la Muerte (Coast of Death) seascape.

Kim and I at the monumental Mile 0 marker in Finisterre.

(*Top*) Popping champagne at the "End of the World" in Finisterre, Spain. (*Bottom*) Chorizo and quail egg tapas on baguette rounds.

lining as the hours inched on. Meanwhile, it had made a clean snap and unhinged when I was flossing and Kim found it shining on the tile floor.)

"I just broke my retainer," I said, wanting to have a big meltdown cry. It would be awkward, but I knew I could wait out a dentist visit. The broken wire would be a total nuisance, but so were the Swedes. I could handle it.

"This fucking baguette is like a Dentabone for a dog." Instead of a dentist visit, you could eat one of this guy's baguettes and remove tartar in one sitting.

Kim made a pile of her bread, unable to digest it either. I folded up pieces of salami and shifted chewing to my left molars. It wasn't the first time I'd done this, and it wouldn't be the last. We didn't bother to kindly return the plates inside and set off again, knowing things had to improve.

The sky was a brilliant blue, the same kind of sky with balloon clouds in the opening credits of *The Simpsons*. We had entered an area of unique mud and hay brick construction. I'd have to tell our neighbour, Donna, who lived in a straw bale home. In Moratinos, hillside bodegas appeared again, visible only because of their tiny chimneys poking out of the hills.

Kim and I ended up on an alternate route into Cazadilla, not intentionally. Once again, we were completely alone. So much for Luis's promise that we'd always have someone ahead of us and behind us! Kim turned back around several times, hoping to see another pilgrim to ensure we were on the right path and not heading south to Portugal.

Of course, the one time a car did trundle down the eerily empty roadway we were crouched on the road taking a piss. There was no sense trying to hide, we hadn't seen anyone for two hours. The old Lada screamed past – they had definitely seen us, shorts down, and the entire family had the silly grins that proved it.

In Cazadilla we had two budget options or another fancy-pants Hotel Rural property to contemplate. If we hadn't had such expensive baguettes at lunch, we could have splurged on a room instead. We crossed the road to the municipal St. Bartolome first and watched two Irish nuns jump up from their sunny seats on the curb to beat us to the door.

The hostel was by donation and nobody was there. Kim said, "We could get lucky and have the place to ourselves."

It was worth the gamble. The volunteer nuns said they only had one guest the night before. We told them about our last eight kilometres of pure solitude and they nodded along.

"Not too many take the alternative route here."

We grabbed lower bunks with crossed fingers at the far end of the left wing. There were only 22 beds in total, so even with a full house it would be more private with the dividing walls between every four bunks.

There was a communal kitchen at the municipal hostel but no supermarket. This was usually the pattern – you had one or the other, rarely both. The town was shockingly quiet. We walked every street until we accidentally found a men's bar where cards were being shuffled as fast as drinks. Waiting for service, I was given a sharp "tsk tsk" for touching a bottle of strawberry gin.

"I just wanted to read the label on the back!" I shrugged.

We received snotty service after that and opted to sit outside, away from the glare of the pursed-lip bartender.

"Rye bread! Wow!" I remarked.

Kim took the first bite and gave me the go-ahead. "Your retainer will be fine."

The pretty pinchos had a layer of thinly sliced potato topped with a delicate curled Galician pepper all drizzled in golden oil. In Spain, there is a distinct geographic name change from tapas to pinchos, but they are the same delicious thing, no matter how you say it, spell it or layer it.

At the only other game in town, Albergue via Trajana, we had the most amazing refuel after our trying day. Kim ordered an "appetizer" of macaroni, which was really penne in a velvet cream sauce. I had the "lamb stew," which was really stewed lamb served on fries and so divine despite having to fiddle with my silly retainer with every bite.

Tomorrow would be better, we were certain.

Bunk Bed Deception

Calzadilla de los Hermanillos to Mansilla de las Mulas
(23.6 km)

- -

"Shit."

I sneezed once and felt the catch in my lungs. I coughed once and felt the tightness of a probable cough. Kim immediately said, "That didn't sound good."

I felt completely fine and didn't experience any precursor scratchiness in my throat, but I could feel a cough sitting there. "Maybe it's just the Meseta dust," I hoped. It was a probable cause – it had been 100 kilometres of dusty track with combines and tractors kicking up even more particulate. I chose to ignore it and hoped the sticky feeling inside my ribs would magically vanish with karmic prayer.

It was another spectacular sunrise of soft pastels that lit up the bottle-blonde fields of hay. The mountains ahead were looming now, pulling us toward the Cantabrian range with an invisible tow rope.

Knowing there would be a hungry 18-kilometre haul before the next possible provisions stop, Kim and I walked back to the albergue where we'd enjoyed the lamb stew and mac hours before for a pricey coffee and football-sized croissant with strawberry jam. The gaps in grocers along chunks of the Camino necessitated buying a few breakfasts, as we could only carry so much yogurt and bars. We boiled eggs when we could, but they had a lifespan too.

We followed the earthen split through ditches charred by controlled fires. Resilient little magenta flowers bloomed bright in the Oreo crumb xeriscape of ash. Later we realized we were also following an old electric rail line. The only traffic for miles was combines humming through the fields.

"It feels so Alberta, doesn't it?" I said to Kim. My sister brags about Banff's bluebird skies for good reason; most of the province is saturated in sun almost 330 days of the year.

The sky was that special kind of Banff blue, with whispery clouds mimicking a school of fish swimming north. It was the most beautiful day in the Meseta, winding through bleached corn and hay. Our spirits had rebounded from the sour state of the day before, even though the ground underfoot had become dicey. We moved from pavement to tractor tracks to an endless stretch of stone that was akin to walking on rolling golf balls.

Again, we were on our own for most of the morning. We had a glamorous private picnic standing beside a bird-shit-splattered picnic table along the trail. An entire flock of something must have used the table as target practice. Kim ate her leftover macaroni from a Ziploc bag with her fingers, while I chased a tin of tuna with day-old baguette. I was reminded of summer camp and the annual cracker-eating contest. Participants had to cram a dozen Premium Plus crackers in their maw and then try to whistle. It's a guaranteed hot, dry mess. I wasn't a whistler to begin with, and after hearing a few avid whistling types on the Camino, decided I never would be.

It was a ghostly, desolate stretch into Reliegos, where the town's only claim to fame was being struck by a 17-kilogram meteor in 1947. Apparently, it was on display at a natural science museum in Madrid. We didn't see evidence of the strike along the old Roman road but imagined it caused a stir of palpable anxiety and more than a few Hail Marys. Or Bloody Marys.

As we entered the fortified city of Mansilla, and the protection of its medieval walls, the only modern-day marauders were sheep and they were rather busy on the grazing front.

We checked into El Jardin del Camino, close to the Río Esla, lured in by its sunny (and empty) courtyard. Curiously, half a dozen captive turkeys paraded around an overgrown parking lot across from the hostel. Inside, the deli counter was jammed with locals (where did they come from?), drinking short glasses of wine, focused on a televised soccer match.

The dorm had 32 beds divided into two rooms. We tried a new approach, placing items on the bunks above our chosen lower beds to suggest that four bunks were taken.

"Why didn't we think of this before?" I said to Kim.

It was rather annoying in dorms with dozens of empty beds to find that of *all* the vacant bunks, someone had to choose the one directly over your head in your absence. Not one of the five empty bunks in between. Directly overhead. Maybe this was un-Camino-like behaviour, to rig the beds to appear occupied, but my immune system was compromised. And this same reflex annoyance is triggered on empty buses or coffee shops when someone believes the seat directly beside you is the very best option. If the hostel ended up being 100 per cent full, obviously the staff would figure out our hack as they documented the numbers that had checked in and react accordingly. It was worth a try, selfish as it was.

We were probably due for another private room, as the closeness and habits of fellow pilgrims were beginning to ride on us. I had a few coughing bouts during the day, the kind that cramp up your stomach and leave you gasping for air like you've been held underwater for too long. Kim and I were so conjoined in hearts and minds that she decided to start coughing too. Her throat felt raw, though, like she'd swallowed razors.

The bunks all around us had pilgrims in various ill states. There had been talk that this was normal. Usually two weeks in, it was rumoured that "everyone" on the Camino had diarrhea or some stomach thing. I didn't want to be everyone. This crew was barking and snivelling on pace with us. Something evil had descended and it wasn't a surprise. Despite being fanatical about hand washing, 95 per cent of the public washrooms, restaurant sinks and hostels had no hand soap. It was inevitable. It was the equivalent of sneezing directly down someone's throat, or being back in snotty-nosed kindergarten.

At most hostels, pillowcases were issued. Some were thin and flimsy one-time use cases that seemed to be made out of fabric softener sheets. Others were a standard, starchy affair. But I had yet to see anyone disinfecting any surface – bunk bed or sink. Some of the communal kitchens would have been glowing neon like Las Vegas from space under a black light inspection.

Downstairs, we found pints of our "afternoon medicine." One or two cold beers seemed to take the stiffness out of my bitchy right Achilles and the throb out of my left collarbone. Kim used it to nurse her shin splints that seemed to flare understandably on the longer stretches.

Flip-flopping out to the courtyard with some socks to wash out, we heard a familiar voice.

"My friends, my friends!" Gudrun approached us with open arms and we gave her skinny body a squeeze. Her weight and age were probably the same. Teresa was in tow and they both joined us in the courtyard after grabbing sandwiches inside. Gudrun emerged with a pint, while Teresa opted for a soup bowl of hot chocolate. Hot chocolate! They were staying at the municipal hostel that night and were envious of our backyard.

"We even have turkeys here," I said, pointing out the fowl across the way.

While we thought we'd have the afternoon to catnap in the sun, the courtyard abruptly closed at 3:00 p.m. for no particular reason. So Kim and I walked some more, around the periphery of the walled city, looking for a grocer. We took our picnic fixings to the riverside until the sun had set and bats whistled past. We weren't keen on heading back to the hostel, as the only flex space was under the stairwell where a few tables and plastic chairs were assembled.

It was notably nippier, so we were happy to find a tiny restaurant that was as bright and warm as a tanning bed. Wine was less than a euro per glass and we were plied with generous hunks of chorizo. We were the only patrons and it truly felt like we were sitting in a local's living room. There were several family pics taped to the walls, and we spent the next hour watching a toothy toddler be pulled around in a milk crate, squeezing his own bald "Bebe." The grandmother sat at a table in the corner, talking in Spanish to us full tilt. The grandfather was the puller and round and round he went. When the milk crate stopped, the kid screamed for more, in a happy way. Granddad took a slug of wine and continued while we enabled the act by waving *adios* at each turn.

Soon we said adios for the night, wondering how many chorizo links we'd eaten since we arrived in Spain. It was only 8:30, but I had a good night of coughing ahead of me to get cracking on.

Zombie in León

Mansilla de las Mulas to León (17.9 km)

Gudrun had kindly informed us that the walk into León would be a boring one. I liked how she classified a day mostly by elevation. It was either "Down, down, down," or next we go "up, up, up." Or "boring."

According to my notes, León might not be boring at all due to a mole and the Santa María de León Cathedral. I'd noted that this church was worthy of a visit for the fable alone. When the Gothic church was being built, mystified workers would return to the construction site only to find their previous day's work in ruins. Surprisingly, the suspect was a giant mole, so the frustrated workers set a bear trap to teach it a one-time lesson. The mole was captured and the skin hung at the door of San Juan. This very skin was finally subjected to tests for authenticity and the evil moleskin was actually the skin of a turtle. What the greater message of this fable is, I'm not sure, but A+ for creativity to the creator. Great marketing and branding! The Fiestas of San Froilán was also supposed to be ramping up with chess competitions, a big-headed people parade, marionettes, jugglers and the like. There were supposed to be fireworks, falconry, wandering folk bands and a medieval feast. Even though it was touted as one of the important events on the Galician calendar (held annually October 4–12), nobody in León seemed to know or care about it. The only other cultural to-do I had on my list was to visit Casa Benito, the oldest tavern in the city. We were amazed to find it so easily, and not amazed to find it closed. The roller doors were down, much like the rest of the rolled-up, siesta-ensconced city.

It was a frosty start following the roadway and mighty aquifer into León. Gudrun was right, it was a fast, easy, well-marked passage into the city, but it was boring on the overall Camino scale.

Kim had an Oprah aha moment as we left the dregs of the industrial scape to the urban spread. To find the city centre and, in turn, the path of the Camino, wayward pilgrims only have to look as far as the church spires and belfry. They were usually the tallest spikes on the horizon. The Camino was a footpath of churches, and while a backcountry hike might involve following the flow of a river or path of the sun, here it was the gong of church bells when in doubt.

Jointly, Kim and I realized having too many choices for sleeping was as trying as only having three options. We stomped in and out of six scary hostels, the last three of which I looked at alone while Kim held ground outside, losing enthusiasm for all the stair climbs to stuffy third and fourth floor dorms.

At Hotel Albany, we found Colin and Cathy hurriedly claiming a private room.

"This is nuts," Cathy said.

They had tried to pre-book at a few hotels, but they were all full. We had just come from the Hostel Globetrotter, which had one bunk left. Shame, because it was totally our speed with the funky touches of floor to ceiling mural wallpaper, neon-lit signs and hot air balloon motifs.

"Are you guys going to book here?"

We wanted to, fearful that we'd blow our entire afternoon walking in circles and up and down stairs. Colin waved a key at Cathy and she apologized for rushing off. "I just can't wait to have a hot bath and a bottle of wine and long nap."

It was pretty close to our agenda and we wished them a sweet night of luxury. It was the first private room they had booked. Meanwhile, Kim and I were on a private room streak.

As soon as they disappeared up the stairs, so did the staff. An agitated guest barked for the manager, complaining that there were items missing from his laundry bag and he wanted to be compensated. Kim looked at the clock. This guy's sock rant had eaten up 20 precious minutes. A woman behind us gave up waiting with an audible sigh. Finally, there was an apology to us for waiting. Would we like coffee? A seat?

"No, we'd prefer a beer," Kim said.

We were whisked to the bar area, unsure of whether the beer was complimentary or going to be tacked on our room. Our bartender looked exactly like a Hispanic Jann Arden and I told her so. Her English was as patchy as our Spanish, but we tried to convey that this was a good thing. I asked to take a picture with her and she shrugged, agreed and returned with a business card with her name on it: MAR CASTRO. Maybe she thought I was the head of a talent agency?

Nearly 45 minutes later, we were tended to at reception. The hotel was now fully booked – but it had a satellite property "just down the alley. Someone can take you in one hour." One hour? Kim was ready to combust. Colin and Cathy were probably already deep in their REM cycle and we were stuck in our dusty boots, half-starved, only to learn we would need to wait a little longer to be granted this room in the alley, sight unseen. It was too risky to have a much-desired tantrum and leave. For where? We'd seen the other options. So we huffed and puffed, paid for the room and found some cans of beer and corn nuts to pass the time. Gudrun appeared, all smiles and shower fresh from her municipal hostel lodging. We didn't bother launching into our truly boring tale of woe. She was eager to see Antonio Gaudi's modernist Casa Botines on a building that now operates as a bank.

"Are you going to the organ concert tonight?" she asked.

I said no, safely, without need to confer with Kim. Organ music was on par with singing nuns and singing for meatballs for both of us. "We might try to see the hanging moleskin and find a place called Planet Mongogo. It's supposed to be some Hellmex, psychobilly voodoo bar. Whatever that means. And if that doesn't pan out, there's a place called La Trébede that is supposed to have stuffed reptiles and old farm implements on display."

Gudrun frowned and wasn't sure what to make of my reply. I was just being honest. That was the stuff I wanted to see. She carried on, shaking her head, eating a giant apple.

We were lucky to take in a free concert as we worked through corn nuts so stale I felt like I was eating my own molars. Two buskers had set up across the road and the acoustics nearly matched Toronto's historic Massey Hall. Both had guitars and I recognized the first chords immediately.

"'Zombie'!" I shouted, startling Kim. "I love this song." Kim couldn't place it.

"'Zombie'! The Cranberries."

I forgot about everything, charged by the lyrics and power of this woman's voice. "That was an awesome send-off," I said to Kim as we headed back to the hotel desk. The song would run on repeat in my head for the rest of the week.

Seeing so many freshly scrubbed tourists made me realize how filthy we were. Our clothes had reached the Tide commercial punk level and I felt like a germ ball, now internally too. I had a good coughing jag and laughed.

"Oh my god. I have kennel cough!"

Dog owners will know that this dreaded affliction is common in boarding and daycare facilities and dog parks. It's contagious and it usually runs rampant from the first cough-honk to the last. It's treatable but annoying for innocent pups and their owners.

And now I had it and passed my kennel cough to my daycare partner, Kim. I was looking forward to a proper hotel room, not another night in a petri dish.

I kept thinking of Marzia. Damn her for instilling the physical-mental-spiritual modus operandi in my head. Kim and I started joking about issuing yellow cards on the Camino as warnings, like they do in soccer matches. I was due for a yellow. Patience infraction. Things were mildly compounding, as they do. Kennel cough. Busted retainer. On the flip side, my hysteria about having appendicitis or a hernia was diminishing the longer we walked.

We followed a suited dude with wildly swinging arms to our alley location.

"How the hell are we going to find our way out of here?" Kim said.

We zigged. Zagged. Circled. Zig. Zag. I tried to make note of landmarks, but every business had security roll shutters in place. Above, every Juliet balcony seemed to have identical placements of blood red and candy-striped trailing petunias.

Our room was on the third floor and rather lacklustre for the price. The walls were menthol green. A 24-inch flat-screen TV was precariously mounted two inches from the 12-foot ceiling. The pillows were seemingly made from the collected ends of 2,000 Q-tips and the bed looked like it had the ability to fold into a taco. We collectively sighed and dumped our bags. Yellow card.

Psychobilly Planet Mongogo didn't open until ten. My second pick, with the taxidermy reptiles, was closed until Tuesday. Instead, we circled the core a few times and settled on barstools at the shiny new San Miguel Tasting Station. The barista slid us a flight of beers and a bowl of spicy popcorn.

Even hungrier after a lean day of mostly corn nuts and popcorn, we ordered an "Oriental" pizza at Kadabra versus the "Nordic," which was topped with smoked salmon and onion. The Oriental ingredients were oddly curried chicken, jumbo

Gordal olives and mozza. Very Oriental! We schlepped the international pizza back to our room (once we found it again) and were sleeping/coughing by nine.

In the darkness I said, "Crap. We forgot to go see that moleskin hanging in the church."

Kim said she'd try to get over her disappointment.

No Slippers, No Service

León to Villavante (31 km)

- -

I felt like a snake shedding unwanted skin as we left León
and its populated throngs (population: 129,000). We were both
groggy from another night of half-hour cat-like sleeping stints.
The bars that lined our alley pumped out music and people
until 4:00 a.m. Half an hour later, bar staff dumped an endless
racket of glass bottles into dumpsters with a nonapologetic
crash. Then the recycling truck came. Diesel-delivery trucks.
Then the street cleaners with their rumble and hissing spray.

"Oh my god, I give up," Kim said.

We both pulled on our familiar clothes and ate cold Oriental
pizza with glugs of peach nectar.

It was a winding eight-kilometre walk out of the city to
Virgen del Camino, where the Virgin Mary told a shepherd to
slingshot a stone and build a shrine wherever the stone landed.

And then, just past the fateful slingshot, we were in the
midst and comfort of cornfields and rural aquifers again.
Some guidebooks actually suggest skipping the dull city exit

by hopping on the A1 bus. It seemed sacrilege to us to skip over any part of the Camino due to the bore.

Our intended destination was Villar de Mazarife (21.5 kilometres) and we were there by 11:30 a.m. With the energy to press on, especially after seeing the area, we kept going. It was much like Hontanas and Boadilla with zero amenities. The only place for us to sit was in a tiny playground on a bench that was ready to give way. At the deli we asked for some Gouda and *caña de lomo* (pork loin). Kim was ecstatic to find individual tubs of mayo for ten cents. We had endured a lot of dry sandwiches, so I was thrilled with her find. Another highlight was a six-pack of Bimbo hamburger buns. A reprieve from the baseball-bat baguettes. The Bimbos were definitely broken-retainer friendly. I would keep my dental hardware intact a day longer! We were the only ones in the playground, save for the blackbirds that made a sound not unlike gravel being shaken in a tin can.

It was another nine and a half kilometres into Villavante and Albergue Santa Lucia. Kim was on a mayo high that escalated when she spied spaghetti Bolognese on a blackboard menu.

This town was equally desolate, but with two bars occupied fully by men. After a 30-kilometre day, it was such a reward to park ourselves in the sun. I asked the bartender if we could carry two chairs into the sun and he shrugged, sure. There was zero traffic to contend with, so we actually sat in the middle of the road where the sun was beaming strongest. All the men in the bar turned to observe us with dancing eyebrows that indicated "two women in the bar!" They were playing hot games of dominoes for pennies. Kim nudged me to look at the table closest to us.

"They're all wearing slippers."

My god, they were. Awesome.

We took our beers into the sun and cheered on the two Australians who limped past. They asked if we knew where the Hotel Rural property was. We wished we did! It was a guaranteed beautiful stay.

A stream of cyclists muscled past next, asking if we had seen a guy who fit a particular description. We hadn't but promised we'd be stationed there for another hour at least, and would extend their message.

We didn't see their cyclist friend – they were worried he'd taken the alternate variant route. Hopefully, they would cross paths ahead.

Instead, we watched all the men pile out of the bar around the same time. Kim laughed, "Supper time, I guess."

They shuffled in all four directions in their plaid slippers, linking arms and singing. Who knew dominoes were such fun?

We shuffled back to Santa Lucia for spag Bol and Al Jazeera coverage of the deadly flash floods in Mallorca, Spain, that had killed ten.

"Are we in trouble here?" Kim said with a hard swallow.

I was mostly sure we were fine, but was more positive that my parents' neurons would be lit up at home. Any mention of Spain in the headlines would have them pacing.

"Ta-da! Wet. No Wet!"

Villavante to Astorga (22 km)

We left Villavante in a steady spittle. This was my optimistic take on what Kim would call full-blown rain. I didn't want to dig out my rain gear, but two minutes from our hostel we tucked into someone's front porch to pull it out. Was this the Mallorca system already?

As we passed our favourite men-in-slippers bar, the headwind was high intensity. It would be our first official rain gear test. Naturally, another two minutes later, it was over and we removed everything rainproof with confidence. A rainbow arched across the sky…and then rain dumped down again. The sky turned to a committed ominous. Clouds ran across the bruised sky and we ate the last of our Oriental pizza on the fly, losing a few precious rolling olives on the way.

In Hospital de Órbigo the rain was still being a nuisance – especially when trying to take a photo of the dramatic Gothic bridge that spans over the Río Órbigo. Now here's a crazy story:

A knight was ghosted by a woman way back when and, in his lovelorn state, he locked an iron collar around his neck (the medieval version of listening to Sarah McLachlan on repeat). The knight refused to take the collar off until he defeated 300 knights in jousting. Knights loved the challenge and came in droves in the Holy Year of 1434. The knight succeeded in his mission and carried on to Santiago, without his iron collar. He left a jewel-encrusted bracelet in memory of his heartbreak that can still be seen at the Cathedral Museum in Santiago. The bridge is also known as El Paso Honroso (The Honourable Pass).

With the storied bridge in view, we had coffee and massive, sticky, butterfly-shaped pastries called *palmeras* (or "palmier" or "pig's ear" in France). We nodded to relatively new but familiar compadres we were now on pace with: a twentysomething German woman with short hair always on end, and a determined French madame who wore her rain cape most days – as a preventative? With her blue cape billowing over her pack, she looked like a giant hunchback from afar. We called her "Lynda" because she looked identical to our friend Lynda (who doesn't have a hunchback but is of similar height and greying hair).

The Camino cut through sturdy apple orchards, a sole (and fragrant) dairy farm, cornfields and a stretch of hop vines intertwining six metres in the air on an efficient pole and cable system.

We crossed countless stone bridges; the kind that have been memorialized in thousands of oil paintings. I could see the typical scene: moody sky, a torrent of water sluicing under the bridge, a stout man carrying a quail by its limp neck with a hunting dog at his heels.

As we climbed the steep hill into Astorga, I stopped dead in my tracks. At first, I thought it was a hummingbird, but its flight pattern didn't make sense. Kim was a few steps ahead and I called her back.

"Look, it's a hummingbird moth!" I'd never seen one before and it seemed like a good and gorgeous omen. Its wings were a blur as it pulled nectar from the colourful blooms just like a hummingbird.

Astorga was a window-shopping dream for those inclined, with trinkets, patisseries and chocolate shops boxed around open plazas filled with tableclothed tables and cut flowers. At Albergue San Javier, our random choice for the night, Kim was happy to kick off her soggy boots. My Vasques had repelled the drizzle well, but Kim was left with wet socks. The cranky innkeeper shooed us into a covered outdoor area with our footwear and rammed newspaper in our hands. I'd been longing for a nice daily, but this wasn't his intention.

"Here!" He reacted to our blank expression by crumpling several sheets and forcefully grabbing Kim's boots.

"Like this? Ta-da! Wet. No wet."

He stuffed the balls of newspaper into the toes of her boots and did the same to mine. We guessed it was like the wet iPhone rehab of white rice in a Ziploc.

"Thank you for the hot tip," I said and received a grunt in return.

I rolled my eyes at Kim. "What's with Daddy Warbucks?"

He wore an ascot and a rather rumpled suit, his hair a wild mess upon his head. We took cautious seats when he summoned us to his old-school desk.

"It's like being in the principal's office all over again," I whispered to Kim.

He issued us a pillowcase and shooed us upstairs, vaguely pointing out the communal kitchen and clothesline. It was a lovely building, with exposed beams and stone walls. The customer service was lacking though.

The sun finally emerged and, after inspecting the questionable sanitary conditions of the communal kitchen, we decided on just boiling eggs for the coming days. We renamed Daddy Warbucks "Ebenezer Scrooge" as he brusquely ushered new pilgrims in. He had started a healthy fire in the woodstove, and with the dodgy skies outside, Kim and I settled in with a bottle of wine, salted peanuts and an egg. High romance and gourmand dining here. We were perched on the end of a lumpy couch until Ebenezer hollered at us.

"No! No wine on couch."

Strangely, he was okay with the clearly unbathed grubby feet at the other end of the couch. We were ready to leave, but instead Ebenezer pulled out a small bistro table for two out of nowhere and told us to sit, like dogs.

It was a strange night, one that ended with Ebenezer snoring on that same lumpy couch behind us. And he was there in the morning too.

FOUR

Cantabrian Mountains El Bierzo

The Camino is an ever-changing path of cobblestone, tractor ruts, highway shoulder and often, single-track trail.

Sleeping in the Clouds

Astorga to Foncebadón (25.9 km)

- -

We left the burnt sienna Meseta for the verdant mountains and there was a collective twitchy rumble about a return to the punishing elevation ahead in El Bierzo valley. Thankfully, the Bierzo region was also known for its neatly terraced Garnacha and Mencía grapes and harvests occurring a full month earlier than other vineyards in Spain due to its low altitude.

At walking speed (even our jackrabbit setting), it was easy to see the slow transition in architecture, crops and landscape. There was a subtle change from tile to slate roofs. The doors adorned with symbolic dried *eguzki-lore* (flower of the sun) sunflowers in the Basque area gave way to beaded entryways instead. The Basque believed the sunflowers helped ward off evil spirits, witches, disease and storms. The beaded curtains helped ward off pilgrims afraid of losing their teacup and saucer and tortilla upon exit to the patio.

In El Bierzo, the Celtic influence was prominent and I was looking forward to the transition from mud and straw dwellings to mystical circular thatched buildings.

Midday, we found prime picnic real estate in the adorable tree-lined hamlet of El Ganso. It had been a Goldilocks morning of too hot, too cold. My pack felt too heavy – was I piggybacking someone instead? Kim was shifting hers around a lot too. This was par for the course. Some days our packs fit like a favourite pair of jeans, and the next it was a constant adjustment to not feel some strain.

In a small, stone-walled courtyard I watched dozens of cats emerge from the recesses as Kim unpacked our lunch. This band of wild cats of all colours and stripes were not picky. I'm sure if we tilted our bottles of Mahou to their whiskered lips, they would have taken a slug of beer too. Who knew cats loved egg salad sandwiches? They weren't of the petting kind, but Kim had distinct flashbacks of her visit to Hemingway's house and museum in Key West, where 40 to 50 polydactyl (six-toed) romp around.

The elevation kicked in as we neared Foncebadón, and lyrics to Buffy Sainte-Marie's "Up Where We Belong" played in my headspace reflexively.

"We'll be sleeping in the clouds tonight," I said to Kim, coughing with the extra altitude squeeze on my lungs.

There was a bit of rock and roll underfoot, but the distraction of the valley vista was unreal. Fog clung to the lower valley and moved in defined sheets across the town ahead. Shirley MacLaine and Paulo Coelho had both made note in their Camino memoirs about aggressive dogs in this area, but we failed to see any. Instead, it was a populace of mewing cats. They were everywhere – like one of those drawings where you have to find the hundred hiding cats at a carnival. The mountaintop hamlet was a crumble and jumble of stone with a few albergues, a cafe/pantry and skinny pizza and Prosecco joint advertising a happy hour. Many of the town's residents left in the '60s and '70s, seeking employment.

We walked to the end of the abandoned stretch (two minutes?) to examine all the options. Monte Irago was a little too hippie for Kim's liking. The bunks were situated in a way that meant somebody's feet were at your head. Talk of bed bugs had been crawling around and this albergue with vinyl-covered mattresses looked like a prime suspect.

"I can't believe the number of cats here," I said to Kim. "Look at this kitten! He has a little dream catcher on his neck!"

Of course, I had to try and snap a picture, but he kept up his kitten roly-poly antics, hiding his precious necklace. I started coughing and couldn't stop. Just as my lungs were completely deflated, Kim started to laugh at me, bent over, unable to breathe, but still trying to get the ultimate picture of this silly kitten. Then I wheezed, laughed with her, half-pissed my pants and made an involuntary sound like I was going to throw up. I got the Nat Geo capture I was looking for and coughed for two minutes straight, nearly blowing my eyeballs right out of my sockets. I had tears down to my collarbone and couldn't stand up from cramped stomach muscles. It was the worst cough I'd had in my life. Kim was on par – it was the sudden attacks and sprees that left us breathless and usually laughing at each other, all snotty and crying, unable to function, crossing our legs to not pee.

Natural breathing resumed, we checked into La Cruz de Fierro and were thrilled to be placed in a tidy, modern room with just six bunks.

"We might get lucky tonight," Kim said. And not meaning *lucky* in that way. Several pilgrims we'd chatted with were choosing to spend an extra night in Astorga and it had been a rather thin day on the trail. A Rotterdam couple was waiting for the arrival of new hiking boots for the husband via the post.

"Plus, he has had diary for three days," his wife explained.

Diary? Oh, diarrhea. The husband sheepishly smiled and Kim warned me not to share such diary disclosures with anyone, if that became the case.

"Maybe we'll have the room to ourselves," Kim hoped aloud.

It was modern, cozy and had an in-house restaurant and bar. The wind had turned a bit wicked on the ascent, and with the fog we were happy to hunker down for the afternoon. After all, I had the award-winning cat photo, so I was content.

"Let's have hot toddies," I suggested, as my throat was clenched and needed some liquid soothing. I glanced at the menu while we waited and said to Kim, "They have Russian salad, but only in the summer season. What's that supposed to mean?"

"Kind of like the Oriental pizza with curried chicken and olives, I guess."

I asked the bartender if he had lemons. Yes! "Could you mix hot water, rum and honey together for us?" He hadn't heard of a toddy but understood our direction.

I found an English copy of *The Red Bulletin* (a magazine produced by Red Bull) and read it like a starved person. Kim was happy to stare out the window. I was like her audiobook at the best of times, reading the best bits aloud. There was a feature on climbing Yosemite's El Capitan and the soon-to-be-released documentary, *The Dawn Wall*. Free climber Tommy Caldwell's heartbreak and ordeal somehow downgraded my kennel cough to a mere nuisance.

"We should drink tea more often," Kim said. "It's so good."

"Babe, it's not tea," I laughed. "It's hot water and rum!"

I tore through a few back issues of a German travel mag and dated *Vanity Fair* as the day dimmed. We had planned on dinner at La Taberna de Gaia Cocina Medieval, directly beside our albergue. And not because the Russian salad at our albergue was seasonal. La Taberna had a circular thatched building behind it and everything dripped with medieval. The stone walls were insulating and the stoked fire in the main room made the space sleepy warm. Candle wax ran in rivulets down tabletop wine bottles stuffed with candlesticks. Heavy metal sconces glowed and made the room of mismatched chairs, heavy tables, hides and dried gourds feel truly ancient.

It was so convivial, and the smiley staff were quick with a ceramic jug of local wine. Loreena McKennitt's ethereal

"Greensleeves" pulled the experience together in a tightly knit bow. I loved that her rendition popped up in such unexpected places. The last time we heard it was on a boat on the Yangtze River in China.

Kim knew I'd go for the venison stew and I guessed that she'd opt for the pumpkin soup. The vessels that were set on our table could have fed six knights. My stew had half a deer in it and at least 12 potatoes. Whole. I counted them. Our stomachs were topsy-turvy from sucking on cough candies, but the stew was the best thing I'd eaten in years. Our server returned, wondering why we had pushed our clearly unfinished bowls away so soon. We apologized, said we both had terrible coughs. Hell, we couldn't even finish our wine. She assured us she'd be able to pack up the leftovers. Even the wine! We wondered how we could manage take-out containers with our packs. I didn't want to walk with a plastic bag swinging in one hand until lunch the next day.

She returned with Kim's soup in a glass jar and my stew in a Ziploc. The wine, well, it was in a corked bottle and would have to do. We would be true pilgrims on the way to Ponferrada in the morn, carrying our deer rations and plonk!

Back in our room, we met our bunkmates. It was a full but happy house. The women were all from South Africa – all of them related but one. Sonia from Capetown introduced her crew and told us how they came to land on the Camino. She had owned a bookstore called Graffiti (now called Upper Case) as a professional dalliance and had decided to return to her previous life as a lawyer. Her friends in tow hiked somewhere different each year as a group.

"You must do the Fish Bone in Namibia. It's the world's second-largest canyon, along the Fish River. It will blow your mind," Sonia insisted.

The women were such refreshing company. They weren't walking all the way to Santiago, though, and had decided on a relaxed pace of 15 to 20 kilometres a day. We would lose them as well, which may have been a positive. Kim apologized first and said they would hate us by morning.

"We both have the worst coughs of our lives and sleeping triggers it more than anything. I get that tickle and can't stop coughing."

They promised not to hate us and genuinely felt sorry for us. This was the part of the day that made Kim and me both anxious. Lights out and the pressure not to cough. At least while we were walking it was just us, and we both agreed to cough it out, as much as we could.

I fell asleep with two lemon cough drops under my tongue, shallow breathing in my sleeping bag with crossed fingers.

Atomic Sunrise

Foncebadón to Ponferrada (27.1 km)

- -

The sunrise! It was difficult to make any headway as we both kept turning to say, "Oh my god, look at it now!" The sky was bleeding orange and candy pink. Clouds swiftly rolled through the valley below in a mesmerizing way, revealing the green velvet of the mountains. Pilgrims who shuffled out just ten minutes behind us would have missed the stunning show. The stone silhouette of Foncebadón against the atomic tangerine sky was otherworldly. Though I am a self-identified sunset-over-sunrise kind of gal, this one was a heartbreaker.

Almost immediately, the famed Cruz de Ferro appeared. It marks one of the highest points on the Camino Francés and was in the limelight of *The Way*. I'm not sure what I was expecting, but here it was, left to my vibrant imagination no longer. As in the movie, and the centuries before it, pilgrims carry a stone along the Camino (from home, or one that felt significant from the trail) to add to the growing pile. The stone represents a burden with the intention of leaving the pilgrim lighter after doing so. We both thought of Clara and her bag weighted with favourite rocks and tuna tins. She'd feel a difference, for sure.

Kim and I had selected rocks from Spain, waiting for this fabled iron cross atop a tall pole. With every dropped stone, though, the pile height was gaining ground on the mighty cross above. Soon it would be within reach!

I was supposed to be thinking about a burden, something to shed, but I hadn't really nailed anything down. Kim had ideas, but suddenly the stone pile was at our feet and I hoped the burden could still be removed after placement. Was there an expiry date? We waited patiently for a group of three that had gathered around the cross at the top. Kim zipped the legs off her pants, overheating already in the queue.

Kim realized that one of the pilgrims at the cross was the squirrel she had yelled at a few hostel stays ago.

"That night with the Swedes. That's her up there. She was the one stirring around for an hour and we still managed to leave before her!" Kim said in a hushed but amplified voice.

We tried to be courteous, as this is a very emotional stop for many pilgrims. There were pre-painted rocks with loved ones' names inscribed, ribbons, laminated photos and tiny crosses left as tributes in this sacred place. Our intention was to climb to the base of the pole, but Kim was ready to move on.

"Are you sure, babe? We can wait it out." Then the guy at the top bent to his knees and confirmed that it was going to be a while.

I figured Kim was thinking about her parents and didn't want this symbolic moment to be lost. She placed her rock and I followed suit, more concerned about Kim than trying to think up something to unshoulder. She had tears in her eyes and I was a bit miffed that this moment had been a bit tainted by the three hogging the iron cross. Oh yeah, patience. Yellow card for me again!

I hugged Kim tight and squeezed her shoulder, walking in contemplative but comfortable silence.

Rubik's-cube-sized rocks changing to smooth rolling potatoes caused a few skids and near tumbles (mostly on my sleep-disturbed end).

"Weird," Kim said, picking her poles among the rocks. "Now the rocks are totally square."

We navigated granite Pop-Tarts and then big sheets of tree-bark-like rock that began flaking in shale hunks with our weight.

There was a lot of fancy footwork involved in the dodgy descent into the slate-roofed, drystone buildings of El Acebo (Holly) at the 11.5-kilometre mark. Population 37! This is where the South African girls were contemplating staying if their legs were giving way. They had just started in Astorga and wanted to take things slow and steady. We stopped for some stew, jarred soup and a sock change, temporarily enjoying the sweet village.

The final quad-busting descent into Ponferrada ended in a big sweeping circle. It had been our favourite section of the trail since the Pyrenees, with a good dose of scenery, elevation and awe.

Trying to find a place to stay was a swear-inducing venture. We had passed the 174-bed San Nicolas de Flue to be in the heart of the city. Plus, 174 beds! It was huge. The Alea hostel (the only other one listed on our accommodations sheet) was sold out. Apparently, it was a national holiday. Even though the streets were totally empty. A newer albergue that wasn't on our coveted list only had one top bunk left.

As much as we wanted to drop our bags, it was a cutthroat, time-sensitive search for lodging. In the town hall plaza, we tried the Bierzo Plaza Aroi Hotel. The lobby looked impressive and chic enough as it had just been renovated in 2009. It occupied three old restored houses fronting the square. However, the only room left was in the unrenovated basement.

"The basement?"

"Yes, but it is adequate."

For 60 euros, it was a private room, but one that belonged along a highway road stop in northern Ontario in the '70s. We

bit the bullet as we'd already walked in three circles unsuccess-
fully. The location was ideal, in the beating heart of Ponferrada
and Plaza del Ayuntamiento. We were able to nip out easily
and find a grocer for breakfast stuff.

"Organic fairy cakes?" I asked Kim, holding up what looked
like pound cake muffins.

She shrugged, "Sure."

I grabbed a carton of our go-to peach nectar. We must have
downed 60 gallons of it already.

Afterwards, we wandered around the perimeter of the
Herculean Templar Castle with its 12 towers. The towers are
said to represent the 12 months, or possibly the 12 disciples
(depending on which historian you confer with). Originally
built in the 13th century, it was erected on the grounds of a
destroyed Visigoth fort that had been built on a previously
decimated Roman fort, and so on, and so on.

By the time we walked down the River Sil and back, the
squares and plazas were beginning to vibrate with locals of all
generations. Half imbibed while the younger set whistled the
start of pickup soccer matches, dangerously close to the tables
heaving with wine bottles and pinchos.

Kim and I joined the mix (imbibing, not playing soccer – too
risky with the wild kicks of the munchkins!). Our San Miguel
beer was served with a "Filipino" (a chocolate-glazed biscuit).
Beer and cookies – it was like a Homer Simpson fantasy!

Before an early self-imposed bedtime (in an attempt to kill off
our coughs for good), we had *jamon* (ham) and *pina* (pineapple)
quesadillas at El King Kong, a wildly painted and art-plastered
"rhythm and booze" Mexican bar next to our hotel.

The rhythm continued as the lobby above our basement
heads became the focal point of the national holiday and tables
and chairs scraped to and fro in preparation and take down.
Oh, sleep. I give up.

Tester #16 and Mystery Meds
Ponferrada to Villafranca del Bierzo (24.2 km)

‑ ‑

Looking out our gloomy basement window at 6:00 a.m., Kim made an executive decision to postpone our departure and crawled back into bed. Around eight we stirred again and the sky was still milky with rain. We ate our fairy cakes in bed with robust coffee that was offered to us gratis only after I grumbled about the moving furniture of the night before.

We started out in drizzle across the wet square that had been clotted with tables and revellers the night before. I thought it was funny that no pilgrim was unaware of this national holiday, but the famous week-long Celtic Fiestas de San Froilán that I *did* know about, none of the locals seemingly did.

It was a worried walk out of Ponferrada as we couldn't find any markers. A guy from Seattle caught us when we stopped at an intersection to ask if we knew where we were going. We carried on as three lost people heading in the direction of the highway. It felt wrong, but we hadn't passed any arrows or signature shells since we left the hotel. None of us felt like walking back to the town centre to recalibrate.

"Seattle" told us to press on; he had a slower pace. He was with another American who had left much earlier, but they had reservations in Villafranca and would reconvene then. I noticed an open cafe that was hot and ripe with fried eggs. I asked a server if we were travelling in the right direction for the Camino.

No comprende. But did I want to order breakfast?

An older gent shuffling along more sideways than forward was my next target.

"Camino?" I gestured, pointing ahead and behind.

"*Si, si, si!* Camino!" He copied my hand gestures and seemed quite confident. What followed I'm not sure, but he had a lot to say. We thanked the little chap and pressed on. Seattle was nowhere to be seen. Had he cut off and not whistled to alert us?

For the next two kilometres we didn't pass a soul. The endless blocks were a drowsy repeat of hardware and paint stores and vacant houses. Kim spied the stream of pilgrims from the right, cutting diagonally toward us.

"What the hell?" she said, pointing to the pilgrims feeding into our route.

We had accidentally taken some kind of variant and were glad to be connected again. The sight of a half-dozen backpackers let us fill our diaphragms a little more fully.

We dipped back into rolling vineyards, reminiscent of Osooyos and the wine nirvana of Naramata Bench in British Columbia. A misty rainbow arched and spilled into the top of the Galician mountain range, another cheery omen after an anxious walk out of Ponferrada.

The hours to an impromptu lunch pit stop in Cacabelos were flat and gorgeous. We passed trees weeping with pears and golden apples. The fig trees were practically leaning with ripe fruit. Churches from the 13th and 17th centuries and a former leper hospice were necessary stops for many pilgrims. I was disappointed to learn later that we missed seeing one of the oldest cypress trees in Europe at Convento de la Anunciada.

It was said to be 400 years old. Soon all that was ancient and desolate gave way to a very modern and thriving Villafranca.

Though we longed to stay at the lovely Albergue Leo, with its roaring fire, creaky floors and stone wall interior, it wouldn't have been fair to our bunkmates. Still coughing, Kim and I retreated to the outskirts of town, across the river, and checked into a private room at El Cruce Hostal. Colin was in the lobby, trying to tap into the Wi-Fi, and was quick with a hug. Cathy was upstairs napping and they were chugging along all right, save for Colin's knee that had him hobbling most days. The hostel had welcoming ambassadors at every turn: a puffy cat with avocado green eyes and a waggy golden retriever.

Our private room fit the bill for the price tag. We had a funny, ancient TV the size of a cereal box, a flesh-coloured toilet and sink and a three-quarter tub that was out of the question.

"I'd have more parts out than in in that thing," I said to Kim. Instead, we played with the flimsy curtain and hand-held shower that we never really grew accustomed to. This was a working holiday after all, not everything could come easily.

We went on a tapas hop around town, starting at the very cool, industrial lower-level El Benito. Plates of ham drizzled in olive oil as golden as the beer were placed in front of us. As we looked closer at the stonework inside, we began to notice all the coins lined up along the individual stones. We added to the collection, and if someone was ambitious enough to collect them all, there was some money to be made!

Rain slid in again in fine spits as we wandered back to our hostel's vending machine that sold both cans of beer and sachets of a spicy corn nut mix that had become our Camino staple. It was a moving gallery of graffiti and tight, flower-punched alleys. I loved so many things about Spain, from the quirky vending machine offerings to the verdant parks with riverside pizza ovens for public use.

I also loved that our only daily responsibility was to walk. What a golden way to live out a day! Cimmy the Dane might have cottoned on to something brilliant. Why not just keep walking? From wherever you are!

I worried that my inner inertia would have me convincing Kim to sell our SUV so we could only walk. Hell, we could sell the house and walk down to Belize for the winter. Kim sensed I might be feverish and delirious from coughing with my/our new-found life goals.

At the forefront, I was thinking about Villafranca and the Puerta del Perdón (Door of Forgiveness), a welcome passage for pilgrims who were too sick to continue to Santiago. Walking through this door at Iglesia de Santiago was deemed to be the equivalent of arrival in the heralded but unattainable Santiago.

Back in the day, Cacabelos had been the location of six pilgrim hospitals. In 2017, 301,036 pilgrims received their Compostela (certificate of achievement). In the Holy Years, when St. James Day (July 25) falls on a Sunday, a "Holy Year" or "Jubilee Year" occurs. With leap years factored in, this means Holy Years occur in five-, six- and eleven-year intervals. Next up? 2021, 2027 and 2032. Eligible pilgrims can walk through this Door of Forgiveness gate and receive a Jubilee. Only here and in Santiago can the Jubilee be received.

As I laid flat on our baguette-hard bed, waiting for Kim to preen her pretty self, I made note of a few recent observations:

Spain has a lot of cigarette and gambling machines in the oddest places.

Stop signs say "STOP" not "*DETENER*," which is Spanish for stop. Why?

Restaurants love cafeteria-style bright lights. Someone needs to introduce the dimmer switch and the soft light of Edison bulbs. However, on the flip side, 75 per cent of bars had one, if not two, zero beers (0 per cent alcohol) on tap.

Where are the condiments? Kim hadn't stopped talking about her ten-cent mayo find – and we hadn't found it since. Canadian resto tables are eaten up by skull-labelled hot sauces, lazy Susans of barbecue sauce, sticky ketchups, HP and the like. So far, I'd only seen cinnamon in the cafes. Our quesadilla from El King Kong came as dry as kindling. No guacamole, no sour cream, no salsa. Not even a snipped chive or chili pepper flake dusting.

This is an unofficial observation, but residents of Spain must have teeth like camels and beavers to eat baguettes on a daily basis. I still had half of my retainer attached, but it was just a matter of time before I swallowed the wire and brackets with some salami.

There are out-the-door lineups at every local *panaderia* (bakery) of mostly men picking up a daily baseball bat of bread. Confession: I had begun experiencing serious naan bread fantasies.

There is a lot of siesta going on and everyone seems to have individual, regional hours that puzzled as much as the Filipino cookies, Oriental pizza and seasonal Russian salad.

Since Ponferrada, there had been a huge surge in the number of establishments offering pizza and burgers. The pinchos of the Basque region had slowly turned into tapas with slim difference. A toothpick had been replaced with a piece of baguette as a vehicle for the chorizo or cheese somewhere around León. Now knee-deep in tapas land, we had entered a zone of pig-heavy menu that included everything from fried tails to pig ear tapas. I wondered what my late pig farmer grandfather would have to say about that.

As much as I fancied a pigtail, we needed drugs. Stat. We were forced to steer ourselves into a pharmacy because the cough thing was annoying us both to no end. In lieu of a doctor's visit, the pharmacist kindly diagnosed us and ran through all of our options. One-stop shopping, thank you! We went with the lightweight alternative of an over-the-counter Cinfatos Expectorante. I copied out the mile-long ingredient list appearing in a font suitable for mice (in particular, mice who wore glasses). *Dextrometorfano Hidrobromuro*. I'd have to ask my brother Dax about how legit it all was. I was turning into my grandmother, who treated my brother's PhD in biotoxicology and microbiology as the equivalent of Telehealth Ontario (Telehealth Ontario is a free, confidential health advice service answered by a registered nurse, 24 hours a day). My grandmother would phone Dax with questions about her latest blood pressure medication, expecting my bro to be able to address her concerns. And usually he did. So I would do the same.

The sachets were filled with magic powder that had to be added to a half cup of water. Kim was already shouldering the added weight of an industrial-sized conditioner bottle on my behalf, since I'd left our skimpy tube behind in the godforsaken hostel with the Swedes. Spanish grocers didn't carry anything smaller than a litre-sized bottle of anything in the body care department. Even our new tube of toothpaste was as big as my forearm and tasted more like mint pudding than the triple-action *pasta de dientes* advertised.

Our clothes officially smelled like chorizo and Gouda. Mine, a little more like stewed deer and El Bierzo wine. Maybe our sweat composition had changed? I'd have to ask my smarty-pants brother about that too.

Luckily, most grocery stores had a huge selection of cheap cologne on display with testers. After several cities and nourishing spritzes, we had become fans of tester #16. It smelled mostly like cloying cotton candy and unicorns but much better than #12, which had us reeking like forest fungi and root cellar.

As shower-fresh as we could be in our flesh-coloured three-piece bath, we lost ambition to cross the river back into the city core. Instead, we joined a gabby throng at the restaurant on the corner. Colin and Cathy waved again and gave us the universal "sorry" signal that their table was full.

Venturing out, I ordered the garlic trout, as the region was known for this fish. Kim smiled to see spaghetti Bolognese on the menu, so it was a no-brainer for her. Our flustered server flapped around the full house, rolling her eyes at a group from Britain sliding tables together without permission.

She dropped a bottle of very chilled red juicy wine at our table and disappeared again until the trout and spaghetti steamed in front of us. Bonus? Rice pudding without asking.

Again, we were knocked out by nine, hoping our magic sleeves of cough medicine were magical, not poisonous.

A Night with Nigel at the Tree House

Villafranca to La Faba (23.7 km)

It was an indulgent ten hours of sound sleep. I nearly had bedsores from not budging all night. We had two more fairy cakes in our pack, which, day-old, were a crumbly mess. I finished my chocolate milk drinking box like a bratty 5-year-old, sucking out every last droplet as we turned left at the bridge. A fine mist clung to our GORE-TEX and cheeks like wet static cling.

It felt like a quintessential fall day with the heady whiff of woodsmoke in the air. It curled out of every chimney, making me long for a woolly blanket, more coffee and that smiley golden retriever from El Cruce at my feet.

The leaves were turning a spun honey gold. Fallen aspen leaves stuck to our hikers like pieces of tape as we cut through century-old forests with giant ferns up to our hips. The trail was as flat as my chest and paved all the way to our first coffee in an eclectic stone house with the same coin-lined wall decor. To boot, there was a stuffed warthog head with olive-sized eyes and tusks that were well worn from photo ops. There was a taxidermy civet cat as well, or something to that effect. (It had seen better days.)

Our next stop was even more curious, inside a tiny grocery store that had a table for two in the centre beside the nearly bare shelves of biscuits, crackers and pâté. There was a small cooler with fresh goat cheese and the local microbrew stout for an even stouter price. A local couple flitted in, downed espressos with the shopkeeper at the skinny bar, laughed in our direction and carried on. We had purchased two bottles of beer and unwrapped our sandwiches, realizing we were the daily spectacle. Nothing like the ambience of a grocery store table for two!

After a few more hours of criss-crossing snaking rivers, the final four-kilometre ascent into La Faba was a rocky road into and out of a dense jungle of moss and gigantic fern fronds. The tiny hippie pocket of a few buildings actually had a vegetarian restaurant adjoined to our hostel, Albergue de la Faba (now called CaminArte). Those with better/younger backs made a beeline for the cheaper hammock stay. The bunks in our room were of clever design. I could practically stand on my bunk and not hit my head on the one above. A German owned the establishment, and given all the tall Germans we had encountered, this ergonomic, tall-friendly design made sense. However, the miniature en suite that ten of us would share was at the top of a small staircase. You had to perform a Cirque du Soleil move to get inside, and once the door was closed, you had to angle yourself just to sit on the toilet and wash your hands in the bird bath sink at the same time. The shower was a comical affair and possibly designed for a surfboard, not a human body. I had to skip soaping up anything below my knees, as the tight quarters didn't allow for bending. As demonstrated hours later, the 13-centimetre gap from the floor to the door offered zero soundproofing and perhaps enhanced acoustics.

The curios were everywhere – ornate, carved elephant trunk door handles, stuffed animals and mermaid hardware. There was a kiwi tree outside the front door. To mark our bunk, we were instructed to choose a "stuffie" and place it on our pillow. Kim wasn't too sure about certain elements but appreciated the Hobbit-inspired room. We had narrowly missed out on the sole couple's bunk that had a double mattress.

We sniffed out beers at Casa el Árbol (The Tree House) only because the veggie restaurant was packed with pilgrims slurping soup and lentil burgs. It had a Nordic feel, with playful red chairs and a rouge vintage bike hung on the wall. The energetic barkeep from the UK with powder blue eyes and a well-groomed lumberjack beard was eager to entertain. He stoked the fire and served us samples of Portuguese moonshine as scorching as the flames. Kim and I fell into Nigel's trance easily. He was an *extra* extrovert and laid out his life story in neatly wrapped parcels. A new customer failed to interrupt his stream of consciousness. Nigel swiftly delivered the order and resumed his tale about traversing the west coast of Canada in a birchbark canoe like Alexander Mackenzie in search of a northern trade route through Bella Coola.

"You must buy my friend's book about it all, *Voyageur.* Robert Twigger. Write it down."

The stories came as fast as the drinks (and, oddly, as the bartender – he was keeping equal pace with us). Nigel had climbed ice walls and scaled walls of a nunnery in Spain. The previous year he met a wolf pack of pilgrims and they decided to walk the Camino at night, by the light of the moon. They slept and drank by day, and traversed like the Three Kings of Orient. I could see Nigel's infectious spirit luring even the most sound, practical mind into a haphazard adventure. He found "his people" at a commune along the Camino that had a pop-up, free hugs and a "Pissy Palace." We couldn't miss it and Nigel refused to divulge further details for risk of spoiling the great duct tape surprise.

"What do you want to hear? Let's Spotify something Canadian," Nigel insisted. We requested Jann Arden and he had a dozen of her albums on instant rotation – even the Christmas one. Listening to Jann Arden singing carols as we drank San Miguel by the fire while Kim applied mascara for Nigel, on Nigel, was just the innocent beginning of events that night.

When the crowd inside thinned, Nigel dragged us outside to play an ancient game of tossing metal washers into a wooden drawer with sectioned boxes and slots. In the centre of the drawer sat an iron frog with an open mouth.

"Get it in the frog's mouth and I'll give you a free drink," Nigel offered, triggering Kim's competitive spirit.

Kim tossed three rings into the frog's mouth without practice. Nigel couldn't believe it and decided to change the reward to a points system. He tossed washers with us until a few pilgrims entered the bar. "I'll be back!" he promised, sashaying inside, a yellow feather boa tossed over his shoulder.

Back inside, the frog toss game mastered, we sipped our potent free drinks and decimated a platter of thin baguette slices brushed with garlic and drizzled with olive oil, artfully presented salty sardines and wilted greens. Jann Arden was rockin' around the Christmas tree when the chef offered us more free samples of her croquettes and blackened El Bierzo peppers.

I felt that small pull of wanting to stay in La Faba for a week, maybe months. Nigel had stayed on for that same reason – and would continue the Camino when it felt right again. But maybe it was the 40-year-old gin that was presented to us, overriding my rational thinking.

We had another herb elixir and some local hooch that surely took the enamel off my front teeth. At this point, it felt like maybe Nigel had forgotten about his staff status. We watched the chef take off with a wide lipsticked smile, her body like fondue in the arms of the German hippie who owned the hostel where we were staying. He bled cool with long silver hair combed with fingers. A magpie or raven feather was braided in his hair. Not too many people can pull that look off.

The randy chef was supposed to be back for 6:30 to prep for the dinner crowd. Nigel was still feeling responsible, surprisingly, and ushering pilgrims in, plying them with drinks. And Jann Arden carols.

When a low-lying rumble about the absent chef surfaced, a confident hobby chef from Nova Scotia offered to take over the helm. Barry disappeared into the kitchen with Nigel to take stock. They hammered out a menu that would not be as advertised.

Just as orders were filtering in, the sultry chef oozed back in, smiley and satiated from a shag.

"Nana Mouskouri! That's who she looks like!" I said, sharing my gin epiphany with Kim.

Nana blew our table a kiss and, despite no order from us, more salted El Bierzo peppers were placed on our table with equally salty and oily potato chips, hot from the fryer. Then she delivered croquettes filled with a silky potato bacon mousse.

Our true order was delivered about two hours later. The Tree House was empty, save for the chef, Nigel and us. We had ordered the "Kevin Bacon" and "Vietnam" sandwiches, but when we referred to the blackboard descriptions, they contained none of the ingredients outlined. Instead of beets and guacamole, I had pineapple. Kim wasn't even sure what she had, but after a full day of grazing both Nigel's shelves and the chef's freebies we were stuffed.

We wrapped our mystery sandwiches in serviettes, hugged wild Nigel goodbye like an old cherished friend and safely fell into our German-sized bunks.

"We have to get out of this town," Kim said.

"I know. It's too dangerous."

FIVE

↓

Galicia

A familiar sight along the Camino behind the hostels and albergues. Sour clothes are renewed with suds and line-dried in the sun at day's end.

Pink Gin and Flaming Eyeball Rituals
La Faba to Triacastela (25.7 km)

In a murky gin haze, we left La Faba in squeaky morning light. Ten steps in we were faced with an Everest climb to O Cebreiro that made us question our frivolity and thirst the night before. Nigel!

It was an Ansel Adams sunrise and luckily our heads cleared with the milky fog. Every living thing was bejewelled with dewdrops that sparkled in the shafts of sunlight.

O Cebreiro is the first official Galician town on the Camino's route, and the circular stone dwellings with thatched roofs are a giant step back in time. Three of the nine remaining *pallozas* have been spun into casual museums. Again, the hours didn't jibe with our passage through.

Rain is guaranteed for 150 days a year in O Cebreiro, but it seemed like the kind of place where that level of gloomy grey and monsoon would be doable. Wood smoke lured us into a lower level cafe for coffee where two delivery men were drinking short glasses of red wine. It felt like Ireland with the same kind of forecast that permitted hearty meals, welly boots, picky wool sweaters and wet dogs.

"I wonder how Martina's witch ritual went?" I said to Kim, enjoying the caffeine injection into my bloodstream.

"Oh yeah! That was supposed to happen in O Cebreiro!"

Martina was a spunky twentysomething from Poland walking the Camino with her boyfriend and another guy they picked up along the way. She asked if we planned to do the ceremony that was intended to help ward off witchcraft.

"You have eyeball that gets lit on fire and then you swallow it."

I'd convinced Kim on many questionable things over the years, but even I wasn't so keen on eyeballs.

"It's only two euro, and you are safe from the witches of Galicia," Martina explained. Her quieter boyfriend nodded along when she explained that he had done it when he walked the Camino a few years before.

"It's no big deal," he said.

We said we'd wait for Martina's report when we crossed paths again. We first met at a grocery store in the town with the singing nuns. She was looking for strawberry gin at the time. We had a tutorial on both the pink gin and eye-eating ceremony in one swoop. From that point forward, Kim and I called her Pink Gin.

The coffee helped enormously, but maybe I did need an eyeball to ward off all evils. The morning still felt strange and I was baffled even more when I saw a woman walk out of her house with a cow on a lead. I had watched her emerge from a front door and call back – and I fully expected a dog at her heels. Instead, it was not one cow but three that she led out of her home. I would later learn that houses in this area are typically built with room for livestock below, which in turn heat the upper level of the home. Still, it was an odd moment.

It was a big ask for a morning climb with a steady cerebellum-pounding ascent to 381 metres. Again, Kim and I had taken an unintentional variant and were walking alone for several kilometres before we caught wind of pilgrims again. Reunited, we followed switchbacks "down, down, down" (as Gudrun would say) to Triacastela. The sheep bell tinkle of the Pyrenees had morphed into the deeper dong of cattle bells and potent manure.

This is where we met Nona (not to be confused with Nana, the runaway chef in La Faba). We were following a dozen cattle that also used the Camino as their "Way." A sun-weathered woman in tall rubber boots and a long black skirt cracked a single-tailed whip and nudged the most wayward of the bunch toward her barn. Footing became dodgy with not only mud but wet cow patties as big as medium pizzas.

As we patiently waited for the cows to collectively turn right or left, we entered a narrow passage of houses in serious need of shoring up. Nona appeared out of a dark entrance like an apparition, all smiles, holding a plate to her chest with something wrapped in a tea towel. She had a cute, well-floured apron knotted around her waist.

"English?"

"Yes," we nodded in synchro.

"Pancake?" She opened the tea towel on her plate to reveal a neat stack of thin pancakes, like crepes.

Kim and I smiled at our good fortune. We had heard of random strangers supporting pilgrims in this way. Like the guy who had offered us a bundle of grapes while we wrote postcards. Another shopkeeper had insisted on filling our palms with a free scoop of nuts and raisins for energy. And, here, free pancakes from this kind woman.

We said, yes, please, in gracious tones. She deftly rolled the pancakes like cigars and pulled out a shaker of sugar from her apron. She shook a generous amount on the two rolls and Kim and I gave her praise in our limited conversational Spanish: "*Muy bueno!*" (very good). Human kindness! Wow. We'd have to tell Martina that there was no need to eat eyeballs. The Galicians were a genial bunch.

But then our hopes and faith were dashed. Nona made the universal signal for money by rubbing her thumb and index finger together.

"Donativo? Donation?" She smiled even wider. She lifted her tea towel back enticingly.

"More pancake?"

Kim knew we only had big bills. We had tried to break them earlier into coins. I knew I had ten euros in my pocket, but that would make for super pricey pancakes without genuine maple syrup. Kim and I exchanged glances – we certainly couldn't walk away in good conscience.

I held out the ten and asked if she had change. Nona provided a quick mitt of coins and automatically charged us four euros. Which was fair. They were the most authentic pancakes we could possibly have. In the middle of the road in a tiny hamlet with no name. A town with more parked antique tractors than people. Where we had to wait for cows to merge so we could continue on the Camino.

Nona waved us goodbye, resuming her position in the dark entry of her home, ready to pounce. Kim and I agreed she must be sitting on a mattress full of millions. Like the entrepreneurial kid with the lemonade stand.

After our nourishing pancakes, we didn't stop until Triacastela, which is named for the three castles built in the tenth century – that no longer exist. Apparently, medieval pilgrims would voluntarily carry large pieces of limestone from the limestone-dense area to the limekiln in Santiago. These stones were used to build the cathedral. I was glad to not be medieval.

Triacastela had seven albergues to choose from and our lucky find was at A Horta de Abel. The stonework alone was a powerful draw. A fire was roaring here too; the night temperatures had started to creep lower. We interrupted a woman ironing sheets to book bunks.

"Do you want private room?" she asked.

For just a few euros more, we were game – and what a delight. She showed us the silo-like room and we couldn't believe our Camino windfall. It was much colder in the turret, but she was happy to bring us more blankets. The silo was off the main dorm room, just a few steps down, but with a door to close off the commotion. I heard Cathy's voice.

"How did you two land that private room? I didn't even know there was a bed in there!" Cathy stepped inside and admired the space. "And look at the ceiling height!" She was equal parts happy and jealous of our sacred find and we called it even as I reminded her of our bust of a stay in León.

"Remember when you and Colin had a bath, a bottle of wine *and* a nap, all while Kim and I were still waiting for our room down the alley with the beer bottles smashing all hours?"

With the sun still stroking the backyard of the albergue, we washed out socks and added them to a long, sagging line of dripping clothes. We picked up fixings for crude quesadillas. It was difficult to find fresh produce in the tinier towns. There were always potatoes, onions and mealy cabbages, but we had to make do with a small tin of sweet corn and a not-quite-ripe avocado. We had learned a week earlier (after a scolding) to take produce to the attendant in charge of weighing all fruits and veg and "slaps." (They unceremoniously slap price stickers – often bigger than the item – onto the produce, which is then scanned by the main cashier.)

"Hey, pink gin!" Kim said.

Naturally, I looked for Martina, but Kim had found a spark plug of strawberry gin for two euros.

"Same price as the witch eyeball," I said. "And the exact same price as this roll-on Nike deodorant. Is Nike really making deodorant now?"

"Knock-off," Kim said with confidence, especially after smelling it. "Oh, and check this out. Now they're selling Coca-Cola with coffee! Coke *and* coffee in a can!"

We left the grocer, leaving the Coke and coffee combo to the imagination, even though we wanted to hear what song the store was going to play next. First it was Rick Astley's "Never Gonna Give You Up," and then a heart skip to Chris de Burgh's "Lady in Red." I felt like I was back in Grade 8 at a lunchtime dance in the gymnasium.

My attempt at quesadillas back at our quaint albergue was another confirmation that Spain needs more no-stick pans. Urgently.

Pissy Palace and the Mad Hatter
Triacastela to Barbadelo (23 km)

- -

We had crepes to start the day, marking another crossing of Spain's invisible breakfast boundary line from tortillas to churros to pancakes and crepes. We smeared the crepes with little tubs of something similar to Nutella that we found in the albergue kitchen and they were almost as good as Nona's.

Kim and I slept like dead pigs in our private stone silo cave until 8:15 a.m. A sleep-in world record by Camino standards.

Roosters serenaded us out of the town named for three castles that were no more. Skinny kitties and sleepy German shepherds resided at every house we passed before slipping into the wet shade of a giant green forest that was a hybrid of Sleepy Hollow and *Where the Wild Things Are.*

It was cattle country now and the manure-splattered trail was a reminder. There were no coffee stops, not by choice. The trail was a steep roller coaster with as many ups as downs through empty farming hamlets. I admired Kim's butterscotch legs from behind, her calves having definitely refined to the point that I could see the impressive lines of her medial and lateral gastrocs.

"There's Pink Gin – Martina," Kim said, to clarify. We caught up to the Polish crew and asked about the voodoo witchcraft night. Martina was quick to pull out her camera and show us the whole scene.

Clicking through, she stopped and said, "And here is a bowl that they light on fire."

"A bowl?"

"Yes, a bowl," she confirmed. But with her accent, it sounded like "eye-bowl." Or "eyeball" as Kim and I both heard the first time round.

"Not an eyeball."

"What?" Her eyes widened.

I explained, "I thought you were doing this witchcraft thing where they lit an 'eyeball' on fire. I totally thought you said 'eyeball' not 'a bowl.' Kim and I were having a great debate as to whether it was a cow eye or sheep's eyeball even! Oh god, and I even told Colin and Cathy all about it. No wonder it wasn't in their guidebook! O Cebriero is going to have this influx of kooky pilgrims asking for flaming eyeballs now!"

Martina had a great Santa-like laugh. "You didn't miss much. And it was three euros, not two like we were told. But we drank much gin after to make up for it." Kim told her that we'd found a bar shot of pink gin that we were saving to commemorate the last 100 kilometres.

"Ah, very good. *Okrzyki!*"

After sharing our unexpectedly wild experience in La Faba, the Polish trio was disappointed they had pushed ahead and missed the antics of Nigel for witchcraft elixir. Martina and Nigel would have been a very lethal duo.

Kim and I parted with the Polish and took the San Xil variant to Barbadelo. The alternate route, which was 6.5 kilometres longer, passed by the Samos monastery that also had an albergue. But the route involved more pavement, and after bedding down in a monastery already, we had a strong visual for the monastic experience. San Xil asked a little more in terms of elevation, but the forested walk was utopian, until Sarria at least.

We'd heard a lot about Sarria, especially from Colin. He fed us all the pertinent info we needed for legs ahead, knowing (and unbelieving) that Kim and I could travel without a guidebook, maps or a phone. Though the Camino had its variants, there was truly only one way to Santiago, and we were okay with the surprise element of where we landed and lunched, or starved.

Sarria is a major starting point, as those who begin here, at the 100-kilometre mark, qualify to receive a Compostela in Santiago. Colin warned that the Camino was going to be suddenly overrun. Albergues were going to be sold out. We tried to remain relaxed about our tech-free commitment and hoped it wouldn't backfire with 98 per cent of pilgrims being able to pre-book the nights ahead.

We felt the seismic shift, more in commercialism, not pilgrim numbers. Every other building in Sarria advertised a hostel or retail catering to pilgrims. All the kit was suddenly available – hiking shoes, walking poles, buffs, Tilley hats. I couldn't imagine buying and breaking in a new pair of footwear en route like bra-less Cheri-Lyn did after her Yorkdale Mall retail spree.

"I wonder if the Dutch guy was able to get his boots in the mail?" I said. We hadn't seen the couple since León.

"Hopefully, he didn't get diary again," Kim smirked. Then we hoped we wouldn't get a bout for making fun. I could hear my Nan scold, "See, the Devil got you for that!"

We bought a few snacks and more cough drops for our cling-on cough in Sarria and were ready to march on out of the bustle of the city for the rural aromatics.

But first we found Nigel's hippie commune with the celebrated "Pissy Palace." Kim was not impressed, and though I took a picture, it was a little too grunge for even my rustic-leaning self. The palace was a crude outhouse that had been adorned with a shiny duct tape seat, prayer flags and a crown that you were to wear while engaged.

"Gross," was our tandem commentary. Others filtered down the hill, anxious to see this world-famous crapper.

The place was all about feelin' groovy and livin' off the land. The commune dwellers had various homemade bikes in states of disrepair. The gardens were wild and untamed but healthy, the scent of rosemary (thankfully) thick in the air.

Waves of pilgrims were thrilled to find this hippie joint. The Hugging Zone sign was prominent among the love and inspo quotes and amateur paintings. We dodged sweaty hugs and contributed to the donativo, happy for a boiled egg, ripe bananas and a few sweet dates. Kim skipped the egg, not trusting the sanitation level and expiry dates observed at the commune.

The route beyond the commune was a marvel of giant pumpkin patches like I dreamed our little community garden plot was producing back home while we were away. In adjoining fields, broccoli bounty had been stripped, but tall corn sliced the horizon view in half.

In Barbadelo, Camino marketing was suddenly a thing. The previous 700 kilometres had been akin to an extended scavenger hunt, searching out albergues without an address. Our precious sheet only provided the name, phone number, number of beds, cost, season and whether or not there was a kitchen available. Most often the establishments were just to the right or left of the main road, but in bigger cities like Pamplona or Burgos it was a feat. For *feet* that had already walked 30 kilometres.

Prices were now being advertised trailside. There were souvenirs, postcards, English translation! Newbies to the Camino, all fresh-legged and perfumed, breezed in to a fairly flawless enterprise. Kim and I weren't charmed by any of the hostels we peeked in, so we continued another half-hour to Casa de Carmen, which was supposed to be right around the corner. It was a big corner, let's just say that. Maybe another two kilometres. We probably wouldn't be walking back into town for dinner, especially given the remote road and our mini pen light. At Casa de Carmen, several dogs and chickens greeted us.

"That dog looks exactly like Fozzie Bear," Kim said. It was uncanny!

Ocean blue hydrangeas were tipping with heavy heads. Crimson flowers cascaded from a box planter on the handlebars of an antique bike. It was definitely worth the extra grind to get to. The owner flitted about much like her chickens. In and out of the kitchen, cursing, wiping her furrowed brow. Checking in was like an encounter with Mr. Bean. It was a long, drawn-out affair, but we were glad not to be stuffed in the last room we looked at in Barbadelo where six out of eight beds were filled with people fast asleep.

We had a beer in the last bit of sunshine with one of the many dogs at our feet before clouds marched in and the wind bit at our bare legs. We were the only ones at the albergue – so far. Inside, I found chess and checker boards and Kim and I took turns with tutorials. Though I remembered chess rules less than Kim did checkers.

Dinner with the Mad Hatter owner was a colourful affair. More pilgrims had trickled in, but our dorm still had just five occupied beds. Bonus! Who were we kidding with our coughs? We were the annoying ones everyone was trying to avoid! I'm sure we had a reputation all of our own. Potential bunkmates probably saw our signature black and blue Osprey bags outside a hostel and detoured for somewhere with snorers versus hackers.

For a reasonable 14 euros each, Kim and I compensated for some missed calories. We had pork ribs and chicken breasts, both heaped with fries (we had also entered the "fries with everything" region). A bottle of wine was included, in addition to a rather lovely pineapple flan. The Mad Hatter was running the show – the entire show. Cutlery was slammed onto tabletops, wine was delivered with a dangerous swirl and my chicken breast was served nearly on my lap, in addition to half the fries as they skidded off my plate with her hurried service.

After dinner, we retreated to the lounge area and flipped through an old *National Geographic* atlas and some 2012 Spanish issues of *Peregrino* magazine until we started to fade. We had 30 kilometres on our docket in the morn, making my eyelids heavier than my footfall in a few hours. Should have bought a can of Coca-Cola + coffee.

Wendy's Hello

Barbadelo to Hospital Alta da Cruz

(29.5 km and 1.2 km further to Ventas de Narón)

"Ooh, god."

I was still in my bunk and wondered what the hell was happening. The room was as black as an inkwell.

"Ohhhh myyyy." The moan was guttural, animal-like.

That signalled the end of my sleeping. Was the woman next to me dying? She rolled and yawned with more audio and finally slippered her way over to the light switch.

Really?

Lights on, I glared in her direction. Kim gave her an indirect "WOW."

We ate lime yogurt and granola bars on my bottom bunk, watching this dramatic woman shuffle around. What a production! She was already knocked out when we came to bed the night before, so we had no idea what kind of whinging had happened already. Was she at dinner? We didn't recognize her.

She beat us to the shared washroom and was already moaning in the steam of the shower. Her performance was something else. We weren't certain whether she was stiff or possibly pleasuring herself.

"Ohhhhhhhhh, god."

It was nearly obscene. We brushed our teeth, practically gagging with the questionable acoustics.

This woman was in her late 50s, but still. I couldn't imagine publicly moaning like that. (As much as I wanted to.)

Outside the hostel, tightening our straps, I began the day in a new and appropriate way. One that we would never tire of.

"*Ooh, god!*" I moaned in mockery.

We laughed until we were delirious and left the open expanse of the pastures for an impenetrable forest.

"I keep expecting to see Robin Hood pop out," Kim said. We were in the middle of a truly enchanted forest of century-old oaks. While I can wholly appreciate the history of the city, it's the architecture of a forest that floors me. We moved from the canopy shade to the seared remnants of an old forest fire. Scarred and charred pines would be the foundation of nature's powerful regeneration and resilience.

We found tortillas and coffee inside a roadside cafe with sweating windows. Locals ate slabs of walnut cake while standing, all of us in warm silence, save for the purr of espresso beans.

It was a monumental day, cracking the sacred 100-kilometre mark. The decline to the marker was so steep my kneecaps wanted to unhinge. Kim was doing her zigzag technique and I copied. Just as I zigged, I felt a heavy hand on my shoulder and a push. It was with enough force that I turned to see who it was. There was nobody there. I wasn't startled as it was broad daylight. If it had been dusk, I'm positive I would have fainted, but I knew exactly who it was.

When Kim and I first bought our stone house in Galt, a friend of a friend dropped by to pick up two slipper chairs that we'd posted for sale on Facebook. It was a fruitful transaction, as Wendy not only brought us a dozen still-warm chocolate chip cookies but she also "read" our house. She had psychic abilities and had often been called upon by the police to help locate missing persons. Wendy could hear the echo of an anvil being hammered in our master bedroom. It must have been William Webster, the stonemason who built our home in 1861. In the kitchen, Wendy paused, suddenly keyed into the otherworld.

"If you ever feel a push here in the kitchen, don't be afraid. It will come from behind; you'll feel it in your shoulder."

For the four years that we lived in that stone house, I waited not-so-subconsciously for that push. A year after we moved in 2016, Wendy died. It made sense that she would give me a playful shove at some point, seeing how I didn't get it in the kitchen as she promised. It seemed even more fitting on the Camino, where I'm certain many spirits smile, tease and play.

"Wendy just said hi," I told Kim as we reached the bottom of the hill and walked toward the 100-kilometre waymark.

"Wendy?"

"Yeah, the psychic. Remember she told me to expect a shove from behind in our stone house? I totally felt it. I know it was her."

Kim wasn't surprised by my assumption. I seemed to attract ghosts, spirits and the odd UFO.

I dug the ceremonial pink gin out of Kim's pack. There was no need to lean in to ensure that the waymark said 100 km; it was obvious with all the graffiti and adornments that dangled from it. While stones were commonly placed on top of bollards (stone or concrete markers) along the Camino, graffiti and stickers seemed to be trending, unfortunately. The celebrated marker was looking more like a rubbish bin with flowers and tchotchkes, old holey hikers, key chains, weathered flags and the like.

It was only 10:15 a.m., but it made sense to do a gin shot then and there. Every tendon and muscle fibre would be called upon until we reached Ventas de Narón. I felt like we were on an extended garden tour with the harlequin blooms. Crimson zinnias, soft pops of lavender. The visuals were nonstop and staggering. It was awesome to experience each day without expectation. Yes, we had been held captive in the towns that didn't have a supermarket, and were forced into dining out. Some of the picnics we had were very patchwork and failed to resemble any part of Canada's Food Guide. We ate unrefrigerated yogurt four-days strong and boiled eggs that had bounced around in our packs even longer. We were at the mercy of the vacancy gods for accommodations, but, considering, we had fared exceedingly well, despite a waning interest in baguettes.

Midday we joined the weary leagues pausing for a beer and some chorizo at a bar with a generous patio. Beside us, a jovial bunch, fresh from Sarria, carried on like an improv group. There were four women and two guys in the comical crew and we were soon looped into their animated conversation. They all had their boots off and were complaining about the speed torture their friend had put them through already. They wanted to hear of the stories beyond Sarria, and we were happy to share the highlights over Amstel pints before we realized we'd better carry on, otherwise hours later we could still be gabbing with this fun crowd and have to bed down at the pub. One of the women sounded exactly like Catherine Deneuve, and every time she spoke I was swimming in her honeyed voice spell.

"We'll find each other ahead," I promised, hoping that we would. While many pilgrims who had started in France poo-pooed those who jumped on the Camino bandwagon in Sarria, we didn't care. We'd rather keep company with this lot!

In Portomarin, we crossed an intimidating bridge that instilled instant heebie-jeebies in both of us as we leaned over the railing. The spooky view below was of the submerged former town. In 1956, dam construction flooded the former city that flanked both sides of the river. Remnants, like skeletal remains, can still be seen provided the river level is low.

The current city still appears historic, as many of the buildings were relocated upstream and downstream stone by stone. The entire city seemed impeccably whitewashed and efficiently gridded out. There were endless pharmacies (more cough drops), supermercados and albergues. Amstel beer replaced the usual staples, San Miguel and Estrella Damm. Clapboard signs advertised omelettes instead of tortillas. "Matrimonial beds" were available at every other albergue. Change was underfoot.

Leaving Portomarin, we dodged hairy chestnuts galore. I'd never seen anything like them. They were like urchins all over the trail, and in some sections they were as wet and slippery as slugs to cross. We slowed down to check out the pop-up store selling boomerangs of all things. There were painted scallop shells en masse, bananas, beer and painted thimbles. Of course. One-stop shopping.

Hospital Alta da Cruz was one of the tiniest hamlets yet and smack dab on the highway. There was a dumpy albergue and hotel with a restaurant and that was it. I don't think Kim and I even spoke out loud – we just knew we were carrying on.

In Ventas de Narón, we were happy to find the pastoral stillness of Casa Molar. We splurged on a private room with a shared bath, as somebody had already fashioned a sign indicating that they snored and hung it on the dorm door. Smart move. We hadn't tried that deterrent yet!

We had sheep in the "front yard" of our hostel and the tinkle of bells and bleating was soothing. We circled around the dirt path town to see what else was on offer. Albergue O Cruzeiro had beer on tap and served pints with a bowl of gumdrops. Gumdrops! My great-grandmother would have been thrilled. A subtitled Carol Burnett movie was on mute behind us, and again, the juxtapositions of Spain made me shake my head.

Just as I had finished trying each colour of gumdrop, a blind man barrelled into the bar with his dog and a wheel of fresh cheese bigger than a birthday cake and insisted we buy it. I tried to kindly explain that we were on foot and didn't want to carry another nine kilograms of cheese. He barked at us (not the dog), angry at the rejection. The bartender, who had slipped into the kitchen, heard the commotion and returned, yelling rather aggressively at the blind man until he turned and left, hugging his cheese wheel.

"He do this all the time. Come in here with his cheese and try to sell to customer."

Dinner was 100 per cent beige but amazing. Kim had spaghetti and was delighted that it tasted exactly like childhood Heinz Alphaghetti pasta. I had grilled pollo and *frites* (fries) with mayo.

Kim held up her glass of gratis wine, "Do you think we've been drinking grape juice all this time?"

It was possible. Some of the pilgrim wine tasted rather juicy, but the placebo effect worked.

Still barking, we ordered hot toddies and sat in the bar watching the *Property Brothers* in *español*. We had become so cultural in such a short amount of time.

Kim dished out our latest attempt to overcome kennel cough. A pharmacist in Portomarin had recommended tablets that dissolved in half a glass of water like Alka Seltzers. The swill left my teeth furry, so I was thrilled when the bartender offered us a slice of the Tarte de Santiago I had read about. It was on the to-eat list I'd crafted back in Canada. I'm not a cake person by any means, but this skinny slice was divine. It was dusted with icing sugar, dense and lemony. We would have to take advantage of this regional cake before it disappeared. And, with less than 100 kilometres left, our cake clock was ticking.

Corncrib Crypt Lessons

Ventas de Narón to Boente (32 km)

We started walking under the pinpricks of stars, from the paved road to woodsy hollows. There was a low hoot of an owl invisible in the sky-high plane trees. The trees looked as though they were in various states of disrobing; long perfect strips of bark hung limp at the ankles of the tree. It was a nonstop reel of IMAX visuals until our first coffee stop.

We squeezed into a cafe for luxurious, velvety coffee. The croissants were as big as travel pillows and the thistle-coloured hydrangeas in the adjacent garden were soccer-ball-sized.

We had crossed paths (and croissants) again with the British contingent. They looked even wearier than the first day we met but were still jolly and well spirited. Over double espresso shots they hadn't skipped a beat with roasting each other. I opened myself to fair and deserved roasting after sharing my goofed interpretation of Pink Gin's flaming eyeball witchcraft story with the crew. I was about to learn of my next accidental story fabrication.

Since we had entered the Galician region, Kim and I had passed by dozens of elevated structures made out of red brick, wood and stone. Most had crosses on them. Plausibly, this is where the dead were buried. These crypts were in every backyard and of varying sizes. My heart felt heavier seeing the smaller crypts that were obviously housing an infant. The wooden mausoleums were most creepy – I even pointed out the shadows of bony remains to Kim. It was a larger mausoleum and probably contained several family members – perhaps the whole family tree. You could see the outline of their bodies!

There was a newly painted mausoleum directly in front of the albergue we were staying in that night – had a pilgrim died right then and there? I asked the innkeeper what the story was. Why were these raised tombs only found in Galicia, and not throughout the rest of Spain?

"Tombs?"

"Yes, tombs," I confirmed, pointing to the obvious red one out front.

"That is a *hórreo*. A…granary. Corn. Corncrib," she said with a frown.

"Hórreo? Corncrib?"

"Yes, to store corn, grains and keep out the rats."

Ooh. This also made sense. The shadows of bodies I'd seen were actually dead corncobs all along.

I whispered to Kim, "Did I tell anyone else about these mausoleums?" Who did I have to share this updated corncrib intel with?

After days of not seeing many familiar faces, Boente pulled them all out of the woodwork. I hadn't talked about raised tombs to any of them, so I was safe.

Kim and I had decided in Estella to not take any more rest days, unless totally necessary, just to keep the momentum going. It made more sense to bank the days for the end, or Muxía, where we hoped to hang out for a few days after Santiago. We had veered off the typical itinerary that most pilgrims were following by a few nights already. Whether we had carried on to the next town in search of a better hostel, or chose a variant, it immediately split us from the pack that went to see the monastery. We hadn't seen Irish Jack in weeks or Capetown Felicity, though we often wondered aloud about their progress. However, Gudrun and Teresa, PEI Mary and Pink Gin all appeared at the corncrib albergue. The French woman from our Airbnb in Saint-Jean-Pied-de-Port was there too – it was like a grand ol' reunion.

Albergue Boente was a squeaky new and efficient Dutch-owned joint that was more hotel-like than hostel-like. There was a definite bump up in quality and for the first time menus advertising American breakfasts: bacon, eggs and brownies! The menu was explained in photos as well, like a typical old-school Chinese restaurant.

Bus tours with lanyard-wearing passengers and tacky gift shops were on the rise. The albergue was packed with a religious group wolfing back fries and beer on the patio. I pointed out the telltale sign to Kim, "Using the toilets without consuming equals 50 cents. Fifty-euro cents!"

The wind whipped our laundered clothes dry in no time, but it was too cool to sit outside as we usually did, though we tried, moving chairs around to find a wind block. Inside, we joined Pink Gin and her duo at a tight booth for a beer and then moved on to dinner. Kim and I split a braised chicken with stewed peppers on a mess of fries. The mixed salad was "mixed" in the same culinary manner as the last few places: tuna, green olives and tomato with iceberg. And to knock the night out of the park? A slice of my beloved Tarte de Santiago. We were two precious sleeps and (probably) just as many slices of tarte away from Santiago.

38 Accidental Kilometres

Boente to Lavacolla, by Accident (38 km)

– –

Pink Gin's boyfriend flicked the light on in the dorm room around seven, spurring a litany of complaints and disgusted huffs. Even though I'd become hardened by nearly four weeks of the communal Camino, I still couldn't imagine being the one to decide that everyone else should be awake too. It wasn't necessary to have an overhead light on to stuff a sleeping bag into a compression bag. I didn't need a light to put on the same thing I'd worn the day before. Our bags were ready to go, save for our sleeping bags and long johns in the morn.

Kim and I had synced our appetite and both of us were ready to roar and run on empty. We would find breakfast along the way and get a head start on the slow-moving mass around us. Pink Gin and her beau were still yawning in pajamas when we left the building.

"It's kind of crazy," Kim said. "Tomorrow we'll be walking into Santiago. Tomorrow! It seemed like everything was going so slow and then we were at that 100-kilometre marker, and now we're here."

"I know. Seeing that woman from Quebec who was at our Airbnb in France that first night – that seemed ages ago."

Our dreamy musing was interrupted by an a cappella group singing the worst possible earworm to hear on the Camino: "The Ants Go Marching." It appeared to be a father, adult son and two tow-headed kids with spindly legs. Dad was using the dictation app on his iPhone and dictating loud enough about his authentic Spanish breakfast for the stragglers in Boente to hear. It was far too early for the ants to be marching. Kim's eyes widened when the grandfather moved to the front of the line and they started into the lyrics again, this time with walking sticks to the air, ant voices booming.

"This is why my brother can never do the Camino," I said to Kim. "The Ants Go Marching" made *my* hippocampus itchy. This kind of singsong would not fly with Dax.

We watched the ants march past Albergue Milpes and knew we were safe to stop for breakfast without the soundtrack. Music was booming through the outside speakers despite the patio being empty. Kim and I were the only two inside and still repelled by the music penetrating the windows. We were reminded of a B & B stay in Samana, in the Dominican Republic. A parallel street to our accommodations had more speakers than people, and I could feel my internal organs vibrating at night in bed.

An aproned chef came to the counter within a few minutes.

"What's *mixta* and *huevos*?" I asked. I knew huevos were eggs, but mixed what?

"York. And queso."

I deduced that "york" was pork and ordered two. "Wow, and ketchup on the tables," I said to Kim.

It was ketchup's first appearance in Spain.

I was quickly lost in the impressive collection of snow globes the chef had amassed. He had globes from Amsterdam to Hong Kong and a dozen other places he had travelled. The space shuttle launching inside a snowy Houston sphere was a quick favourite.

Our mixta and huevos arrived in less than five. "It's Eggs in a Nest!" I tried to communicate my thrill with the chef, explaining my childhood staple. Eggs in a Nest was the Canadian take on mixta + huevos, or vice versa. In Grade 2, I had attended a workshop where I learned how to make the gourmand entree. Eggs in a Nest would become the only "dish" that my dad could confidently make. (Outside of scorched toast that he'd scrape free of char and mask with butter as thick as wedding cake icing.)

Kim and I both moaned like the ailing woman in Barbadelo. Who knew ketchup could be so missed?

Well fuelled, we carried on free of the a cappella group into another plane tree forest. The scaling bark, not unlike a sycamore, made me wish we lived just a little more south to enjoy their tall, surreal presence. The leaves were like thin green fish and the ribbons of bark lifted in the breeze. Holly bushes, with leaves so shiny they seemed to be freshly coated with a brush of urethane, began to make up a vital part of the greenery.

A pop-up donativo appeared just as we needed a sweet kick. We grabbed two fragrant just-scrumped figs and plodded on with measured steps. We knew we were carrying on to Muxía and Finisterre, another 120 kilometres beyond Santiago, but still, Santiago felt like a finish line of sorts. Beyond Santiago we both believed the extension in walking to be of the celebratory, honeymoon variety. A vacation walk, if you will. All of it seemed to be coming at us fast and hard. We wanted more days. More bunk beds even! Maybe we were delirious.

When we happened upon a surprise beer garden around the 30-kilometre mark, it was natural to wonder if the oasis before us was really a dream. Brown bottles were suspended from trees like Christmas decorations, they were stacked in pyramids, piled up with butt ends facing out – all with white glass marker messages of love and goodwill. The Peregrino lagers were a five-euro sting for two skinny bottles, but the atmosphere of the garden was not to be missed. The white marker made its rounds as pilgrims commemorated their visit and scaled trees and fences to create the next tier of the garden. The collective fever pitch was double that of Saint-Jean-Pied-de-Port. While France's fever was one of anxiousness to begin the dream, the beer garden so close to Santiago was a reminder of the proximity of an actualized dream. We were all so close we could almost taste it. Or was that yesterday's chorizo?

Upon turning right toward O Pedrouzo I almost collapsed with the sound of gunfire. Was it cannons? Were we under siege? Kim thought a car blew a tire behind us. We never did learn what the 21-gun salute was all about, but my heart flipped to hummingbird speed. Maybe the gunfire had left us rattled (or the beer garden beers to be fair), but somehow we completely missed our intended town: O Pedrouzo/Arca do Pino. There were seven albergues in this area – Xunta de Galicia had 120 beds even. We didn't see any of them. Upon fuzzy reflection, I do know precisely where we made a sharp right instead of left.

Two kilometres beyond the town, we were in the thick of the forest, meandering along the gentle path. Our legs knew we had already logged 30 kilometres.

"The albergues must be just after this forest," I assured Kim (and myself).

We mentally retraced our steps and decided we were still on the right track. There was no option for us to go wrong. We had come to one desolate T-stop in the road and "life" seemed to be to the right, not left.

Of all days, we had decided to dump our lukewarm water bottles shortly after the beer garden. We congratulated ourselves on finally getting smarter, on, like, day 30. Why were we lugging around water we weren't going to drink? Even though we had arrived at our hostels a few afternoons with still-full bottles, now we were psychologically thirsty. Sahara thirsty. Our only food source was a small packet of six salty olives and some cocktail peanuts. We could drink our urine – I was certain we'd watched a Bear Grylls episode that involved that.

Further into the woods, we chatted with a German couple who were backtracking. They had walked a half-hour into the woods and realized that O Pedrouzo was definitely behind us, not ahead. I pulled out our only resource of hostel listings and had the same fainty feeling that the 21-gun salute instilled. From O Pedrouzo, the next advertised "stop" was Monte de Gozo, 15.5 kilometres away. There was supposed to be another Xunta de Galicia with 400 beds. I muddled through the fine Spanish print: "*Centro europeo de peregrinación Juan Pablo II.*" Kim shook her head, sensing ill fortune ahead.

"That sounds like a place for religious tourists, like when the Pope comes to visit," Kim guessed.

She was dead right and it didn't sound promising. The Germans decided to detour back to town. The wife was limping with hot blisters and bone-deep fatigue.

(Insert swear words here.)

"What should we do?"

We had six olives and thinning patience but enough daylight to see us through. The beer garden revellers were probably already at a satellite patio with bunk beds secured in town, celebrating the last night before Santiago.

"Let's keep going," Kim said. "It doesn't make sense to backtrack at this point. Maybe we'll find a private hotel or something before that Monte de Gozo."

We carried on, parched, going through the motions. The only hotel option was 55 euros and the cafeteria alone depressed us. There were no pilgrims; everyone was in car-rumpled suits drinking Pellegrino in the parking lot patio. I couldn't even decide on a much-needed sandwich. I looked at granola bars with disinterest and Kim insisted I go for something more substantial.

"We don't know how far we're walking after this, Babe," she reminded me.

She was right and my "veggie" sandwich was wrong. I laughed and showed Kim the guts of it once I'd cracked into the cellophane.

"It's tuna *and* egg. Totally vegetarian as promised."

After our weird sandwiches and a quick beer to rebalance our smudged moods, we sped forward toward Lavacolla.

It was a shithole highway town, worse than the tuna and egg sandwich place. The airport was at the edge of it and the roar of plane engines shook our eardrums from afar. The first albergue was like a YMCA. Kim was wilting fast and needed to stop. I went to look at the dorm room while she slumped on the lumpy couch in the lobby, sweating profusely.

The light was hospital blue and grim, it smelled like unwashed hair and was so sterile I wanted to cry. We could *not* spend our last night before Santiago here. At this point, Kim didn't care where we slept, but I reported that the hostel looked like the kind of backroom you'd go into and have your organs harvested in your sleep.

"Now what?" Kim was losing interest fast. Our elevated Camino spirit was rubbed raw.

"Can we just look at this other place? I can see a hotel down the road here. Just a few minutes away."

Kim was reluctant.

"Okay, give me ten minutes, I'll go check it out," I offered.

I half-jogged down the dirty highway to Ruta Jacobea. It was even more expensive than the tuna and egg hotel at 69 euros. I slumped out of the hotel lobby, my hikers squeaking on highly polished floors that hadn't seen the dusty likes of pilgrims.

The only other viable option within our walking radius was Hotel Garçon. I felt terrible to the core, dragging Kim across the multi-lane highway to another hotel. Did it really matter where we slept? We'd walked over 38 kilometres and I couldn't even form words let alone sentences – the fatigue was that deep.

"Let's just do it," Kim said. "It doesn't matter how much. I'm whipped."

I pulled out our Visa and cringed at the 50-euro charge. It would have to do. It was better than the organ removal hostel. It was cheaper than the Ruta.

Our room was to the left of the lobby and Kim couldn't wait to collapse on a bed. She opened the door and my heart dropped.

"Oh my god. I wouldn't even kill myself here."

I thought of Jann Arden's melancholic song, "Unloved." Maybe she wrote it here, at Hotel Garçon?

It was an instant time warp to the worst part of 1968 with orange and yellow floral sheets and dark walnut four-poster beds – three of them no less!

Kim was actually on board. It was ridiculous for 50 euros. I wasn't sure if I wanted to cry or throw up when the assistant manager refused to process a refund. The battle royal began.

"We are *not* staying here. We want our money back, just refund the funds to our Visa or we'll take cash if it's a hassle," I fumed. My head felt like a popcorn maker ready to blow lava-hot kernels into puffed corn.

"Do you want to see another room?"

I couldn't imagine any improvement, but he was being so starchy about the no-refund policy. I followed him upstairs into the dark gloom, letting Kim sit for five in the air con.

The second room was worse than the first. It had four beds and said bed bugs to me.

Back to our standoff.

"Please," I begged, whining now. "I'm sorry, we do not want this room."

He matched my whine. "Sorry, I cannot undo transaction."

"Call your manager then!"

I'd worked in several hotels and knew there was room for movement, everywhere. All you had to do was keep asking for someone more important, with more authority.

Why the hell would we stay in this rundown barfy hotel when we could pony up 19 euros more and sleep on pillows stuffed with emu feathers? With turndown service and truffles and someone to fan our flushed faces? Feed us seedless grapes?

I had a long stare-down with the assistant, which was totally unlike my general cool as a cuke modus operandi. I never snapped.

"Staring at me is not going to change anything!" I spat out as my heart pounded out of my eyeballs with shitty hotel rage.

I didn't want our last night to be this – but maybe it had to be, to teach me some vital lesson?

I hated lessons.

The manager was called, reluctantly. No go.

Rage.

I took in the scene. A murky guppy tank bubbling in the corner. A neon El Dorado gambling machine looking for some vulnerable sap. Budweiser signs. Ugh.

"Please. Call. Your. Manager. Again."

He did. Our money was refunded to our card (although we wouldn't believe it until we were back in Canada and could see it on our monthly statement). I grabbed ten business cards to ensure I had all the contact info for the godforsaken place.

We crossed the death highway one last time, beelined our bodies to Ruta Jacobea and happily paid the 69 euros that included breakfast! Small joy.

While we could still move without seizing, we went to the gas station beside the hotel and bought a six-pack.

"How about a cassette tape?" I asked Kim. "They have Ricky Martin, Janet Jackson and Madonna. Cassette tapes! "Oh, wait – how about a porno?" The gas station inventory was a riot: porno DVDs, dusty Barbie dolls with hair that needed a good blow-dry. And plastic-wrapped pound cakes iced with big gaudy icing flowers from (plausibly) 1985.

We surveyed our gas station dinner options, as we were ready to unlock our hotel door and not move again until morning. There were glazed donuts, a lovely selection of cakes and meatballs in a tin. The gas attendant was less than helpful when we asked about nearby restaurants and pointed to the tinned meatballs. Lavacolla was giving me hives already.

I looked out the window of the grubby gas station and noticed a Rent-a-Car business. "Can we just go in here for a minute? I have a brainwave."

A young guy in pencil pants with well-gelled hair asked if we had a car reservation.

"No, but could you help us order a pizza?"

He laughed, "Yes, of course."

I *loved* the Rent-a-Car dude. He ordered a chorizo pizza for us, from somewhere, and had it delivered seamlessly to our hotel. There wasn't even a delivery charge.

I thanked him profusely and we walked at our slowest pace yet back to the hotel.

The pizza arrived like it fell out of heaven. We were beyond hunger at this point and slumped in chairs in front of the TV, listless, watching roller hockey. Roller hockey!

We'd be in Santiago in no time – and here we were, at some fancy-pants highway hotel, eating pizza courtesy of the Rent-a-Car employee who should be employee of the month.

Everything smelled so sanitized and bleached and pretty, which was ironic for a town whose Latin name – *Lavamentula* – literally translated to "wash private parts." I drained the hot water tank after Kim, showering away the scum and crankiness of 38 kilometres. I applied every free flowery lotion and potion that was provided, and when we fell into bed we didn't move for a solid nine hours.

The End of All Ways

Lavacolla to Santiago de Compostela! (10 km)

- -

It was after eight when we finally stirred. There was no need to fly into action, as we were just ten kilometres from Santiago. We were well ahead of the pack, which had bedded down in O Pedrouzo. It was a hedonistic night and the crisp linens and bouncy pillows mellowed us incredibly. The blood in my calves felt like setting pudding. After so many weeks of nonstop walking we were incredibly stronger and had the endurance of pack mules. But we could also feel our bodies breaking down. Microtears, twitching muscles, lactic-acid-packed fibres desperate for a long, hot soak and massage. Our immunity was on the upswing and the kennel cough that put us on our knees had cleared, save for the times we laughed too hard and triggered the remnants sitting on the bottom of our lungs.

It was difficult to pull on punky clothes after feeling so purified and expensive-hotel clean. I had already abandoned a T-shirt a week back, Kim did as well. Even with extensive soaping and spritzing of our #16 grocery store cologne, our cotton tees were deeply steeped in sweat, tapas and vino.

Breakfast was like an oasis; it was overwhelming and indulgent. The hotel even offered Tarte de Santiago as a breakfast option. The orange juice was freshly pressed and pulpy. "White coffee" (as we were informed) arrived steaming with cute little sachets of raw sugar. I walked up and down the buffet offerings, unable to commit to anything. There was a platter of salmon with capers, cup-a-soup mixes, chipped gherkins, pepperettes, a dozen cheeses – I returned to the table with corn flakes. Kim couldn't believe it.

"Corn flakes?"

I surprised myself. I just felt like cold milk and the crunch of flakes in a proper bowl, seated. So many of our "meals" had been on the fly, swallowing dry granola bars in the dark or slurping yogurt out of tiny tubs with no utensils in our bunk beds. I drank tepid boxes of chocolate milk whenever I found them at a grocer.

The opulent dining room had seating for 100, but Kim and I were the only two at a round table set for ten. I read the dinner menu aloud while Kim sipped a second cup of white coffee.

"We could have had baby eels and onions last night!"

"Barf," was Kim's reply.

I walked the buffet line again, disappointed to not have an appetite for the motherlode, and grabbed some pepperettes and a yogurt for the road.

We looped out of the town that nearly broke us and found a pension *and* albergue at the foot of the hill.

"What the hell?" Kim said.

"Yeah! How could that woman walking her dog yesterday not know about these places? Surely, a hundred pilgrims pass through every day asking the same question."

On a road parallel to the highway, where the Camino feeds in, I had asked the dogwalker about hostels or hotels. She only knew of the Ruta Jacobea and patted me on the arm, saying, "It will be very pricey for you."

I've always believed that wherever you live, hometown or adopted hometown, you should be the very best ambassador for that place. If a stranger slowed down to ask me where to buy shampoo or a fish taco in Lion's Head, or where to sleep for the night for that matter, I would know.

It was a peculiar walk toward Santiago, probably the least scenic and most bland of the entire Camino, save for the industrial pounding of pavement into León. My stomach felt a little furry with excitement (or maybe it was the lactose), and I could sense the anxious skip in Kim's step too. Had we really done it? The soupy August days of the Ferndale Flats when we first strutted out on fresh Vibram soles seemed so, so long ago. I kept focus, conscious that now would not be the ideal time to roll an ankle or flip on an exposed tree root.

It was a nonceremonial route through the suburbs and kind of a shame for the "grand finale." For those who had begun walking in Sarria, I was sorry they hadn't seen the very best bits of the rolling vineyards, carpeted mountain ranges and pastoral panoramas. We had seen the world awake under creamy sunrises cross-stitched with jet streams.

The outskirts of Santiago were clotted with industry, the racket of the airport replacing bird sound and babbling brooks. I wanted to enter Santiago through a swath of eucalyptus and plane trees...not like this. We passed by the 400-bed Xunta de Galicia barracks, situated in a park the size of several football fields. It looked rather closed, for months, not hours.

We followed the now familiar bronze scallop shells toward the great beacon, again, alone. We were in the company of a few stray cats, but no pilgrims.

"Look, there's even a cat crossing sign!"

I was reminded of the yellow turtle and snake crossing caution signs of our Bruce Peninsula, but for cats? Yet I could see why. They wormed out of every nook with a mew and yawn.

While I counted all the cats milling about, Kim noticed the church spires ahead. We were close.

As we arrived not so dramatically into the beating heart of Santiago, early risers were meandering around in sandals, backpacks noticeably absent from their backs. They had arrived the day or days before and were now privy to watching the parade of new dusty pilgrims spilling in. It would be strange to drop our packs for nearly an entire day once we checked into a hostel. A ten-kilometre walk didn't even register for us. It usually signalled the first coffee stop.

"Is this it?" I said to Kim, slowing in front of the cathedral.

"I think so."

"It can't be. It doesn't look anything like the movie."

Kim agreed, but it was definitely the fabled cathedral. A flush-cheeked bagpiper piped us in as we cut through the stone archway to the square ahead, continuing our investigation. The shrill skirl of the bagpipes made all my heart chambers flex. It was impossible to resist the hot tears that came with the enormous accomplishment of it all. Kim's eyes were wet too, the drone of the bagpipes adding to the drama of the moment.

"We were at the side of the cathedral!" I said with a laugh, recognizing the iconic, prodigious facade of the church before us.

"Imagine if we started celebrating at the side of the cathedral. Good thing we watched *The Way* to have a visual!" Kim said.

It was ten o'clock, making us very early arrivals. Most pilgrims would land in the early afternoon from O Pedrouzo and beyond. We asked a jaunty Swede to take our picture before the crowd thickened, even though the front of the cathedral was under construction and blocked by scaffolding and green safety netting.

Still unbelieving, we hugged and dropped our packs to take it all in. School groups were being herded into tighter groups as coach buses crept in for closer parking. Throngs piled off the buses with selfie sticks and hurried toward the "Fun Train."

"Oh my god. A Fun Train? That definitely was not featured in the movie," I said with disappointment.

A few day-old pilgrims were perfecting Instagram leap photos and/or pouty expressions in the Praza (plaza) de Obradoiro.

"Odd pose," Kim said, watching two South Koreans take turns making love to the camera with the cathedral in the background. We found sunny front row seats to the square's activity, absorbing the landmark moment, happy to become spectators after enjoying our own limelight. The relief of arriving in Santiago in one mostly solid piece was unmatched.

Kim tipped her head back on the pillar and closed her eyes. "I really can't believe we did it."

I squeezed her hand full of unswerving love, pride and tranquility. The kilometres ahead of us would be a mere bonus. As long as we were in Madrid by October 31, we were golden. I wouldn't have walked the Camino with anyone but Kim, my very best friend and only love. We'd done a lot of crazy and questionable things around the world, but walking 800 kilometres together to this very place elevated everything.

"Should we go get the official certificate?" Kim asked.

I was rather zoned-out, locked into a full-on absorptive sponge mode. We'd been told by those in the know that the pilgrim's office lineup could be hours long. Here we would receive the almighty Compostela and the final stamp. Rumours were rampant. From Sarria onward, pilgrims were supposed to collect two stamps from each town to authenticate the pilgrimage. Typically, a daily stamp verifying your stay in a hostel or albergue was sufficient and acceptable to the powers that be at the pilgrim's office. Now we needed two a day? Kim and I chose not to believe it and chalked it up to 100 per cent speculation and hearsay. As we walked to the judgment grounds of the office on Rúa das Carretas, we decided that if they turned us away because we didn't have the two-stamp scuttlebutt, that would be fine too. Kim and I knew we walked every one of those 800 kilometres from France and a certificate wasn't necessary to prove what our stiff backs and boot soles did.

We'd heard there would be a tough interview, questioning our personal reasons for walking the Camino. Hearsay also suggested that those who weren't doing it for religious reasons were scrutinized even more, and sometimes rejected.

This is all baloney. Still, Kim and I had a few rehearsed statements in our heads. The lineup wasn't as we anticipated – there were 15 pilgrims ahead of us at high noon. We queued up like we were at a bank waiting for a teller. A flashing digital sign indicated what gate we were to go to and, for three euros, we'd be cross-examined and legit.

There was a short form to fill out – did we choose to walk the Camino de Santiago for religious, spiritual, physical or tourist reasons?

Being in the holy epicentre, I didn't want to check off religious for fear of a lightning bolt striking me down, even though this had been advised to avoid controversy. I wasn't even sure if I was Presbyterian or Anglican. What did they even mean? There was no blank space to explain, "I attended a few strawberry socials with my grandmother who went to church regularly and always promised to take us swimming at Earl Haig Pool afterwards if god spared her."

I filled out Kim's form to ensure she didn't check off something that would disqualify her completely as she didn't have her reading glasses.

We went to the gate together, provided our passports for review and confirmed our reasons.

"Spiritual," said Kim. And there was no prompt for more.

"Physical," I replied, and my passport was skimmed through like the sports section of the newspaper.

"Where did you start from?"

"Saint-Jean-Pied-de-Port, France," Kim and I replied in sync.

The stamps came quick and with authority. We had passed, even with one measly stamp a day. So much for all the hysteria! Who was creating these urban myths?

The volunteer used a steady and practised hand to commemorate the moment in calligraphy. And, just like that, we had joined the leagues and centuries of pilgrims who had stood in awe of the mighty cathedral.

"You miss the pilgrim's mass now." She pointed to her watch. "Maybe this evening?"

I had asked Kim if she wanted to go. I was happy to skip it, but if it was a big deal for her, I'd definitely slide into a pew beside her. While there was no guarantee of the famous botafumeiro being swung end to end, the grapevine suggested that a generous 300-euro donation would guarantee it. Not that I'd be ponying up the fee, but certainly with the tactile excitement of Santiago, somebody with deeper pockets might ensure the thrill for all.

Kim was okay to take a pass on it, but we both understood the monumental nature of the Santiago mass for some pilgrims. We all have our leanings and my goal was to find Modus Vivendi in Praza de Feixóo. The bar had an old horse trough in it and it seemed worthy of a visit.

First, we navigated our way to The Last Stamp albergue on Rúa do Preguntoiro for its clever name alone (even though we had more stamps to gather en route to Finisterre). It was in an ideal location in the historic centre, 100 metres from the cathedral, "The End of All Ways," and a soon-to-be-boisterous stretch of restaurants and bars.

The rooms were modular and super modern, with contrasting ancient stone walls. A magnetic card granted us 24-hour access – there were no more curfews to abide by! The six-floor hostel had a kitchen on the lowest level with a glass-ceilinged "chill room." The place had personality plus and the mood was electric. Collectively, frayed nerves seemed calmed by the arrival in Santiago. And The Last Stamp ink design was my favourite in our storied collection.

Our ten-kilometre walk from Lavacolla barely warranted a shower, but we steamed a little just to recalibrate. It was a peculiar feeling to have come to a stop. If you've slept on a boat more than a few nights, you will know of the vestibular tilt that keeps you rocking on land for days after. Stillness, motionlessness is difficult to find. So we kept moving. It was easy to decide that we would leave in the morn again. Prior to landing in Santiago, we thought we'd spent two nights in the city. After an afternoon of the Fun Train and the pushy tourist swarm clogging patios and souvenir shops, we were okay to move on. The horse trough bar was a bust as it was closed, and O Beiro, with its thousand bottles of wine and "best tapas ever," was closed forever.

Instead, we found vacant seats along the very jammed Rúa da Raiña. The local scene was a fiesta that turned into siesta within a two-hour window. At Bar la Cueva, we had two *cañas* (small glasses) of beer and flaky Galician tuna pies.

We wandered the streets to and fro once they emptied, checking out the menus displayed in windows. "It's Hunting Day Menu here at this place," I said, waving Kim over.

"Hunting Day?"

"Yeah – listen to this! Wild boar with chestnuts, quail, deer and rabbit." The menu was also available in photos to ensure no wild boar mix-up.

Trays of razor clams and whole flounders were whisked out to customers by servers in pristine whites. Sangria was on free-flow in the alley.

Chocolate shops were hawking gold-dusted scallop shells and take-home Tarte de Santiago cakes. Gorgeous sweet buns, braided with nuts, raisins and dried fruit, lured in droves. Despite all the sweets and savouries surrounding us, it was impossible to settle on something to eat. It was like my undecided-corn-flakes-at-breakfast moment.

We had a few octopi croquettes and roasted sweet peppers stuffed with queso and moved on. Paellas had jumped to an unaffordable 40 euros (to share), more than we had paid for private rooms along the Way. Bed or paella? Hmmm.

The menus were definitely catering to the tourists that flitted in and out of Santiago on bus packages, not strapped pilgrims eking out a few more days of travel. The pilgrim menus that were posted didn't really tempt. Cod pie with melon? Spaghetti Bolognese with yogurt for dessert?

We gave up on food and found magical mini burgers, half-expecting the version we had at a Red Sea resort in Hurghada, Egypt. There the "*ham* burger" was actually ham on a bun. These hamburgers were the real deal, with caramelized onions and goat cheese. For less than two euros!

As we made our way back to The Last Stamp on our last legs, I noticed the horse trough bar was open.

"Nightcap?" Kim said, knowing I was irrationally eager to go to this bar.

"Let's do it!"

The bar had a pulsating disco vibe and the lower bunker had a mismatched collection of colourful cubes to sit on. To get to the bunker, patrons had to stumble down a cobblestone ramp. I'm sure there had been a few sangria-infused headers over the years.

Kim said, "So where's the horse trough?"

"I have no idea." We could barely hear each other over the *thumpa thumpa* soundtrack. "My beer tastes like horse blankets though!"

"To doing it! Santiago!" We clinked beers and oozed into the charcoal night.

Sleep came fast and furious with merry bagpipes still bleeding sound in my head.

SIX

Camino Finisterre, "End of the World"

In the shadows of ourselves
and the pilgrims before us.

Police Tape

Santiago de Compostela to Negreira (21.9 km)

- - - - - - - - - - - - - - - - - - - -

The square was still and spookily empty as we left Santiago, turning once to see the spires of the great cathedral poking into the peony pink sky. Where were the Fun Train and bus passengers in chinos, falling over each other to get hurried pictures and jiggly iPhone video coverage?

The mood was relaxed. We were still riding on the relief of making it to Santiago and accomplishing that enormous leg. Now it was Finisterre or bust. We had lots of days to play with, allowing us to plot two nights in Muxía, two easy mileage days before Finisterre and then two nights at the End of the World before jumping on a train to Madrid.

As we snaked our way out of Santiago, we couldn't help but adopt Brit accents and narrate the scene.

"Oh, Piers, look at this marvelous gated entrance to this spectacular Spanish colonial!"

"Caroline, did you know true Spanish colonial homes are devoid of glass windows?"

"Go on, Piers!"

"That's right. Instead, these homes were built with small holes for the entry of light and air and the passage holes would be shuttered."

Kim and I adored Caroline Quentin and Piers Taylor, the animated hosts of BBC's *The World's Most Extraordinary Homes*. Their banter was always a guaranteed riot as property enthusiast (and actor) Caroline fawns over (and often interrupts) architect Piers's analytical commentary.

The homes along the approach to Sarela were all jaw-droppers, with shamrock green grass seemingly trimmed with scissors. All the houses were manicured and pedicured and elaborately gated with loyal, regal watchdogs on duty.

We ran on empty, eating up only the scenery until the 12-kilometre mark of Alto de Vento (high wind). We knew from our time in Quebec's Magdalen Islands what *vent* meant. Every B & B and pub on the breezy island had *vent* in its name. *Vent* is French for "wind," while *vento* is the Spanish. They weren't exaggerating here at the Alto, either. French or Spanish aside, it was universally windy.

Again, we had nothing but olives and some corn nuts in our packs. Had we learned anything on the Camino? We had anticipated a coffee shop somewhere sooner and chose to get out of Santiago before the circus began without caffeinating ourselves.

We waited patiently at Formica tables, draining giant soup bowls of coffee that were served with sugar cookies while absently watching a football match on the telly.

"I guess we're in omelette territory now," I remarked.

No more tortilla, no more mixta + huevos – and the coffees had grown substantially in size. The omelette was so large it didn't even fit on my plate.

"And toast! Real toast," I said, ready for less baguette to challenge my still dangling retainer.

It was a steep day. It was windy and we were winded. When our half-dozen-egg omelettes finally wore off, we stopped for

Amstel radlers in the sparkle of the midday sun after crossing Ponte Maceira's storybook 13th-century stone bridge over the Río Tambre.

There was a distinct page turn, like we were following a dreamer's path now. It was a different pursuit, to seek out the End of the World by foot. However, Albergue Turístico San José was apparently at the *other* end of the world, and after repeated stops for directions, we finally found it in the most unlikely spot on Rúa Castelao. Negreira was a hopping town with giant supermarkets and restaurants every which way – and no signage to indicate the whereabouts of anything. Naturally, Kim and I walked the complete opposite direction first, across the Río Barcala, and then doubled back. A twitchy antique shop owner told us there was nowhere to stay in the town. A fruit vendor with lipstick on her teeth said there were rooms above the pub on the corner – a pub so gloomy that we turned on our heels merely one step in. Another woman with wild hair that kind of matched her dog's fur sent us under the bridge – but cautioned we would have to walk *too far*. Another ten kilometres, for sure.

"I call you taxi. My husband have taxi."

Hmmm. Smelled like a dirty but clever ploy. We resumed our aimless searching.

At Turístico San José, the dorms were well polished and barely occupied. A no-fuss manager handed us the standard issue: sheets (!), a pillow case and two towels. Towels! I was really beginning to miss the luxury of a cotton towel – my travel-size, quick-dry chamois was efficient but utilitarian. And barely big enough to cover a guinea pig. In an attempt to shave off unnecessary pack weight, Kim had cut a healthy chunk off my already-too-compact towel. I longed for that chunk.

In the dorm area, we counted eight backpacks scattered about. I asked the manager if we could take the bunks in the lower room that was obediently empty due to the yellow police-like DO NOT CROSS tape barricading the wing.

"No."

He couldn't explain why we couldn't, and I couldn't explain why we shouldn't. I felt entitled. Kim is more of a rule abider, but I felt we should be able to choose whatever bunk we wanted. I surreptitiously removed the tape as he left the room and reapplied it behind Kim.

"If we take these bunks in the back, he won't know. You can't even see them from the stairs."

Most hostels weren't staffed 24 hours. The majority were unattended after six o'clock (aside from Ebenezer Scrooge, who oddly slept in his suit on the no-red-wine-allowed couch in the communal lounge area), and we knew we would be out the door by the time anyone returned for the morning shift.

We felt like thieves, taking over the room of 12 empty bunks for ourselves. I unclipped flip-flops from our packs and flopped outside to the sun-soaked yard to test out all the unergonomic chairs that were available.

"Great idea, babe. It would be nice to have the space to ourselves."

When we finally went back inside to grab long sleeves, we discovered we had company – even though the police tape was still up. Four others had the same brilliant idea as I did. At least they dispersed and chose bunks well away from the occupied beds.

We attempted using the albergue kitchen again, eager for a salad and some crunch. We took a health risk on a bottle of leftover garlic dressing. The freebie section of the fridge also had a solo can of rum-flavoured beer. Kim figured one would counteract the other.

A woman as skinny as a whippet offered us some of her rice in exchange for some of our pesto. Deal. I did a hack fry of chicken and an onion that cost eight cents in pesto oil (in yet another sticky pan). We were the only three in the sparse dining area, all aglow and abuzz with the neon lights of the vending machines selling alternate ramen noodles and Snickers.

We had a super sleep in real sheets in our illegal quarters, laughing at our mischievous police tape removal. Our T-shirts had been refreshed with our cologne tester #16. My sleeping bag was definitely ready for a spritz of something.

Feeling the Pinch

Negreira to Olveiroa (33.3 km)

I was feeling the pinch of our remaining days in Spain. After spending four months volunteering in Uganda at the Jane Goodall Institute in 2008, I developed an unusual mindset that I haven't been able to shake since. When travelling, I completely forget about having a real job or house or anything "back home." On the Camino, I did think of our bed fondly, but at the same time totally failed to think about my upcoming obligations at *Harrowsmith* magazine or elsewhere. Wasn't this our nouveau way of life?

At the 12-kilometre waymark in Vilaserío, we ordered colossal coffees and a monster French omelette sandwich at Albergue O Rueiro. The rowdy table of bohemian pilgrims beside us ordered wine and beer. At 9:00 a.m.!

I still felt like I was in the Indy pit. Sock change. Coffee. Omelette. Water fill. Go! It was hard to shake off the jackrabbit speed we had become accustomed to.

The topography morphed again to fields edged with heather, harvested corn stubble, turbines slicing the denim sky and a hush of wind through the pines. The corncribs had also changed face from wood to thoughtful stone construction.

In Lago, we took refuge in undiluted sun and enjoyed a glacial beer on the patio at the arresting Monte Aro hotel. We shared bites of Galician pie stuffed with tuna and tried to mop up the last of the endless summer days that Spain had provided. We were coming to a sharp end of two lovely things: an extended summer and the Camino, in one delicate fold.

The 33 kilometres felt fluid. Maybe it was the injection of subliminal energy, knowing that the edge of the world was near and the Atlantic spray and brine would be deep in our pores in days. We checked into Casa Loncho (there were only two albergues to flip a coin over), adding to our new passport book offered to pilgrims continuing to Finisterre. Another certificate would be available, indicating a successful journey to the End of the World. I'd add it to my eclectic collection of certifications, from completion of orthodontic treatment to Best Scarecrow at the Bell Homestead Scarecrow Competition when I was 8.

At Casa Loncho, we were privy to bumpy bunks and breaded everything on the menu. Breaded pork, chicken, hake and deep-fried croquettes for good measure. There was nowhere else to eat, so we went for the gusto and guiltily enjoyed the hot, oily, salty fries and fried portions of hake.

"Well, I won't need lip balm for three days," I said to Kim, licking my greasy lips.

We watched Real Madrid challenge Paris Saint-Germain until our heads felt as heavy as the fried stuff in our gut.

It was the quietest night on the Camino yet. Was everyone too exhausted to snore? It felt strange and addictive, like the irresistible feel of brushing velour in the opposite direction. What a different Camino it would have been had we been able to sleep like babes.

The Undiluted Magic
of Muxía and Marzia

Olveiroa to Muxía (31.8 km)

Muxía had stitched its way into my brain's fantasy fabric since Marzia's big sell. There are two routes to Finisterre and most pilgrims swing south to walk from Olveiroa to Finisterre in one clean coastal shot of nearly 32 kilometres. By jagging north to Muxía, we were adding another 60 kilometres. I had eavesdropped on earlier debates about what route was most traditional, challenging and/or scenic. Some pilgrims went to Finisterre first and then reserved chill time for Muxía. It seemed backwards to us – the End of the World should be the end, so we routed to Muxía. The path was increasingly less travelled after the not-so-official *F* (indicating Finisterre) scrawled on an arrow pointing left and opposing *M* (representing Muxía) arrow splicing right.

It was a day of downhill sliding on a fine pine needle carpet through both towering pines and palms. There was a churr of distant tractors and whir of turbines mixed with birdsong and my own happy, pounding heart. A few startled bow-wowing dogs serenaded us as we cut into tall grasses that waved like bounding golden retriever tails.

Surfacing in a two-bar town, we were drawn to the well-swept entry of a tiny home-slash-rum-bar. I investigated beers while Kim set us up at a table at the side of the stone building in the slanted sun just as a dozen shaggy sheep in dire need of a shear galloped down the "main" road with a herder hot on their cloven heels.

I poked around the empty space and wondered if I was actually inside someone's house. There were crayon drawings of big-nosed people and sideways houses taped on the fridge. Framed photos of family members here and gone hung on walls in desperate need of a coat of paint.

"¡Hola!"

I heard a "hola" response from the back and out shuffled Nana in an apron. It was rare to see a woman *not* wearing an apron in these parts. I asked for two Amstels and she raised her eyebrows.

"Dos?"

"Oui," I replied, perennially mixing my minimal French and Spanish into one hot linguistic mess.

She handed me the beers, almost reluctantly, and then glanced out the window toward Kim.

"Oh, you have friend. I thought, two beers just for you."

That wasn't as strange as she made it sound, but it meant I received a plate of chorizo for two, not one.

"Pincho, for you and your friend."

She held up a baguette and I waved her off, happy with the chorizo. As I carried the cargo out the door, she launched into a heated blast directed at the albergue owner across the road. Apparently, he was an unapologetic poacher and lured pilgrims in from her side of the road to his bar across the way. She shook her fist in his direction and thanked us for choosing her.

"Sure, no problem."

Kim blew out her cheeks at the sight of more chorizo. "I'm still stuffed from that omelette sandwich." I was too, but Nana would be displeased if we rejected her chorizo. I wrapped it in a serviette, thinking of my dad's sneaky moves at the Chinese buffet. It was amazing how many almond cookies and egg rolls he could pull out of his pockets, Copperfield-style.

Our arrival in Muxía was just as magical. I couldn't help but think of "Surprise Corner" in Banff, Alberta. My sister and I were running around Sulphur Mountain on one of my first visits to the area. We popped out of the lodgepoles to the main road and jogged toward the Bow River. Kiley announced the "surprise" with a sweeping hand gesture. Here the Fairmont Banff Springs hotel appears in all her majesty, a peerless castle nestled in the pines, like a thoughtfully curated model train layout.

Muxía hit us with the same impact. I was preoccupied with my footing, as was Kim, but the aromatic sea air curled up into my nostrils and registered in my olfactory, replacing the manure smell-track of the last jag.

Houses moved from stone to stucco and unafraid, confident colours like flesh tone, periwinkle, Kraft Dinner yellow and rouge. An elderly couple sitting on the steps of their home called us over, insisting we take a handful of just-roasted chestnuts from their cast iron pan. There was fleeting apprehension: Is this another sweet Nona and "free" pancake scenario?

It wasn't! They genuinely wanted to share some chestnuts with us, which were molten hot inside. I took two, but they pressed me to fill my pockets. Would we do the same if someone wandered off Ontario's Bruce Trail? Kim and I lived ten kilometres from the trailhead, but I think our North-American-instilled paranoia about serial killers and kidnappers would get the better of us. The untainted kindness of Spain was unmatched. Maybe they didn't have serial killers?

We waved and bowed and did all sorts of grateful charades in the direction of the toothy couple, as we raced to get closer to the coastal view at our boot tips.

Gulls screamed and careened overhead. I could see a ribbon of honeyed sand and the Oxford blue Costa da Morte (Coast of Death). I felt an instant charge and surge – this is probably how 90 per cent of pilgrims felt seeing the penultimate cathedral in Santiago at long last. I had reserved my wow for this moment. The coast! Kim experienced parallel excitement – we were both suckers for a gorgeous beach.

We walked along the boardwalk that skirts the town and marina, starry-eyed. A dozen prismatic boats bobbed or motored along to fishing grounds.

There were lots of sleeping options in Muxía, so we were carefree in walking several loops around the town to ensure we found the very best digs. And we did, at Albergue Bela Muxía. But, of course, fate would worm its way in first.

"Girrrrrrrrrrrrrrrllllllllllllllllllsssssssssssssssss!"

We turned around, assuming the catcall was for us. The alley was empty, with the exception of a skittish ginger cat, but we didn't recognize the voice. Before we could register a face, we felt the hot squeeze of arms around us.

"I can't believe it! You came!"

It was Marzia! She was as brown as a coffee bean, and though we had only met her once back in Burgos, it was fun to see her smiley face. I wondered how her philosophies were panning out. If she had set her mind to just "be." She looked so content in her skin that something was definitely working.

"I have to jet, I'm on a wine run," she said, holding up a bottle of plonk. "But tonight, let's meet on the rocks by the lighthouse at sunset. I'll find you." She hollered back the name of the hostel she was staying at, but it was lost in the wind.

"Marzia!" Kim said. "I can't believe it. How is it that you can follow the same itinerary and path with the same people but lose them? And then you meet someone once, like Marzia, and, after three weeks, cross paths in Muxía of all places."

It was a brain grinder.

We grabbed some beer at the store Marzia had pointed to and planned to camp out until sunset. The albergue had a private room, and we were all in for some private real estate and an uninterrupted ocean view. From our suite the sliding doors opened to a terrace that overlooked the first view we had of Muxía. Terracotta roofs surrounded us. Turbines spun in the haze of the day's heat. My eyes were spinning like Vegas machines, taking in an owl-like 360-degree that the Camino didn't always permit due to constant cow-crap watch and loose rocks underfoot. The tide was miles out and we were about to experience another full moon. Ah, Clara. Where was she?

The room at Bela Muxía was a sensory overload. Space. Silence. The Nordic vibe was tactile. I loved the smooth, buffed cement floors, white walls and sterility. A Spanish poet's stanzas were painted on the walls, adding to the creative juice of the property. A chatty mustachioed innkeeper named Ramon asked us what ink stamp we would like in our passport – a cat, an octopus or a rooster?

"Please, have some welcome cake and chestnuts." *Everything* was cool here. As we booked our two-night reprieve, a jarring fellow Canadian rippled the calm.

"I heard 'eh' – must be Canadians checking in here," he leaned on the desk counter so close to me that I could feel his breath on my arms.

"Is this your first Camino?" He didn't even wait for a response. "It's my fifth. Yep."

I thought of our brief night with the lovely South African crew in Foncebadón. Sonia asked, "What's with people doing the Camino five times or ten times? Why not do it once and do it right?"

It was our new philosophy. Move over Marzia!

Fellow countryman or not, his tone was insulting. Why can't you walk the Camino once and be just as accomplished? Five times gave you more cred? My nerve endings were recoiling.

Kim and I were equally annoyed and scrambled away from the guy as fast as we could. We were ready to go all Keith Richards in our hotel room and spread our shit everywhere. No bunks! A bed, sheets, towels! Our only mission was sunset at the lighthouse at 19:41 sharp.

We quickly found an upper terrace that gave us a bird's eye of most of Muxía, and we didn't move from the sunbaked stone and arresting beauty of it all.

As the day drew to a close with a hush, we found picnic fixings: pickled onions, gherkins, skewers of olives. We had Nana's chorizo, a wedge of cheese and some blueberry-studded Melba-like crackers.

At "the rocks," pilgrims had set up for the show in style. It was like a drive-in, but for a nature's one-time never-to-be-shown-again film. We didn't see (or hear) Marzia. Maybe the afternoon vino had immobilized her into sleep.

The huge flat rocks accommodated every dreamer. There were small cross-legged groups, some introspective singles and a few smoochy couples like us. The turbulent sea heaved and crashed in front of the iconic lighthouse as the sun dipped and blurred the horizon with shades of sherbet. In the same peaceful breath, a full-bellied moon inched up the slate sky. The moon's beam was otherworldly, striking a bone white path across the Atlantic. Church bells sounded and bounced from the sea to the stucco, with no rhyme or reason. The brawny chap at the end of the bell-ringing rope had entered a calculated dance of physics, tugging on a thick rope with devoted might. The bells didn't signal seven o'clock. There were more than 40 gongs of the bell – following the unpredictable pattern of bell ringing across most of Spain. They sounded 15 minutes after the hour or before the hour, or just because.

The moonlight was so vibrant I could see Kim's expressions. We returned to our room, sunset soothed, and uncorked our picnic wine. There was a cauldron of free pumpkin soup for pilgrims in the communal kitchen and some roasted walnuts, so I stocked up. I'd also found a back issue of *Cosmo* from April 2018 that remedied my detachment from books.

Kim flipped to tennis on the TV as I tore through *Cosmo*. I was half-crying in no time. It was a letter from the editor that left chestnuts sitting sideways in my throat.

"You have to listen to this." And then I couldn't speak.

"Okay." I tried to clear my throat of the sadness clenching it.

"This editor went to Provence years ago and was totally smitten. It always stayed in the back of her mind, you know, as places do. She decided to return, with the man she loved then, who is now her husband. The B & B was all faded and tired. There was a disco across the road – totally not how she remembered it. The poolside loungers were broken, the grass burnt, paint peeling – that sort of thing. All the reasons why we don't go back to the same places, right? Like Caye Caulker – we could never have that time back again, as it was."

I paused for wine, cleared of tears for the moment.

"So the old innkeeper's wife who used to make the best coffee in a copper kettle was now tired and frail. Only her husband showed his face and tiredness showed in his movement too. So this editor," I swallowed hard, "she asked, 'And what about the dog?' He said, 'You just missed him. He died last year.'"

I wasn't sure why I chose to read aloud this silly letter, but I pressed on.

"She asked, 'Will you get another dog?' And the innkeeper said, 'No. The love affair cannot be repeated.'"

Kim hugged me, smiling at my sensitivity. Any old dog story stabbed me in the heart at the best of times, but there were so many truths to this letter. I thought of the Canadian goof downstairs being a blowhard about walking the Camino five times. Some places need to remain only in your heart and mind. As the tired innkeeper believed, "The love affair cannot be repeated."

I closed *Cosmo* for the night, clearly not in a stable state of mind. I finished off the ashy chestnuts, leaving charcoal residue on everything I touched.

We had a big sleep-in ahead of us (if it was possible). I'm not even sure if I brushed my teeth before slipping into delicious REM.

A Backpackless Day
Muxía (5 km?)

- -

What a sweet, decadent sleep. I stared at the white walls and minimalist space, distilling the days in quiet yawns. Bela Muxía nailed the branding of its hostel with an artistic injection. The rooms and communal spaces were an education, with mural-sized photos and text by Anton Castro, retelling shipwreck disasters and the lore of the Costa da Morte. Castro established "the hostel as an identity." From the 360-degree terrace to the tranquil outdoor foot baths – right down to the unconventional square business card – I felt like we were "in the know." This is where the cool kids hung out.

Kim was happy to unload and decamp, her backpack was emptied out within minutes, all inventory spread about our square footage. We had a treasured day to wander without agenda or mileage. Though we wanted to embrace a John and Yoko Bed-in for Peace and stay put for a week as they did at the Hilton in Amsterdam and the Queen Elizabeth Hotel in Montreal, we righted ourselves for coffee by the marina.

It was a slow and hot two cups in the cozy confines of Noche y Día (Night and Day). Coffee was served with individually wrapped sugar cubes that I admired for their cute ridiculousness. We watched small boats ending and starting their days, captains and crew crossing fingers for a safe return. A man in a cap pulled low reeled in squid from the pier with sinewy forearms and decades of finessed skill.

Perked, we picked up a few breakfast items and returned to our hostel's kitchen to boil some eggs and make a picnic lunch to go with Emmental, plum tomatoes and the ever-present baguette.

The blonde sand of Lourido beach pulled at our tired bods from the coastal road. Pilgrims were just arriving from the "opposite" direction, making their way to Muxía via Finisterre. Knowing smiles were exchanged. Even though we were backpackless and well scrubbed, there was a look and silent communication – the kind that Jeep and VW owners share. The ebb and flow of the beach with its ribbons of kelp and polished stones offered a sensory reward different but as satisfying as Santiago. Those who agreed abandoned packs and heavy boots to run headlong across the dunes into the steely waters for a bracing welcome.

The sun was sensational, sitting high above the horsetail clouds that stretched across the water. We had another full-blown hunter's moon to bathe in later.

"I bet this is what Newfoundland feels like," Kim said as we set up camp on the deserted beach.

Muxía was a stack of distant colours, the sea was ripe and haunted with lost men and cargo. The chilling echo of church bells carried out into the Atlantic, an audible beacon to the lighthouse's glowing guidance. So many dreams and loves were submerged in Muxía's depths and I was certain just as many had emerged too.

We loved Muxía instantly. Like red velvet cake and huskies with two different coloured eyes, it was distinctive and surprising. It was exactly the kind of place where Kim and I would open an albergue. Many hours were spent hammering out the blueprints of our perfect hostel. We knew of all the elements that irked us and the easy refinement that could be made. I'd worked at a half-dozen hotels in Ontario: the Fairmont Royal York, Le Royal Meridien King Edward, Sheraton Centre Toronto and Langdon Hall Country House Hotel and Spa. As travellers, we'd slept in so many beds, but I could spout off our top ten without blinking. It's such minutiae. It's individually wrapped sugar cubes. It's a rental cottage that stocks your fridge for arrival with milk, orange juice, a dozen eggs and a jar of homemade granola. It's a hotel offering warm chocolate chip cookies at reception, tiny handcrafted lemongrass soaps or a bamboo toothbrush. It's a cool towel and rum-kicked cocktail "hello" after a long-haul flight, a pillow menu, cut tropical flowers with an inspirational quote…

Our albergue would definitely piggyback on all those thoughtful flourishes. We'd have shipping containers stacked and situated for an optimal, private Atlantic view. There would be deluxe coffee machines in each private room, so guests could have a Bed-in like John and Yoko. We'd provide tall pitchers of watermelon-infused water and hot ginger tea at day's end. Jars of macadamia nuts, dried mango and trail mix would replace gumball machines. Candles reminiscent of warm pipe tobacco or sheets on a clothesline would burn like pheromones. On the bedside table, a selection of aromatic massage oils – sandalwood, bergamot. There would be good books – only good books and magazines like *Kinfolk* that make clocks stop.

We had a lot of time to furnish rooms as we walked through the meseta, with paramount attention to the bed that would have to feel like a hug and a Japanese soaker tub to cure all. I voted for a red cedar barrel sauna and vitamin-D-loaded banana cocoa smoothies 24/7, just like the kind Toronto's Body Blitz Spa served.

I loved dreaming out loud with Kim, and the scenery we were steeped in was a giant motivator. Already we were thinking – what next? What does one do after the Camino? I had no interest in the altitude sickness associated with climbing Kilimanjaro. Were we ready for Japan's ancient pilgrimage route, the熊野古道 (Kumano Kodo)? What about the Dakar Rally?

We merely swapped out our seaside spots from Lourido for the repose found on the rocks still generating heat by the lighthouse. New faces grinned back – all of us collectively connected by a syrupy sunset. Still no Marzia. The previous night's show had been startling, but heavy purple clouds ate up the sun before the ocean did. Still. The saffron moon readied for the night shift, tilting the equinox closer to winter's reach.

My hairs were on end from the moon's chill and the nervous rush that was inexplicably connected to the End of the World and the end of our Camino.

There was free hot brothy noodle soup and chestnuts when we returned to Bela Muxía. Kim and I filled mugs of both to take to our room.

Heavy with daydreams and thoughts of the already vanishing days ahead, we fell asleep intertwined, church bells serenading us, and the lost.

Santiago's Afterglow

Muxía to Lires (16 km)

We left the sanctuary of Bela Muxía under a still porcelain sky. At Restaurante a Marina, we lingered over coffees thick with alabaster foam and Galician toast, a crostini-style bread that wasn't exactly loose-retainer-friendly either. Hot sugary churros arrived to our table as well, but after a fill of toast I shared them with a lean couple who were probably travelling on even leaner wallets.

Totally restored, we turned south toward Lires, passing the dull pounding of waves on Lourido beach. It was good to shake the fine strands of cobwebs from our rested legs. Walking had become an addictive sedative.

The 16-kilometre route was a steady ascent through vine-clad pines, up and over a ridge that left us parallel with a string of wind turbines. There were dozens of stone hórreos and just as many snoozing Heinz 57 dogs as we skirted the few houses along the Way.

As we entered Lires, showpiece hedges were groomed closer than a Hollywood star on Oscar night. There were only a few accommodation choices and they involved an uphill or downhill exploration. We did both and returned to our starting point at Albergue As Eiras. The uphill hostel, Casa Jesús, was a little too close for comfort, like rooming with Mom and Pop and their extensive plate collection. They had a private room, but as we considered booking we could hear how unprivate it was with walls as thin as a kitten whisker. Plus, the dark panelling made me feel a little time-trapped. Downhill, the enchanting riverside cabins were a reasonable 60 euros, and had we not had our reprieve in Muxía, we probably would have jumped at them. Instead, As Eiras filled the gaps. Coincidentally, according to another well-circulated rumour, in order to qualify for the Finisterre Compostela, we had to get a stamp from cafe As Eiras as proof that we didn't arrive in Finisterre by bus.

The dorm room at As Eiras was delightfully warm and had just six beds. Private rooms were available, but we skated on the chance that we'd have the room to ourselves as we passed more pilgrims walking north than we did south.

Fast-moving deep violet clouds erased the sun and we bucked better thinking by heading to the nearby beach, about 1.5 kilometres from town, hoping the moody clouds smeared overhead would roll over into something better.

"Oh my god. Gross! Look!" Kim pointed at the river's edge. "What the hell are those?"

At first, the wet spines that broke the surface looked like fat eels or snakes. Edging closer, with a lot of trepidation, I could see the gaping mouths of carp.

"Ew, they're carp. I saw this in the Grand River once. I was in a canoe and they were scraping the bottom of the boat like a horror movie."

As our eyes adjusted to the unbelievable sight, we realized that the shoreline was an endless school of near-beached carp, flipping and worming at the edge.

"How much?" Kim said.

It was our favourite game – how much would we need to be paid to do whatever gross dare was presented.

"I couldn't. I'd pass out from the heebies. You?"

"Yeah. No thanks."

Both of us had stepped on flounders in knee-high water in Zanzibar's Indian Ocean. Kim said it best. It was like stepping on a live firehose.

A heron rookery pulled our attention away from the carp riding the surface parallel to us. The whitewash of bird shit tipped off the population dominating a few skeletal trees on the opposite side of the Atlantic-fed Lires River. All the commotion seemed to gather around a water treatment plant. Luckily, as we followed Parroquia Lires road, the riverside carp show was replaced with a craggy shore and the smack of waves thundering in. Kim found a superb spot to tuck in from the wind and watch the wild sea. In the distance we could see a dozen stoked surfers ride in on curlers to the skirt of sand on Praia de Nemiña.

When the chill from the west and the rock underneath permeated us beyond comfort, we retreated to the riverside cabanas, where I had noticed a snug restaurant and bar called A Braña on the same property as the spanking new Ecoturismo Ría de Lires. Simone, an energetic Brazilian, welcomed us like long-lost family. So did Carmelo, a ginger and white cat that was all purrs and twirls. The business had opened in August and the crowds were now thinning with autumn's clutches. Though some of the mountain passes on the Camino close during the winter, many of the albergues are open year-round, catering to those on slower pilgrimages.

Inside, robin egg blue chairs were pulled up to white chalk painted wood tables. The walls were artfully adorned with tiny bird houses and folky birds fashioned out of stones and wire. The owner's young pigtailed daughters were being typically sibling-like. The older one was industriously illustrating her very own comic book, while the younger sister worked on a giant ham panini sandwich, using only molar power as she was missing all of her front teeth. She'd take panini breaks to nip outside and cruise by on her pink bike, screaming across the cafe's riverfront patio, showing off her tooth-free smile each time.

We told Simone about meeting another bewitching Brazilian, Natalia, at the Albergue Estrella Guia in Puente la Reina. Though I was only basing my conclusion on two Brazilians, I definitely was drawn to their shared spirit and vitality.

As the river turned metallic with the day's end, we shared a jug of vino and a whole wheat baguette piled with buttered mushrooms and ripe local cheese. The sisters fought, the younger one cried hot tears of anguish. The cat was scooted out and accidentally let back in. An older woman in rain kit ordered several teas from her window-side perch, filling a notebook with neat, measured scrawl. I wondered if we were both writing about the very same day and place. You just never know.

The wine and wind had tired us. Back at our hostel, we accidentally fell into a needed catnap, both of us occupying one bunk. I missed Kim beside me every night, as we normally slept together like we had a case of static cling. It was rare to be in a dorm room alone for longer than a hamstring stretch. We soon had company and, though we tried to sleep a little longer, an American dude in pants that sounded like diapers opened all the windows in the room and all the warm air took a quick exit at the same time as our sleepiness.

We'd already decided to return to A Braña for dinner. Simone gave us a head's up on the evening fare – pork tenderloin wrapped in bacon. Kim and I shared a mixed salad with real micro greens (not iceberg!), beetroot and tuna. The tenderloin was a treat after so many patchy dinners of cheese and crackers.

The tunes were solid and the atmosphere was quite unlike the edgy, anxious nights of weeks earlier. A table of eight tight-T-shirted guys ordered a round of beers and then moved on to hot cocoa and pound cake. Conversation seemed relaxed. No one was looking at watches or maps, plotting bedtimes or mileage. The afterglow of Santiago was nearly visible. It would have been a shame if we'd had to hop on a plane back home after checking out of The Last Stamp. I couldn't fathom packing up everything so quickly – not just my physical pack but the whole experience. Were we really walking to the End of the World in the morning?

The Infinity of Mile 0
Lires to Finisterre (14 km + 7 km return trip to Mile 0)

I never tired of coffee foam art. If it weren't for the characteristically obscene start times for baristas, I might fancy myself a latte foam artist. Kim and I folded back into our familiar seats at A Braña. The sisters and Carmelo were still long asleep. For one euro we were served botanical coffees with well-honed Rosetta (fern leaf) designs alongside moist pound cake the size of a pound of butter.

"Please take a free apple too. Buen Camino," the barista winked.

While on the Camino proper, 99 per cent were travelling to Santiago. In Lires, pilgrims could be heading to Muxía or Finisterre, or walking in what we perceived to be the opposite direction back to France and beyond.

"Could you imagine turning around and walking back to where we started?" I said.

Kim couldn't and neither could I. It would be like sleeping on Kim's side of the bed or wearing jeans backwards.

It was 8:30 a.m. when we set south toward the tiger-orange-tinged horizon. Surprisingly, though the sole American was trying to deep freeze us by keeping the windows open, our night at As Eiras was as quiet as a tomb. Our bunkmates failed to stir, rustle, snore or fidget. Now? Where were the likes of these sleepers for the last month? I could have upped my daily mileage to 40 kilometres had I not been so bone-tired from broken sleep.

A few kilometres in, we realized the orange of the rising sun was coming from the wrong direction. A Zimbabwean woman and her Aussie BFF heading to Lires informed us that there was a forest fire and that we should keep right. Their eyes were wide with the unknown, but an update on their iPhone app suggested rerouting to the coastal road to avoid danger. We didn't want to come off as cavalier, but we intended to keep following the trail instead of the road. If we were in such grave danger, the albergue would have alerted everyone. Or that's the notion we trusted. Twenty minutes later, an unalarmed Canadian said the fire was on the next ridge and we were totally safe to carry on. We trusted our countryman and split through the planes and pines, inhaling the cleansing deep menthol hit from the silvery eucalyptus forest. Ferns were starting to rust and curl with the season. The forest floor was a trampoline underfoot with so many dropped pine needles cushioning our steps.

In the wind's rush and hush through the pines we could still detect the distinct freight train roar of the Atlantic. The natural carpet beneath us became paved as we cut through a little village with countless stone granaries and catnapping cats. At what appeared to be a defunct bus shelter, Kim and I took seats on the rough bench and divvied up hard-boiled eggs and some cheddar. A resident dragged open a wide metal gate beside the bus shelter and shuffled toward us in homemade slippers. I nudged Kim to take a look. They were old work boots that only had the steel toe and sole intact. Genius! But what an effort to keep on your feet – which explained his shuffle.

He slopped to the bus shelter with a wave.

"Français? Irish? Englais? German? Italiano?"

I understood a *bon appétit* in his excited slur of words and offered him a "*no comprendo*" for good measure. He continued chattering away and then came into the shelter with us. Was there a functioning bus system?

Maybe not. Instead, our multilingual friend stood directly in front of me, so close he could have gently squatted and sat cleanly on my lap. He read the funeral notice taped on the glass of the shelter aloud, and then again, for good measure. Then stood another few minutes, saying nothing, before shuffling off in his custom footwear.

"Could you imagine walking the entire Camino in those!" Kim said.

"I'm not sure what would be worse – trying to hold those on your feet for a day or swimming with those gross carp."

Debating that, we carried on, shaking our heads at our bus shelter timing. Our paths were meant to cross with this multilingual chap for some higher meaning.

Twenty minutes in, the sky drained of colour.

"Rain," Kim announced.

"No, it's just a few spits," I reassured her.

"Remember last time?"

"Yeah," I said sheepishly, stopping to dig out rain stuff.

The "last time" Kim was referring to was when we were still logging training miles on the Bruce Trail in Ontario. I refused to believe the initial spits of rain were going to materialize into anything and I lazily resisted putting my rain jacket on. Or protecting my pack with its rain cover. I waited while Kim suited up and stubbornly refused until I was so saturated with rain it didn't matter anymore. My pack was soaked for the next day's walk too.

Conveniently, there was a Swiss pop-up (or so we assumed by the Swiss flags snapping in the wind). There was a wooden tipi and Zen music that had shades of the Pissy Palace commune offering "free hugs!" We took shelter under a tiny roofed stand with a spread of peanuts, walnuts, coffee and some Arrowroot-like biscuits. I took two to cleanse my egg and cheddar breath. The stainless-steel sky was foreboding, but a giant end-to-end rainbow arched above us and, naturally, as we donned our rain kit, the spits stopped and sunshine bleached the forest trail ahead.

The shorter walking days were strange to adapt to. We were on the edge of Finisterre (also referred to as Fisterra) in no time. Another sandy stretch of beach beckoned, but the Camino took a hard right in the direction of the faro (lighthouse) and a 3.5-kilometre strip of busy road to the cape's dramatic rocky end. I didn't even really "see" Finisterre as we cut through the town's streets to get to the faro. Kim wanted to find a hotel en route so we could drop our bags, but I arm-wrestled her into continuing.

"We've come all this way with them, we have to walk with our packs to the very end!"

The wind was on max speed and rainbows bled colour in and out of the atmosphere. Wild purple blooms turned the grassy slopes to the surf into a Gustav Klimt. The sea was like crinkled foil. We held hands as long as we could before safely walking single file to avoid being clipped by the coach buses. Clothes-wrinkled passengers piled out of buses and hogged the monumental Mile o marker and harder-to-find bronze boot sculpture behind the lighthouse for selfies.

Sure, it would have been great to ditch a few things and brush my teeth and walk out to the lighthouse unencumbered with a bottle of champagne, but the entire Camino had involved flexibility and a heavy suspension on time. Everything seemed closed for siesta anyway.

At Finisterre, the parking lot eats up what could be a very romantic procession. I also didn't expect the stately Hotel O Semaforo 138 metres above sea level. It hides the true prize, the lighthouse that was built in 1853 with a light that reaches 65 kilometres.

In 1999, the former surveillance headquarters of the marina were developed into the tony O Semaforo de Fisterra, which has just five exclusive rooms and endless views. Waiting out the lollygagging bus tourists, Kim and I took in the promised infinity of the suspended tables in the bar area and ordered Estrella Maltas. The rain pounded down, streaking the windows in silver rivulets, and petered out again. The Mile 0 marker was still being mobbed like a celebrity.

"Another beer?" Fat raindrops splatted on our shoulders, signalling an easy yes.

This time we ducked into The Refuge, a more relaxed bar adjacent to and operated by O Semaforo. Soggy and soaked tourists and pilgrims alike jammed in for an eclectic menu of draft beer, tuna pie, tinned sardines, espresso and ice cream bars. The menu was divided into two simple offerings: "Pies" or "Tins."

In the cramped and humid quarters, we chatted with Mark from Germany about the performance of his neon Hokas, a marshmallow-soled shoe that my sister and Dr. David Suzuki both swear by. When I interviewed Suzuki for *Harrowsmith* magazine in 2017, he was wearing a pair and they made for an ideal icebreaker in my sweaty introduction.

Mark had left Saint-Jean-Pied-de-Port on September 24, four days after us. He had endured a few 40-kilometre days trying to keep on a steady track and lost connection with many he had started with. We had a beer's worth of conversation about the tangled dynamics of the Camino and the predictability of not crossing paths again with the people you found the most immediate bond to. Was it some kind of life lesson to keep meeting those you had less affection for? Multiple times, in the most inexplicable ways? Why were they always in the bunk bed directly overhead?

The rain lifted and the buses parted long enough for Kim and I to snap pictures at Mile 0. I had Alanis Morissette's "Thank U" song in the recesses of my head. Mostly, "Thank U" kneecaps and vertebrae and cheap red wine and rain gear.

Kim and I snaked back into the historic fishing village of Finisterre, hearts knitted closer. We stole kisses and hand squeezes the entire way. Eight years strong and I loved her more than ever. It would be okay if it truly were the end of the world, that's how reassuring Kim's love was.

And if it were the end of the world, we would definitely not be spending it in the first creepy hotel we investigated. The Hostal Mariquito didn't look promising from its dated and dank bar entry, but when I checked out the room upstairs, I was quick to usher Kim up for confirmation.

"It's super trendy but tiny and the terrace has a sea view."

I had let my hopes flatline for anything fancy, but this hotel delivered! Mariquito provided a perfect bird's eye perch for spying on arriving pilgrims as they filtered in along Santa Catalina.

Kim was easily sold, even with the blood red and pumpkin orange walls. With futuristic-looking chairs and matching framed pop art of a woman's rouge lips being silenced with an index finger gesture, it was like stepping inside Andy Warhol's brain. I loved it.

In between rain showers and siesta hours, we found our usual grocery store staples of yogurt, granola, corn nuts, chocolate milk, nuts and an avocado. Kim grabbed a bottle of local brut that would do the trick.

"It might taste like Baby Duck, but it's the only bubbly option."

We spent the afternoon drying off the chairs and table on our balcony only to retreat inside to shelter from yet another pop-up shower. Our plan was to return to the lighthouse for sunset, but there was no lifting the bruised cloud bank from the cape. We lounged with chips cross-legged on our bed until my crude mash of guacamole with lime served in a coffee filter wore off.

Galería Bibliotaberna, a bar I had eyeballed earlier, only served sandwiches and we wanted something more celebratory. But the bar was drenched in cool. There were creepy witch puppets, bottles of sand and booze from all over the world, from Syria to Iceland's Brennivín schnapps. Fishnets were suspended from the ceiling to display vinyl records, gold watches, taxidermized fish wearing sunglasses, sun-bleached currency and weather-worn flags. It was like a museum, LSD trip and brewery visit all in one compact place.

Etel + Pan was my second pick for dinner, but the skinny space was already jammed with folks who weren't moving any time soon. I sighed, admiring the list of Galician craft beers and humble offerings of hummus. We poked around the port and had a so-so dinner at O Peirao. Along the marina, there was a very tourist-driven string of massive seafood restaurants catering to busloads of diners. I was hoping for mussels but was informed "*no mas*" (no more). I had stewed lentils and Kim took advantage of a paella, but we'd been disappointed ever since our first temptation in Roncesvalles. Her paella was peppered with tiny clams, minced octopus and calamari fragments with a whole lot of rice to compensate. My lentils were surprisingly good despite the lacklustre menu description. The surprise pieces of fall-off-the-bone pork and succulent fatty bits made me think of my sister. Whenever my mom made a roast, Kiley went for the gelatinous, jiggly bits like a heat-seeking missile. Same with a Heinz can of pork and beans. Kiley would have that fatty chunk fished out of the pot of still-cold beans with surgeon-like skill.

The Tarte de Santiago was disappointing, as it was too fluffy and cakey, unlike the traditionally dense almond integrity of before. I should have eaten more tarte along the Way.

Back in our Warhol room, we sunk into chairs, mesmerized by the twinkling marina. I had my pants and fleece on and still wanted another layer. We had walked the Camino just in time. The rains and biting cold were edging in. Kim cranked the small rad in our room to 28 degrees and we were flat out in no time.

~~The End.~~ The Beginning.

Finisterre (14 km of wandering?)

- -

Another day of lovely leisure! I wondered what Olympians did with themselves after such intense training and physical output. How could they ever adapt to a day without five hours of weights, cross-training, cardio, baked chicken breast diets and five gallons of water? There had to be a mental slump with retirement or the off-season.

Admittedly, I was ready to embrace Camino off-season sleep-ins. I fetched coffee from the downstairs bar, as that was my "duty." Not that I could speak Spanish any better than Kim, but that was my voluntary role.

"You seem to understand what they're saying though," Kim said, boosting my lingual confidence.

Kim was CEO of my dirty laundry and handling currency, so coffee runs and guacamole production were my way of getting off easy.

We spent most of the morning watching new arrivals make their way along Santa Catalina with that fever we knew all too well. I still felt it, so after brunch Kim and I planned to walk to the lighthouse again. When you're that close to the End of the World, you have to see it as many times as you can.

Around the corner we grabbed egg and bacon sandwiches from Bar Canario for six euros. Storm fronts teased us as we licked greasy fingers and pondered the day's direction. Our bottle of cava was on ice in our bird-bath-sized sink, ready for action. Jesus clouds fell to the earth in giant shafts as we walked to Mile 0, tickled by the inevitable déjà vu. I felt like we were cheating, walking without packs, all casual and unburdened ,unlike the very wet pilgrims plodding along with us.

The rain didn't deter the retail-crazy bus population that congealed around the parking lot souvenir shop. Kim suggested we sit on the rocks by the lighthouse and wait for a decent break. She wanted to take more pictures at the Mile 0 waymark to ensure ample coverage of "good hair." She popped the cava as the sun smiled and lit up the ocean like silver glass. Small clusters of pilgrims had gathered to camp out for a few hours. It was a moment you had to soak in – a moment we had walked 920-plus kilometres to experience. An eruption of cheers followed the cork's pop.

"Babe, we can do anything," Kim said, leaning in for a kiss. She was right. There was an invincibility that was earned with walking the Camino. It's a natural pressure cooker for friendships and more so for relationships.

I had read an article in *O, The Oprah Magazine* about a study that suggested it can take over 200 hours together, in person, before someone becomes a close friend. Kim and I both knew full well that 20 hours with certain individuals was enough to create an enemy. I'm not fabulous at math, but in eight years Kim and I had spent over 70,000 hours together. We were so simpatico that we never needed or wanted time apart like couples who crave a "girls' weekend" or weekly "guys night" to survive the relationship. We didn't meet very many couples walking together, and a few singles mentioned disinterested wives or partners at home, content to not walk the Camino ever. I couldn't imagine going anywhere without Kim by my side. I wouldn't let her walk the Camino alone, and she certainly wouldn't let me go to Uganda again by myself!

My head was swimming from the I-love-you-so-much-imbued bubbles. We drank the bottle quickly because of the menacing clouds.

"We better duck inside," Kim said.

The Refuge bar was packed and sticky with wet-rat drifters like ourselves, tuned into a soccer match and sardines. We had a beer in patient wait, hoping for a sunset-friendly night. With rain on pause, we circled around the lighthouse again. I wondered aloud about where they filmed the scene in *The Way* where the cast burned their clothes, a pilgrim ritual that has since been quashed. Posted signs reminded that the tradition was no longer permitted, and fines could be imposed due to the danger of open fires. Also, if the graffiti-spoiled dumping zone of the 100-kilometre waymark was any indication, I'm sure the rocks behind the lighthouse would become a charred mess of half-torched hikers and Dri-FIT gear.

The rain! It came in another wave, so we ducked into the garish souvenir shop and pointed out all the terrible souvenirs. Painted starfish and corncribs (crypts!) of all sizes, carved and painted for posterity.

We used the public washroom, warming our hands with the hand dryers as the lady cleaning the stalls clattered about, dragging her mop and pail with disinterest.

"Should we just go back to the hotel?" I suggested to Kim. We had seen so many matchless sunsets. We lived on a lake that the sun fell directly into. Yes, I wanted an End of the World sunset too, but I was feeling damp and shivery.

"It's brightening up," Kim said optimistically. I was usually the one to convince her of weather-related optimism.

She was right, and I followed her to some smooth rocks, out of the way of soggy pilgrims walking to and fro. We watched a swatch of rainbow appear over the sea and fade. I noticed that Kim had pulled my notebook out of her pocket. I guessed she wanted us to mutually record our thoughts at the End of the World. Sometimes, with prodding, she'd write one or two lines in my travel notebooks. I'd prompt her for a song to describe the day or place – something like that.

"I want you to read something," she said. "But I just need a minute."

I stared out at the sea, not thinking very deeply. I wondered if she was writing something about her parents. Walking the Camino was a big deal, it moved people in inexplicable ways. I was totally surprised she was moved to writing words as I am inclined to do.

I could tell she was doodling something (hopefully, my pen hadn't run out of ink!). Then she was highly focused. Kim had tears in her eyes as she passed my notebook to me.

"Am I supposed to write something now?"

"No, just read what I wrote," she smiled.

"Okay," I said, kissing the salty tears from the edge of her eyes. "Do you want me to read it out loud?"

"No, you can just read it."

I smiled at the curly, looping penmanship I knew so well.

Cheers to our final day of walking the Camino.

I smiled at her sweet drawing of two fizzy champagne glasses and bottle of cava and turned the page.

You are my world, my everything, my love.
I couldn't imagine walking to the end of the world with anyone else and now that we have officially walked to the end of the world in Finisterre, Spain, will you walk to the end of time with me?
Will you marry me?

I hugged Kim like a python and kissed her hard, both of us wet-cheeked from tears, not rain.

"Is that a yes?" Kim asked.

"Oh my god, yes, forever, babe."

Pilgrims walked past, I'm sure. Buses could have collided and I would have had no idea. I was totally blindsided by love.

"When? Where did this come from? When did you decide you were going to ask me to marry you?"

Kim was equally surprised I had no clue. "You had *no* idea?"

"No! Not at all. Especially not here! We've talked about it, but I thought we were okay with just being 'us,' and that was okay too."

"I knew all along," Kim said. "I've always known."

I couldn't believe Kim had walked 920 kilometres with this proposal replaying in her head and heart.

She laughed, "I had a lot of time to think about it and rehearse."

My bloodlines felt full of shaken champagne and I hugged her again.

"That's why I wanted to get a hotel room when we first arrived in Finisterre yesterday. My vision was that we'd drop our bags, get a bottle of champagne and have this amazing sunset out at the lighthouse."

I was happy for all of it, sunset or not. It unfolded as it should, coloured with rainbows even. Still, I was amazed I could spend the entire last month in step with Kim and not have an inkling that she had cooked up such a romantic proposal.

I thought of Sonia, who had instilled such sense into the pilgrimage. "Why not do the Camino once and do it right?"

I thought of the tired innkeeper in Provence when asked if he would get another dog.

"No. The love affair can't be repeated."

I understood.

I thought so many things in my punch-drunk head, but I knew that, just like the Camino, Kim and I would do this marriage thing once, and we'd do it right.

It's a love affair that can't be repeated, and the End of the World was just our beginning.

The most precious commodity on the Camino! The Credencial or Pilgrim's Passport is reviewed in Santiago by officials. Each stamp, obtained at hostels or churches along the Way, provide proof of the journey and kilometers traveled. If approved, the Compostela is issued, confirming completion of the Camino de Santiago.

"FOOTNOTES"

– – – – –

It's almost as daunting to walk the Camino in words as the actual live event (though less taxing on my calves). I naturally fret and worry that some of the colour commentary will come across as insensitive or abrasive. As a pilgrim, you are supposed to be accepting of all sorts of things, but the physical and mental load lends to a natural breaking point. The heat in the Meseta wilted Kim, while diminished hours of sleep poisoned my good nature. We were beyond hunger so many days and frustrated with snorers and pilgrims who seemed to show little courtesy in regard to communal living.

But, on the flip side, it was an extraordinary way of experiencing a place inside and out. It was unique in that we shared it together, as a couple. I'm not sure if this made us more or less approachable on the Camino, but I'm glad we had each other as sounding boards and built-in motivators.

There was meditation in the repetition – and I hope that translated too. Crossing all of Spain on foot slows a reader's pace down to footfalls and a mostly predictable routine punctuated only by coffee, a treadmill of landscapes, welcome beers, sunsets and bunk beds.

It was a daily challenge reduced to finding water, food and shelter. Most days we couldn't remember where we'd left from just hours before. I'd have to check our itinerary to verify our destination a dozen times, renaming villages by their first four letters to keep things simple. Terradillos,

Calzadilla, Villafranca, Barbadelo, Olveiroa – they blended like watercolours with too many vowels.

If we had learned more Spanish than *gato negro* and San Miguel, it would have been a very different experience. Had we stayed only in municipal hostels and embraced the communal pilgrim meals, singing for our meatballs – it would have been different yet again. If we'd had a cell phone, a map or a guidebook, our Camino would have been half-scripted and way more predictable.

We did the Way, our way (which involved a lot of chorizo). The beauty of the Camino is that there is no right or wrong way to do it, though budgets, timelines and body parts will often determine the rhythm.

It's definitely not for everyone (control freaks, take note of this PSA), though no one is discouraged. It takes a titanium mind to overcome the winding kilometres, oppressive heat, snoring, empty stomach, thirst and muscles as stiff as egg whites. If you think the Camino is a feat, you need a little Iron Cowboy in your life.

James Lawrence, the "Iron Cowboy" from Calgary, Alberta, is best known for his crazy 50-50-50 challenge in 2015. He completed 50 triathlons in 50 days in 50 states. The guy is an unstoppable mental and mechanical machine. He's possibly extraterrestrial. When he was 19, Lawrence was fired from his golf course job when he skipped shifts in an attempt to win $10,000 at the Calgary Stampede by riding a Ferris wheel for ten straight days in a contest. His mother attested that, even with the dangling carrot of $10,000, the challenge was terribly monotonous and participants dropped out quickly. The contest was designed for the likes of Lawrence, an individual who could override the scratch-your-eyes-out boredom and repetition easily. He won first place.

There's an unspoken algorithm and union for all who choose to walk the Camino. From the periphery, it might seem like monotony and perhaps a big dose of boredom. For others who identify, it's easy to see the iridescent twinkle of the extraordinary in the ordinary.

This was our experience on the Camino de Santiago, and it can only be ours, though we walked in the ghost prints of Shirley MacLaine and Jane Christmas and, well, Martin Sheen for that matter. It can't be repeated, but we proved that it's possible.

The Iron Cowboy's coach suggested that James Lawrence had to "redefine what he considered impossible."

I suggest you do the same. As "they" say, all it takes is all you've got.

Like expert birders who train their eyes to find movement in a dense thicket or high in the treetops, pilgrims become dialed into finding the yellow arrow that has quietly led the way to Santiago.

SUGGESTED PACKING LIST

— — — —

Our list was refined a few times and will be best determined by your back's response to your intended load. We saw every size of pack, from Cheri-Lyn's plastic bag choice in the Pyrenees to a woman turtled by an 80L pack much like Reese Witherspoon's portrayal of Cheryl Strayed in the film *Wild*.

Be sure to check with your airline's particulars as many don't permit trekking poles in carry-on bags (even if they are folded). They definitely don't permit jackknives, but Saint-Jean-Pied-de-Port had several shops that carry both. Kim and I didn't check our packs, to avoid the hot mess that lost baggage would entail. The expense of a jackknife and new trekking poles for Kim made more sense. We planned to check our bags on the return flight to Canada, so it was a one-way nuisance, buying things we already had.

Osprey Tempest 30 backpack: Kim and I tried on countless packs and this brand felt best. The top zippered compartment is ideal for stashing granola bars, venison stew, Camino passports and maps, if you have them! Kim liked the stow-on-the-go trekking pole feature. The AirScape back panel, unique to Osprey, offers a lot of ventilation – but still expect a sweaty T-shirt by high noon. Don't be shy about asking local gearheads for intel. They love talking shop, and they've probably done the dirty work for you in trialing several products and brands.

Adaptor plug: Spain operates on a 230-volt supply. We used a Type C, which has two round pins. If you forget your adaptor along the way, as I did, ask if the hostel or albergue has any extras to borrow, keep or buy.

Nikon Coolpix camera: It's shockproof, waterproof and a really convenient size, especially for the Osprey Tempest 30L pack's zippered hip belt pocket. I was impressed with the resolution and didn't have to stress about being responsible for a more expensive camera. Of course, if you are travelling with an iPhone, it can do double duty.

Notebook/pen: I had the Nikon snug in my left hip belt pocket and my trusty notebook in the right. Pens can be a scarce and precious commodity on the Camino. Bring a few!

Bandana: With the cooler starts in October, I liked having a bandana knotted around my neck to keep the chill out. Conversely, Kim wore a bandana to keep the blazing sun of the shadeless Meseta off the back of her neck.

H_2O bottle: We opted for cheap squeeze sport bottles that held 600 ml. My sister would have dehydrated within the first few kilometres without her 1.5-litre Nalgene. A CamelBak would probably suit a solo walker best, as full water bottles can be hard to pull out of a backpack's mesh side sleeve on the move without half-taking-off your pack. It was rare that we were flat out of water, as most villages had water taps and we rationed in the stretches that other pilgrims had warned about. Even then, there was usually a pop-up or donativo in some olive plantation offering emergency-thirst cans of warm Coke or beer.

Quick-dry towel and carabiner: Most of these highly absorbent microfibre towels come with a handy loop for hanging. If your towel isn't quite dry when you head out for the day, clip it on a carabiner to the outside of your pack and say thanks to solar power. They can also double as a small privacy curtain if tucked into an upper bunk (if you're in a lower bunk).

Clothespins: With the high winds in Spain, your laundered clothes will dry efficiently, but not if they've blown off the line and onto the ground. Damp socks can also be air-dried on the move – some pilgrims swear by clothespins, but we had bungee tie-offs on our packs to secure socks with confidence (though we did sock checks every now and again, knowing in reality we would definitely not be walking back to find them if we came up short). Large safety pins will also do in a pinch, provided you don't mind pinholes in your precious socks.

Flip-flops: A must for showers and day's end. Most hostels require boots to be shelved at the door, so you will want something to change into. In a perfect world, I would have preferred a really lightweight sneaker like Nike Free, especially when the nights were cooler and/ or dodgy cobblestone roads made my Havaianas a bit of a dangerous choice. Kim took Gizeh EVA Birkenstocks that offered more support and, with their 100 per cent foam construction, are shower-friendly and quick-dry.

Sleeping bags: While many forums will suggest that you can get away with a sleeping bag liner in the summer, I like to have warmth and the weight of a duvet on me at night – regardless of the season. Many of the hostels and monasteries are housed in stone buildings and sometimes you'll be sleeping with bunkmates who open the windows wide, even though it's the end of October. Kim and I bought Chinook ThermoPalm Hooded Rectangle 50°F bags that weighed in at less than a kilogram. Compressed, they were smaller than a loaf of bread and provided valuable comfort. Don't skimp on a sleeping bag!

HumanGear GoToob 3-pack: These 100 ml silicone squeeze bottles are BPA-free and carry-on friendly. And they don't leak, even with accidental compression. The size would have been sufficient for our entire walk's supply of shampoo and conditioner had I not left the conditioner tube in a hostel shower midway.

Backpack rain cover: It's best if you can purchase a cover that is designed for your brand of pack, but Mountain Equipment Co-op and SAIL do sell multi-fit covers that are essential in a mere drizzle. The MEC cover outperformed the SAIL cover by far, for the same price point.

Louis Garneau base layer pants: Kim was okay sleeping in boxers as she runs at a higher temp most of the time. At night, I pulled on my Louis Garneau pants to sleep in. They were stylish enough to do coffee runs in and would have added a layer of warmth if necessary under my quick-dry pants. I had pants on maybe four days near the end and didn't need a base layer. I also had a long-sleeved cotton shirt and pair of Smartwool socks reserved for sleeping only.

Helly Hansen Lifa Warm Freeze base layer shirt with half-zip: I wore this thing every single day. The merino wool kept me cozy and wicked everything away when I became too cozy on an ascent. We had unknown late summer/fall temperatures to consider, and this was a smart, skinny pick.

Smartwool PhD Outdoor Light and Darn Tough quarter-cushion socks: They are guaranteed stink-free and have a lifetime warranty. Trust us, you can walk in them for four days in a row! It would be impossible to get a blister from these seamless socks, as they don't bunch, slip down or ride underfoot. Kim and I took four pairs each.

Columbia Saturday Trail zip-offs (Kim) and Columbia Silver Ridge pants (me): Kim went for the zip-offs due to her rising barometer and wore them twice. We were happy to keep our rolled pants at the very bottom of our bags.

Columbia Saturday Trail shorts (me) and Helly Hansen Jotun quick-dry shorts (Kim): Two weeks before we reached Finisterre, I bought a cheap European pair of Regatta shorts because my Columbias were falling off my hips and the stitching puckered, giving my pockets a pleated look.

T-shirts: I packed two, Kim took four. We came home with two, total. Your T-shirts will be trashed from salty sweat stains, faded from nonstop sun and stretched from handwashing. That said, we went against the hiking grain by wearing cotton T-shirts instead of quick-dry stuff because, well, cotton just feels good.

First aid: There are so many pharmacies en route, though perhaps not necessarily where you need them. You will also find vending machines that stock Band-Aids and Tiger Balm along the Way. However, we travelled with Advil gel caps, some Band-Aids and New-Skin that Kim left behind at a hostel – on purpose. Stock up on Compeed blister cushions upon arrival if you can't buy them in your country, or order them on Amazon. The inside heel of my hiking shoe was wearing thin by the end and the protection of a Compeed as a second skin saved me from the constant abrasion. If you are prone to blisters, fine-tune what works for you prior to the Camino. Forums rave about massaging your feet with Vaseline each night, or using a thread and needle to diminish a blister. We tried the Vaseline trick once but felt like we'd walked around on greasy French fries all day.

Rain gear: Worst-case scenario, Kim and I figured we could walk in wet shorts and save our pants for day's end. I packed my beloved Helly Hansen 77 waterproof jacket and Kim chose a North Face Venture 2 that didn't perform as well. Many pilgrims kept things even lighter with ponchos that did dual purpose by covering their bodies and packs.

Polar fleece: Kim sided with Marmot, while I stuck with my good ol' hooded Helly Hansen.

Headlamp or HybridLight solar flashlight: (See notes within narrative about me stumbling in the dark every morning.)

Trekking poles: I wanted to be hands-free on the Camino, but Kim was happy to have poles to rely on for both steep ascents and descents. Her hands tend to swell with humidity, so the extra movement that poles require helped immensely.

Euros: Cash is still king in the villages and many hostels. And if you find yourself in a lurch, having half-swallowed Nona's "free" pancake with empty pockets, you'll be okay.

Luxury items: Q-tips (for me), hairspray (for Kim). I had a backwards baseball hat or a toque on, depending on the time of day, eliminating the need for hair gel. Also: tweezers, nail clippers, razors (and mascara and eyeliner for pretty Kim).

Vasque Grand Traverse hiking shoes: I loved these low cuts instantly – they fit like a running shoe. The Grand Traverse design is super flyweight and the outsole of Vibram Ibex really held its ground. I'd buy them again. Plus, I like how Vasque describes its colours: bungee cord and rooibos tea.

Keen Terradora mid-waterproof boots: There were days when I could have fried eggs inside Kim's boots. The waterproof nature of the Keens made her feet too hot. She was doing sock changes every few kilometres in the Meseta because there was no breathability. At the end of the day, we fell into the habit of removing our insoles to let our shoes and insoles dry/air out.

The pinch point on the forefoot of both of Kim's boots started to break down and split. Keen replaced her boots, no questions asked, upon return. Kim was happy for the higher ankle, though, as there were several sections that put a lot of demand on ankle joints. However, a year later, she'd choose the Columbia Peakfreaks she currently wears, or La Sportiva Bushido II trail runners.

Other obvious items that need no explanation: Sunglasses, gloves (Kim finally caved when we reached the Galician region as her bare hands felt the bite of the morning using her trekking poles), lip balm, two bras (each), earplugs (Kim, not me), streamline o.b. tampons (me, not Kim), a travel alarm clock (if you don't have a phone), addresses to send home old-school postcards, a few Clif Bars for states of emergency and extra Ziploc bags for lunch leftovers, or who knows what!

For toiletries like toothpaste and deodorant, we didn't pack travel-size portions, as those skimpy toothpaste tubes are good for about five brushings and you will definitely need a lot of deodorant. Kim and I were lucky to share a lot of these items. I was luckier yet because Kim carried them.

Things to eliminate: Underwear, new-age paper soap laundry flakes (they don't work – use hand soap, body wash or shampoo instead), bug spray.

Things we wished we had: A little more patience, our Petzl headlamps (!), a bottle of Burberry Touch or Gucci Envy (thank god the grocery stores had perfume displays with those reviving #16 testers), some bonding glue for my loose retainer, a no-stick frying pan.

It would have been good to have some SPF of any number. We thought we'd have the sun at our backs as we were walking west (which was true), but we arrived at our destinations by one or two o'clock and were outside until sunset.

When we returned home, I read *Camino de Santiago Camino Francés: St. Jean-Santiago-Finisterre: A Village to Village Guide* by Anna Dintaman and David Landis (Village to Village Press, 5th edition, 2018). This book is as comprehensive as it gets, and I realized how fabulous it would have been to have it along at the time.

Speaking of books, it would have been good to have a book along – any sort. Even though it would have beefed up the weight of my bag, I really missed having something on hand. I had to write one instead to compensate!

HOMEWORK

— — — —

If you are seriously considering walking the Camino, read all of these books, in no particular order:

→ *What the Psychic Told the Pilgrim: A Midlife Misadventure on Spain's Camino de Santiago de Compostela* by Jane Christmas (Greystone Books, 2007).

→ *Pilgrim's Road: A Journey to Santiago de Compostela* by Bettina Selby (Little Brown and Company, 1994).

→ *The Camino: A Journey of the Spirit* by Shirley MacLaine (Atria Books, 2001).

→ *Two Steps Forward* by Graeme Simsion and Anne Buist (HarperCollins, 2018).

→ *Walking to the End of the World: A Thousand Miles on the Camino de Santiago* by Beth Jusino (Mountaineers Books, 2018).

For the popcorn set, be sure to watch these:

→ *The Way* (director Emilio Estevez, 2010).
→ *Walking the Camino: Six Ways to Santiago* (director/producer Lydia B. Smith, 2013).

Don't be confused by the likes of *El Camino: A Breaking Bad Movie*. (Which is also good but totally unrelated.)

Surf's Up

There are dozens of Facebook groups like Hiking Camino de Santiago & the World, Radio Camino de Santiago and Camino Francés. There is even a Camino Taco, but it's a boutique margarita and taco bar in Blue Mountain Village, Ontario.

While tacos and margaritas are important accompaniments while researching, here are a few links that will help rev up your adrenalin even more:

→ https://www.caminodesantiago.me
→ https://oficinadelperegrino.com/en/
→ https://caminoways.com

32-DAY ITINERARY

–– –– –– –– ––

Saint-Jean-Pied-de-Port, France, to Santiago de Compostela, Spain (Plus Santiago de Compostela to Finisterre via Muxía)

1. Saint-Jean-Pied-de-Port to Roncesvalles (24.7 km)

Basque Country & Navarra (162.9 km)
2. Roncesvalles to Zubiri (22.3 km)
3. Zubiri to Pamplona (21.1 km)
4. Pamplona to Puente la Reina (23.8 km)
5. Puente la Reina to Estella (21.8 km)
6. Rest day, Estella
7. Estella to Los Arcos (21.6 km)
8. Los Arcos to Logroño (27.6 km)

La Rioja & Castilla y León (123.4 km)
9. Logroño to Nájera (29.6 km)
10. Nájera to Santo Domingo (20.9 km)
11. Santo Domingo to Belorado (22.9 km)
12. Belorado to Agés (27.7 km)
13. Agés to Burgos (22.3 km)

The Meseta (231.9 km)
14. Burgos to Hontanas (31.4 km)
15. Hontanas to Boadilla del Camino (28.5 km)

16. Boadilla del Camino to Carrión de los Condes (24.5 km)
17. Carrión de los Condes to Terradillos de los Templarios (26.6 km)
18. Terradillos to Calzadilla de los Hermanillos (26.4 km)
19. Calzadilla de los Hermanillos to Mansilla de las Mulas (23.6 km)
20. Mansilla de las Mulas to León (17.9 km)
21. León to Villavante (31 km)
22. Villavante to Astorga (22 km)

Cantabrian Mountains & El Bierzo (100.9 km)

23. Astorga to Foncebadón (25.9 km)
24. Foncebadón to Ponferrada (27.1 km)
25. Ponferrada to Villafranca del Bierzo (24.2 km)
26. Villafranca to La Faba (23.7 km)

Galicia (159.7 km)

27. La Faba to Triacastela (25.7 km)
28. Triacastela to Barbadelo (23 km)
29. Barbadelo to Hospital Alta da Cruz (29.5 km) and 1.2 km Beyond to Ventas de Narón
30. Ventas de Narón to Boente (32 km)
31. Boente to Lavacolla, by Accident (38 km)
32. Lavacolla to Santiago de Compostela! (10 km)

Camino Finisterre, "End of the World" (120 km)

33. Santiago de Compostela to Negreira (21.9 km)
34. Negreira to Olveiroa (33.3 km)
35. Olveiroa to Muxía (31.8 km)
36. Muxía (5 km?)
37. Muxía to Lires (16 km)
38. Lires to Finisterre (14 km + 7 km return trip to Mile 0)
39. Finisterre (14 km of wandering?)